The New Beagle

© Ann Mackenzie '88

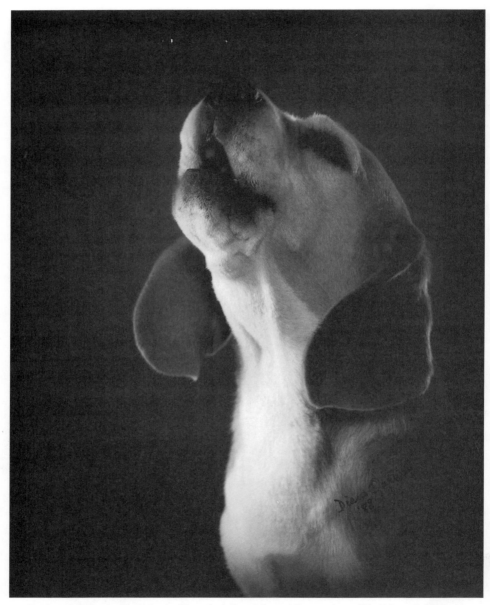

Ch. Page Mill On the Road Again, fifteen-inch Specialty and Group winner (Ch. Fulmont's Flashcube ex Ch. Page Mill Winnie the Pooh), owned by Carroll Diaz. *Diane Quennell*

The New Beagle

by
JUDITH M. MUSLADIN, M.D.
A. C. MUSLADIN, M.D.
and ADA LUEKE

Illustrated by Ann Mackencie

With contributions by
Marie Shuart and Rosalind Hall
Warren Bushey and Nadine Chicoine
David B. Sharp, Jr.
Herman Pyrkosz
Clifford and Edna Warren
Mary Powell and Trudi Reveira

HOWELL BOOK HOUSE
New York
Collier Macmillan Canada
Toronto
Maxwell Macmillan International
New York   Oxford   Singapore   Sydney

Howell Book House
Macmillan Publishing Company
866 Third Avenue
New York, NY 10022

Collier Macmillan Canada, Inc.
1200 Eglinton Avenue East, Suite 200
Don Mills, Ontario M3C 3N1

Library of Congress Cataloging-in-Publication Data
Musladin, Judith M.
    The new beagle / by Judith M. Musladin,
  A. C. Musladin, and Ada Lueke.
      p. cm.
    Includes bibliographical references.
    ISBN 0-87605-025-9
    1. Beagles (Dogs) I. Musladin, A. C. (Anton C.) II. Lueke, Ada.
III. Title.
SF429.B3M87 1990
636.7'53—dc20   89-29080

Macmillan books are available at special discounts for bulk purchases for sales promotions, premiums, fund-raising, or educational use. For details contact:

                    Special Sales Director
                    Macmillan Publishing Company
                    866 Third Avenue
                    New York, NY 10022

10 9 8 7 6 5 4 3 2 1

Printed in the United States of America

To
Nadine Chicoine,
without whom this book
might never have been written

Ch. Keith's Wilkeep Nicodemus, fifteen inches, multiple Best in Show and Group winner; Beagle of the Year, National Beagle Club, 1987 and 1988 (Ch. Starbuck's Full Count ex Ch. Wilkeep's Love Notes), owned by Barbara Cosgrove. *Missy Yuhl*

Contents

About the Authors

DRS. ANTON C. AND JUDITH M. MUSLADIN acquired their first Beagle of field stock in 1959 and their first conformation puppy in 1961. Since then, both have been involved not only with breeding and showing their dogs, but also in associated Beagling activities. They have been members of, and have held various offices in, the Blossom Valley Beagle Club. Both are Supporting Members of the National Beagle Club of America, Judy serving for three years as director of the Supporting Membership from 1984 to 1987 and currently as education coordinator. Tony is licensed to judge Beagles, Basenjis, Basset Hounds, Dachshunds and Whippets.

For three years, together with Nadine Chicoine and David Hiltz, they published a breed magazine, *The American Show Beagle.*

Both Musladins are physicians. Tony, an orthopedist, practices in San Jose, California; Judy, a psychiatrist, is currently retired. Their kennel name is The Whim's.

ADA LUEKE began her Beagling activities in 1967 and has bred and shown her Saga Beagles for twenty-two years. In addition she has served as Bench Show chairman and president of her local all-breed club, as well as a two-year stint as director of the Supporting Membership of the National Beagle Club of America. She has a B.A. in biology, with a special interest in genetics, and has worked in cellular research for some years. Collecting genetic information about our current family of conformation Beagles and advising on breeding choices is one of her many contributions.

Résumés of other contributors appear with their respective chapters. We are very grateful to Marie Shuart, Rosalind Hall, Nadine Chicoine, Warren Bushey, David Sharp, Herman Pyrkosz, Clifford and Edna Warren, Mary Powell and Trudi Reveira.

Acknowledgments

THE AUTHORS wish to express their gratitude to the following for their assistance and contributions to this book:

Ann Mackencie, an artist well known for pen-and-ink dog and cat drawings marketed under the name "Tidings."

W. Jean Dodds, D.V.M., for her editing of, and additions to, the immunization chapter and her technical description of thyroid function.

Jack Pflock, D.V.M., Scotts Valley Veterinary Clinic, Scotts Valley, California, for his review of the dry eye and cherry eye material.

Helen Hamilton, D.V.M., Diplomate American College of Veterinary Internal Medicine, Santa Cruz Veterinary Hospital, Santa Cruz, California, for her review of the intersex material.

James Ticer, D.V.M., Diplomate American College of Veterinary Radiology, Santa Cruz Veterinary Hospital, Santa Cruz, California, for his help with the discussion of chondrodystrophy (epiphyseal dysplasia).

Alan Macmillan, D.V.M., Ph.D., Diplomate American College of Veterinary Ophthalmologists.

Michael J. Kelly, D.V.M., Diplomate American College of Internal Medicine, Main Street Animal Hospital, San Diego, California.

Patrick Gauvin, D.V.M., Chabot Veterinary Clinic, Hayward, California, for his correct diagnosis of chondrodystrophy in our current conformation family of Beagles.

Patrick Baymiller, D.V.M., Central Animal Hospital, Campbell, California, for his advice and help through the years.

Donald Patterson, D.V.M., University of Pennsylvania Veterinary

School, Philadelphia, Pennsylvania, for his help with intersex genetics.

Robert Slike and Dorothy Warren of *Hounds & Hunting* magazine, for their wonderful supply of pictures.

Frank Lueke, for his many helpful suggestions.

Elizabeth Campbell, for her encouragement and help.

Seymour Weiss, Vice President, Howell Book House, for his unending patience and support.

And to all of you who have shared your pictures and your information over the years and offered your encouragement.

Fox Valley Pack.   *William King*

Preface

THE BEAGLE is one of the most popular purebred dogs in the United States.

American Kennel Club statistics show 39,849 Beagles were registered in 1986, 41,972 in 1987. Beagles ranked seventh in number of breed registrations for both years.

During the year 1987, 241 achieved Conformation championships; 17 Companion Dog titles; five Companion Dog Excellent titles; two Utility Degrees; six Tracking Degrees; and 309 completed their Field championships.

The registration figures are staggering. What becomes of approximately 40,000 new Beagles each year?

Fortunately the Beagle is a multipurpose breed and fulfills many of our human needs. It makes a loving friend, a splendid hunting companion, a fine obedience and conformation dog, serves well with the Department of Agriculture seeking out banned fruits and vegetables in airport baggage, visits convalescent hospitals as a "pet therapist" and even aids in termite detection!

This book was written for all who enjoy the Beagle and especially for those who breed Beagles. We have attempted to combine general information about the breed and the many Beagling activities, with more specific emphasis on the breeding of conformation Beagles. We have learned a great deal in the process of compiling the book, especially how much more there is to know. Pooling our experiences, both successful and unsuccessful, can only enrich us all.

Bear with us in some of the technical discussions in the genetic and newborn-care chapters. We feel the information in these chapters is of particular importance in the breeding of Beagles.

The New Beagle

© Ann Mackenzie '88

Beagles, 1835.

Southern Hound, an ancestor of today's Beagle.

Orpheus, oil painting by Giovanni Castiglioni ("Il Grechetto"), ca. 1650.

The Dog Book, *by James Watson*

1

History of the Beagle

"Pour down, then, a flood from the hills, brave boys
On the wings of the wind
The merry Beagles fly:
Dull sorrow lags behind
Ye shrill echoes reply,
Catch each flying sound,
And double our joys."

WILLIAM SOMERVILLE (1675–1742)

EARLY MAN'S association with wild dogs probably began with young taken from dens and nurtured as pets or companions. Thereafter, in his search for food, man began to use the dog as an adjunct in hunting game. The hound, which by scent could track game animals, evolved. The progenitor was probably the Bloodhound. It is likely that, in order to track smaller game, the Bloodhound was bred to a gazehound to produce swiftness and smaller size while retaining the keen sense of smell.

There are references to small Beagle-type dogs as early as 400 B.C. in Greece and in ancient Britain by A.D. 200. These were small dogs that hunted hare and were followed on foot. Exuberant descriptions are given of the clamor and clanging of the pack's cry when in full pursuit.

The Romans, too, had their small hounds and most likely brought some to England, where they were interbred with the indigenous small hounds.

In France, during the 1300s, there is a mention of "Rachys and Brachys," which referred to small hounds brought from England by the Black Prince and John of Gaunt.

William the Conqueror returned from the Continent with a strain of large, mostly white hound called the Talbot Hound, which is thought to have contributed to the development of the Southern Hound, the Beagle and the

Foxhound in England. In any event, by the 1400s the small hounds were popularly established in Great Britain, France, Greece and Italy. It was about this time that the name "Beagle" came into existence. The origin of the word is interesting. There are references to it in both French and Gaelic, the term in both languages being used to mean "useless, of odd appearance, of little value." The smallest of scent hounds in England at that time, the Beagle had probably been bred for many years for amusement and/or hunting game of little significance, such as rabbit or hare.

THE BEAGLE IN ENGLAND

The little Beagle found favor with the British royal family. Chronicles of the reigns of Edward II and Henry VIII contain many references to the small hound. Described as being of diminutive size, the "glove Beagle" (tiny enough to be held in a gauntlet) was also known as the "singing Beagle" for its melodious voice, which was so small in comparison to other hounds; efforts were even made to breed voices that would blend with one another.

Elizabeth I had a famous pack of tiny Beagles for her amusement. Nine inches in height at the shoulder, the "pocket Beagles" were carried behind the ladies of the court on horseback. Paintings of the time show these Beagles to be short legged and somewhat pointy nosed.

Hunting hare with a pack of hounds was a popular sport for the country gentry of the day. Fox hunting had not yet achieved its popularity, and the principal nobles and the Crown hunted deer with a large hound called the Buck Hound.

By the middle of the eighteenth century fox hunting was beginning to attract the younger generation. The English Foxhound, most likely produced by interbreeding the Buck Hound and the Beagle, was used for the faster, more exhilarating sport.

Due to the "vagaries of breeders" (*The Beagle in America and England*, by H. W. Prentice), two distinct types of hare-hunting hounds had evolved. The Southern Hound was slow moving, with long ears and a deep voice; the North Country Beagle was quick and vigorous. In addition to these types, there was a smaller Beagle preferred by some for its small appetite. Though this latter type had a good nose for game, it tended to be playful and full of chatter. In a word, unreliable hunters! Obviously, there must have been hounds of various heights, shapes and colors.

With the advent of fox hunting, Beagles declined in popularity, and it is likely that the breed would have become extinct had it not been for the farmers and small landowners of the southern counties of England. It was the custom in that region to maintain packs of Beagles for the purpose of driving rabbits to the hunter's gun. Were it not for these Beagle packs, also in Ireland and Wales, there would not have been any Beagles left to participate in the revival of the breed.

Giant and Ringlet, two of Mr. Crane's famous pack of "pocket Beagles." Dogs of Great Britain and America

Lap Beagles, painting by Reinagle, ca. 1800.

Blue Bell, a typical early Beagle.   Dogs of Great Britain and America

Rattler and Belle, owned by J. M. Dodge. Rattler, by Charles Turner Warrior (imported) ex General Rowett's Rosy, won first place at Philadelphia, Boston, St. Louis, Rochester and Ann Arbor in 1879. Belle won first place in Philadelphia and Boston in 1879. Both were important winners in the 1829 show season.

First Field Trail of the National Beagle Club, November 3, 1890.

The Beagle in America and England, *by H. W. Prentice*

Waldingfield Beagles' Pack of Four: Oriole, Hermes, Bridget B, and Sergeant.   The Beagle in America and England

4

In the middle of the nineteenth century the Reverend Philip Honeywood was, with the fine showing of his pack in Essex, responsible for increasing interest in Beagles. The emphasis, of course, was on hunting ability, not beauty. With Thomas Johnson's efforts to breed a pack that could not only hunt well, but also excel in beauty, the breed in England began to develop into a good-looking working hound. Hunting with packs of Beagles remains a popular sport in England to the present.

THE BEAGLE IN AMERICA

Little is known of the Beagle in America before 1876, when General Richard Rowett of Illinois imported some from several of the English packs. Though there are reports of Beagles being bred in this country prior to that time, it was the beauty and quality of those imported by General Rowett that brought the breed into much demand.

Southern Pennsylvania, Delaware and Maryland became known as Beagle country. The variety there was known as the "bench-legged Beagle" because of its crooked forelegs. Some of these were undoubtedly crosses with Dachshunds and possibly were even imported from Prince Albert's pack at Windsor, England.

In 1884 the American Kennel Club was established. In that same year the first Beagle specialty club, The American-English Beagle Club, was established by Philadelphia-area breeders, a Standard was adopted, and the breed took a turn for the better.

The early American show Beagles (see chapter 7) were of a rangier type, often were pied or mottled in markings (the best English hunting strains were similar) and ranged in size from "toy to sixteen inches" in height.

The National Beagle Club was formed in the late 1800s, with the object of holding field trial events and for the purpose of improving field qualities as well as type. When the club initially applied for admission to the American Kennel Club as a Specialty club, permission was denied because the American Beagle Club, as the American-English Beagle Club was then known, refused to sanction its admission.

Despite the denial, the new club went ahead with its plans, and in short order merged with the American Beagle Club, thereafter known as the National Beagle Club of America (NBC). Early in its existence a proposal to strike from its constitution reference to improvement on the bench was voted down. Hence, the club was now clearly on record to promote function and type. The Standard was revised in 1900 to increase emphasis on running gear.

The first National Beagle Club field trial was scheduled to be held in Hyannis, Massachusetts, in 1890. However, due to poor terrain, the activity was moved to New Hampshire. The first National Beagle Club Specialty show was held in 1891.

An outstanding Beagle of the period was Frank Forest, bred of Rowett

Ch. Windholme's Bangle, the first Beagle to win a Best in Show.

The Beagle in America and England

Ch. Altopa Atom, thirteen inches, dual-purpose Beagle owned by O. J. Gennett in the late 1940s.

Institute Farm, Aldie, Virginia, home of the National Beagle Club. *Rene Chicoine*

linebreeding by George Reed of Vermont, and shown with great success by his owner, Mr. Perry of Massachusetts. Frank Forest proved to be excellent in field and on the bench.

Derogation of the show-Beagle type was popular in the field trial press of that day. Because of this, in 1896 James Kernochan began to import proven hunting hounds from English packs, thus adding the hound head and body, legs and feet of the good Beagle; these imports were responsible for setting the Beagle type of today. The Hempstead Hounds of Mr. Kernochan, the Windholme stock of Harry Peters and the Rock Ridge Beagles of William A. Rockefeller were the most successful in the early shows. In addition, all of these dogs worked in the field.

Up to 1912 field trials were always held on cottontail and rarely on New England hare. But at that point pack on hare clubs began to demonstrate the endurance of the Beagle on larger game.

The early Beagles performed well in both bench and field. Eng. Ch. Stoke Place Sapper proved himself when he won high honors in both and produced well for both activities.

In 1916 James W. Appleton (president of the NBC, 1910–1942), Harry Peters and George B. Post, Jr. (both directors of the American Kennel Club), Chetwood Smith, Ted Lucas, H. C. Phipps of Wheatley Beagles and C. Oliver Iselin (president of the NBC, 1942–1971) formed the Institute Corporation and purchased the 400-acre Institute Farm in Aldie, Virginia, as the home for NBC activities.

This wooded property, lying about thirty miles west of Washington, D.C., had once been part of Oak Hill, home of President James Monroe. In 1854 a large three-and-one-half-story building was built of stone and stucco for the Loudoun County Agricultural Institute and Chemical Academy. The first agricultural school in the Commonwealth of Virginia, its students and faculty pioneered agricultural experimentation.

The site, with its house, provided good ground conditions for hunting and sleeping quarters for eager hunters. Perimeter fencing to keep the Beagles from straying, kennel facilities and log cabins to afford additional sleeping accommodations completed the project. This then became the site for pack trials, both Beagle and Basset, and brace trials—a tradition that prospers even today.

As the Washington, D.C., suburbs expanded, Institute Farm was placed in 1981 on the National Registry of Historic Places and Virginia Landmarks so the building could be restored and maintained without fear of the property falling to developers' bulldozers. In 1986 the Loudoun Agricultural Chemical Institute Foundation, Inc., was formed to serve as a fund-raising vehicle for restoration of the building and grounds to the original nineteenth-century farm state.

The early National Beagle Club's double emphasis on field and conformation changed over the years as interest in conformation phased out. As early

Eng. Ch. Beacott Buckthorn,
owned by P. J. Tutchener.
Diane Pearce

Eng. Ch. Rossut Foreman,
owned by Catherine Sutton.
Diane Pearce

N.Z. Ch. Merrybrook Jamie
Luck, New Zealand's top win-
ning Beagle ever, with four
Bests in Show and over 100
CCs (N.Z. Ch. Annasline High-
light [U.K.] ex N.Z. Ch. Merry-
brook How Hasty), owned by Mr.
J. Green.

Aus. Ch. Manabay Careless Love, fifteen inches, won the Bitch CC in 1986 at the Melbourne Royal in an entry of 120 Beagles (Aust. Ch. Manabay Midas Touch ex Aus. Ch. Manabay Wun Night Stand). Owned by Leslie Funnell Hiltz and Liz Whitcher.

Michael M. Trafford

Dan. Ch. Black Gold II, sire of many champions in Scandinavia.

Daragoj One Way Ticket, Finnish Beagle with American and English bloodlines, owned by Eeva Resko Heino.

Am./Can. Ch. Terwillegar's Happy Hawker, fifteen inches, multiple Best in Show winner in Canada (Ch. Yarra Belle's Sky's the Limit ex Ch. The Whim's Raise the Roof), owned by Mrs. G. R. Lloyd. *Mikron*

Am./Braz. Ch. Starcrest Brigadoon, fifteen inches (Ch. Pacific Casper of Starcrest ex Mistress Morgan O'Starcrest), owned by Vera Lucia Costa, Brazil. *Fox & Cook*

Braz. Ch. Sto Alberto's Be My Dancer, owned by Alberto Bonofiglio.

10

as 1936, the task of administering the increasing number of field trial clubs and activities grew to be an impossible burden, and a separate governing body, the Beagle Advisory Commission, was established.

In 1970 a small group of conformation Beaglers, also regular members of the NBC, with the encouragement of the secretary, Morgan Wing, held the first National Beagle Club Specialty in many years at Aldie. Virginia Coleman, Evelyn Droge, Louise Marter and Archie Chapman put on eight successful annual Specialty shows.

Growing pressure for representation in the NBC by conformation Beaglers brought about the establishment of a second classification of membership, the supporting membership for those interested in conformation. The annual Specialty show was held in other parts of the United States on two occasions to permit greater participation by exhibitors based away from the East Coast.

Through the pioneering work of Nadine Eaton Chicoine during the late 1970s, the supporting membership was granted permission in 1980 to draw up its own bylaws to govern the Specialty show activities and to provide for the election of a supporting membership director to serve on the Board of the NBC for a one-year term.

The year 1981 saw the inception of a regular rotation schedule for the Specialty show throughout the United States, returning to Aldie at regular intervals.

With the passing of time, there has been a shift from emphasis on the dual-purpose hound of the late 1800s and early 1900s to the breeding of Beagles for specific functions: conformation, brace, large or small pack and gundog. Because of this, Beagles in each of these categories appear sometimes to be of different breeds. However, within the registered Beagle packs, as well as in the more recent gundog movement, there is increasing interest in combining the qualities of a good working hound with the beauty of the conformation Beagle.

As of 1987 the National Beagle Club listed 375 regular members, 162 supporting members. Activities sponsored by the parent club include spring and fall Basset and Beagle pack trials, brace trials and an annual Specialty show. The 1987 centennial celebration of the club's founding provided clear evidence of an active club, committed to its original purpose.

THE BEAGLE THROUGHOUT THE WORLD

Great Britain and the United States are not the only countries in which Beagles are popular. There are active breeders in Australia, Germany, the Netherlands, Denmark, Italy, Canada, Brazil, Colombia, Sweden, Finland (where a conformation winner is required to pass a field test before being granted a championship certificate) and Norway. English and American stock have provided the foundation for the breeding programs in these countries.

An excellent example of the difference between a true fifteen-inch and a true thirteen-inch Beagle. Ch. Foyscroft I'm Triple Terrific is the fifteen-inch, Ch. Jo-Mar's Repeat Performance the thirteen-inch. Both are owned by Marcia Foy. *John Ashbey*

2

The Beagle Standard

THE IMPORTANCE of a breed Standard was clearly expressed in the Remarks section that prefaced the American Beagle Club Standard drafted in January 1884, which with the establishment of the American Kennel Club later that year became the first official AKC Standard for the breed.

REMARKS

Beagle Breeders are aware of the fact that a Standard and Scale of Points are an absolute necessity, so that an authorized type of the Beagle Hound is made apparent for Bench Show Judges to base their decisions upon, as no two are similar in opinion as to merit, and their ideas differ widely in their estimates as to quality and the breed marks of the race.

To avoid having harrier sized dogs recognized at one show and the smallest specimens favored at another, is one of the objects sought to remedy by the compilers of the Standard and Scale of Points of the American Beagle Club, as with an accepted standard the Judge will have a guide to lead him through the difficulties of his position, and the breeder if a novice will be enabled with its assistance to discard those animals that are deficient in quality, and recognize merit where it exists, thus elevating the status of the kennel.

Compiled by Gen. Richard Rowett, Dr. H. L. Twaddell and Norman Elmore, this first Standard was based upon and differed little from the English Standard for the Beagle, or from the English Foxhound Standard. In fact, as will be seen in the pages that follow, the Standard has changed but little to this day. The 1884 standard attributed 35 points for the head (as opposed to 25 points in the current Standard), and specified "a thinly haired rattish tail" or "a short, close and nappy coat" as disqualifications, whereas the current

Standard lists them, in slightly different language, as defects. Re this, it is interesting that the 1884 Standard had this appendage:

NOTE: Dogs possessing such serious faults as are enumerated under the heading of "Disqualifications" are under the grave suspicion of being of *impure* blood. Under the heading of "Defects" objectionable features are indicated; such departures from the standard not however impugning the purity of the breeding.

STANDARD AND SCALE OF POINTS FOR THE BEAGLE HOUND
Adopted by The American Beagle Club—Drafted in January 1884

HEAD

The skull should be moderately domed at the occiput, with the cranium broad and full. The ears set on low, long and fine in texture, the forward or front edge closely framing and inturned to the cheek, rather broad and rounded at the tips, with an almost entire absence of erectile power at their origin.

The eyes full and prominent, rather wide apart, soft and lustrous, brown or hazel in color. The orbital processes well developed. The expression gentle, subdued and pleading.

The muzzle of medium length, squarely cut, the stop well defined. The jaws should be level. Lips either free from or with moderate flews. Nostrils large, moist and open.

DEFECTS. A flat skull narrow across the top of the head, absence of dome. Ears short, set on too high, or when the dog is excited rising above the line of the skull at their points of origin due to an excess of erectile power. Ears pointed at the tips, thick or boardy in substance or carried out from cheek showing a space between. Eyes of a light or yellow color. Muzzle long and snipey. Pig jaws or the reverse known as under shot. Lips showing deep *pendulous* flews.

DISQUALIFICATIONS. *Eyes close together, small, beady and terrier-like.*

NECK AND THROAT

Neck rising free and light from the shoulders, strong in substance, yet not loaded, of medium length. The Throat clean and free from folds of skins, a slight wrinkle below the angle of the jaw however may be allowable.

DEFECTS. A thick, short, cloddy neck, carried on a line with the top of the shoulder. Throat showing dewlap and folds of skin to a degree termed "throatiness."

SHOULDERS AND CHEST

Shoulders somewhat declining, muscular, but not loaded, conveying the idea of freedom of action, with lightness, activity and strength. Chest moderately broad and full.

DEFECTS. Upright shoulders and a disproportionately wide chest.

BACK, LOIN AND RIBS

Back short, muscular and strong. Loin broad and slightly arched, and the Ribs well sprung, giving abundant lung room.

DEFECTS. A long or swayed back, a flat narrow loin, or a flat constricted rib.

FORELEGS AND FEET

Forelegs straight with plenty of bone. Feet close, firm, and either round or harelike in form.

DEFECTS. Out elbows. Knees knuckled over or forward, or bent backward. Feet open and spreading.

HIPS, THIGHS, HIND-LEGS AND FEET

Hips strongly muscled, giving abundant propelling power. Stifles strong and well let down. Hocks firm, symmetrical and moderately bent. Feet close and firm.

DEFECTS. Cow hocks and open feet.

14

TAIL.

The Tail should be carried gaily, well up and with medium curve, rather short as compared with size of the dog, and clothed with a decided brush.

DEFECTS. A long tail, with a tea pot curve.

DISQUALIFICATIONS. *A thinly haired rattish tail, with entire absence of brush.*

COAT

Moderately coarse in texture, and of good length.

DISQUALIFICATIONS. *A short, close, and nappy coat.*

HEIGHT

The meaning of the term "Beagle" (a word of Celtic origin, and in old English *Begele*) is small, little. The dog was so named from his diminutive size. Your committee therefore for the sake of consistency, and that the Beagle shall be in *fact* what his name implies, strongly recommend that the height line be sharply drawn at fifteen inches, and that all dogs exceeding that height shall be disqualified as over-grown, and outside the pale of recognition.

COLOR

All hound colors are admissible. Perhaps the most popular is black, white and tan. Next in order is the lemon and white, then blue and lemon mottles, then follow the solid colors, such as black and tan, tan, lemon, fawn, etc.

This arrangement is of course arbitrary, the question being one governed entirely by fancy. The colors first named form the most lively contrast and blend better in the pack, the solid colors being sombre and monotonous to the eye.

It is not intended to give a point value to color in the scale for judging, as before said all true hound colors being correct. The foregoing remarks on the subject are therefore simply suggestive.

GENERAL APPEARANCE

A miniature fox-hound, solid and big for his inches, with the wear and tear look of the dog that can last in the chase and follow his quarry to the death.

SCALE OF POINTS

	Points
HEAD	
Skull	5
Ears	15
Eyes	10
Muzzle, Jaws and Lips	5
BODY	
Neck	5
Shoulders and Chest	10
Back and Loins	15
Ribs	5
RUNNING GEAR	
Forelegs and Feet	10
Hips, Thighs, and Hind-Legs	10
COAT AND STERN	
Tail	5
Coat	5
TOTAL	100

AKC STANDARD FOR THE ENGLISH FOXHOUND

HEAD   Should be of full size, but by no means heavy. Brow pronounced, but not high or sharp. There should be a good length and breadth, sufficient to give in a dog hound a girth in front of the ears of fully 16 inches. The nose should be long (4½ inches) and wide, with open nostrils. Ears set on low and lying close to the cheeks. Most English hounds are "rounded" which means that about 1½ inches is taken off the end of the ear. The teeth must meet squarely, either a *pig-mouth* (overshot) or undershot being a disqualification.

NECK   Must be long and clean, without the slightest throatiness, not less than 10 inches from cranium to shoulder. It should taper nicely from shoulders to head, and the upper outline should be slightly convex.

THE SHOULDERS should be long and well clothed with muscle, without being heavy, especially at the points. They must be well sloped, and the true arm between the front and the elbow must be long and muscular, but free from fat or lumber. *Chest and Back Ribs*   The chest should girth over 31 inches in a 24-inch hound, and the back ribs must be very deep.

BACK AND LOIN   Must both be very muscular, running into each other without any contraction between them. The couples must be wide, even to raggedness, and the topline of the back should be absolutely level, the *Stern* well set on and carried gaily but not in any case curved *over* the back like a squirrel's tail. The end should taper to a point and there should be a fringe of hair below. The *Hindquarters* or propellers are required to be very strong, and as endurance is of even greater consequence than speed, straight stifles are preferred to those much bent as in a Greyhound. *Elbows* set quite straight, and neither turned in nor out are a *sine qua non*. They must be well let down by means of the long true arm above mentioned.

LEGS AND FEET   Every Master of Foxhounds insists on legs as straight as a post, and as strong; size of bone at the ankle being especially regarded as all important. The desire for straightness had a tendency to produce knuckling-over, which at one time was countenanced, but in recent years this defect has been eradicated by careful breeding and intelligent adjudication, and one sees very little of this trouble in the best modern Foxhounds. The bone cannot be too large, and the feet in all cases should be round and catlike, with well-developed knuckles and strong horn, which last is of the greatest importance.

COLOR AND COAT   Not regarded as very important, so long as the former is a good "hound color," and the latter is short, dense, hard, and glossy. Hound colors are black, tan, and white, or any combination of these three, also the various "pies" compounded of white and the color of the hare and badger, or yellow, or tan. The *Symmetry* of the Foxhound is of the greatest importance, and what is known as "quality" is highly regarded by all good judges.

SCALE OF POINTS

Head	5	Elbows	5
Neck	10	Legs and feet	20
Shoulders	10	Color and coat	5
Chest and back ribs	10	Stern	5
Back and loin	15	Symmetry	5
Hindquarters	10	**TOTAL**	100

DISQUALIFICATION

Pig-mouth (overshot) or undershot.

CURRENT OFFICIAL AKC STANDARD FOR THE BEAGLE
(Approved September 10, 1957)

HEAD

The skull should be fairly long, slightly domed at occiput, with cranium broad and full.

Ears Ears set on moderately low, long, reaching when drawn out nearly, if not quite, to the end of the nose; fine in texture, fairly broad—with almost entire absence of erectile power—setting close to the head, with the forward edge slightly inturning to the cheek—rounded at tip.

Eyes Eyes large, set well apart—soft and houndlike—expression gentle and pleading; of a brown or hazel color.

Muzzle Muzzle of medium length—straight and square-cut—the stop moderately defined.

Jaws Level. Lips free from flews; nostrils large and open.

Defects A very flat skull, narrow across the top; excess of dome, eyes small, sharp and terrierlike, or prominent and protruding; muzzle long, snipy or sharp and terrierlike, or prominent and protruding; muzzle long, snipy or cut away decidedly below the eyes, or very short. Roman-nosed, or upturned giving a dish-face expression. Ears short, set on high or with a tendency to rise above the point of origin.

BODY

Neck and Throat Neck rising free and light from the shoulders strong in substance yet not loaded, of medium length. The throat clean and free from folds of skin; a slight wrinkle below the angle of the jaw, however, may be allowable.

Defects A thick, short, cloddy neck carried on a line with the top of the shoulders. Throat showing dewlap and folds of skin to a degree termed "throatiness."

Shoulders and Chest Shoulders sloping—clean, muscular, not heavy or loaded—conveying the idea of freedom of action with activity and strength. Chest deep and broad, but not broad enough to interfere with the free play of the shoulders.

Defects Straight, upright shoulders. Chest disproportionately wide or with lack of depth.

Back, Loin and Ribs Back short, muscular and strong. Loin broad and slightly arched, and the ribs well sprung, giving abundance of lung room.

Defects Very long or swayed or roached back. Flat, narrow loin, flat ribs.

FORELEGS AND FEET

Forelegs Straight with plenty of bone in proportion to size of the hound. Pasterns short and straight.

Feet Close, round and firm. Pad full and hard.

Defects Out at elbows. Knees knuckled over forward, or bent backward. Forelegs crooked or Dachshundlike. Feet long, open or spreading.

Hips, Thighs, Hind Legs and Feet Hips and thighs strong and well muscled, giving abundance of propelling power. Stifles strong and well let down. Hocks firm, symmetrical and moderately bent. Feet close and firm.

Defects Cowhocks, or straight hocks. Lack of muscle and propelling power. Open feet.

TAIL

Set moderately high; carried gaily, but not turned forward over the back; with slight curve; short as compared with size of the hound; with brush.

Defects A long tail. Teapot curve or inclined forward from the root. Rat tail with absence of brush.

COAT

A close, hard, hound coat of medium length.

Defects—A short, thin coat, or of a soft quality.

COLOR

Any true hound color.

GENERAL APPEARANCE

A miniature Foxhound, solid and big for his inches, with the wear-and-tear look of the hound that can last in the chase and follow his quarry to the death.

SCALE OF POINTS

Head			Running Gear		
Skull	5		Forelegs	10	
Ears	10		Hips, thighs and		
Eyes	5		hind legs	10	
Muzzle	5	25	Feet	10	30
Body					
Neck	5		Coat	5	
Chest and Shoulders	15		Stern	5	10
Back, loin and ribs	15	35	TOTAL	100	

VARIETIES

There shall be two varieties:

Thirteen Inch—which shall be for hounds not exceeding 13 inches in height.

Fifteen Inch—which shall be for hounds over 13 but not exceeding 15 inches in height.

Any hound measuring more than 15 inches shall be disqualified.

Packs of Beagles

SCORE OF POINTS FOR JUDGING

Hounds—General levelness of pack	40%
Individual merit of hounds	30%
	70%
Manners	20%
Appointments	10%
TOTAL	100%

Levelness of Pack The first thing in a pack to be considered is that they present a unified appearance. The hounds must be as near to the same height, weight, conformation and color as possible.

Individual Merit of the Hounds Is the individual bench-show quality of the hounds. A very level and sporty pack can be gotten together and not a single hound be a good Beagle. This is to be avoided.

Manners The hounds must all work gaily and cheerfully, with flags up— obeying all commands cheerfully. They should be broken to heel up, kennel up, follow promptly and stand. Cringing, sulking, lying down to be avoided. Also, a pack must not work as though in terror of master and whips. In Beagle packs it is recommended that the whip be used as little as possible.

Appointments Master and whips should be dressed alike, the master or huntsman to carry horn—the whips and master to carry light thong whips. One whip should carry extra couplings on shoulder strap.

RECOMMENDATIONS FOR SHOW LIVERY

Black velvet cap, white stock, green coat, white breeches or knickerbockers, green or black stocking, white spats, black or dark brown shoes. Vest and gloves optional. Ladies should turn out exactly the same except for a white skirt instead of white breeches.

ENGLISH BEAGLE STANDARD (Revised, 1988)

(Ed. note: All alterations from the previous standard are in italics.)

General Appearance A sturdy, compactly-built hound, conveying the impression of quality without coarseness.

Characteristics A merry hound whose essential function is to hunt, primarily hare, by following a scent. Bold, with great activity, stamina and determination. Alert, intelligent, and of even temperament.

Temperament *(totally new clause)* *Amiable and alert, showing no aggression or timidity.*

Head and Skull Fair length, *powerful without being coarse,* finer in the bitch, *free from frown and wrinkle.* Skull slightly domed, moderately wide, with *slight* peak. Stop well defined and dividing length, between occiput and tip of nose, as equally as possible. Muzzle not snipey, lips reasonably well flewed. Nose broad, preferably black, but less pigmentation permissible in the lighter coloured hounds. *Nostrils wide.*

Eyes Dark brown or hazel, fairly large, not deepset or *prominent,* set well apart with mild appealing expression.

Ears Long, with *rounded* tip, reaching nearly to end of nose when drawn out. Set on low, fine in texture and hanging gracefully close to *cheeks.*

Mouth *The jaws should be strong, with perfect, regular and complete scissor bite, i.e., the upper teeth closely overlapping the lower teeth, and set square to the jaw.*

Neck Sufficiently long to enable hound to come down to scent easily, slightly arched and *showing little* dewlap.

Forequarters *Shoulders well laid back, not loaded.* Forelegs straight and upright, well under the hound, good substance, and round in the bone, not tapering off to feet. Pasterns short. Elbows firm, turning neither in or out. Height to elbow about half height at withers.

Body Topline straight and level. *Chest let down* to below *elbow.* Ribs well sprung and extending well back. Short *in the* couplings *but well balanced.* Loins powerful and supple, without excessive tuck-up.

Hindquarters *Muscular thighs.* Stifles well bent. Hocks firm, well let down and parallel to each other.

Feet Tight and firm. Well knuckled up and strongly padded. Not harefooted. Nails short.

Tail Sturdy, *moderately long.* Set on high, carried gaily but not curled over back or inclined forward from the root. Well covered with hair, especially on underside.

20

Gait/Movement Back level, *firm with no indication of roll.* Stride free, long reaching *in front* and straight without thigh action. Hind legs showing drive. Should not move close behind nor paddle nor plait in front.

Coat Short, dense and weatherproof.

Color Any recognized hound colour other than liver. Tip of stern white.

Size Desirable minimum height at withers 33cm (13 ins). Desirable maximum height at withers 40cm (16 ins).

Faults [*new clause*] *Any departure from the foregoing points should be considered a fault and the seriousness with which the fault should be regarded should be in exact proportion to its degree.*

Note [*new clause*] *Male animals should have two apparently normal testicles fully descended into the scrotum.*

DISCUSSION OF THE AKC BEAGLE STANDARD

General Comments

First, some general comments about the overall look of a good Beagle. Remember, this is a utilitarian little hound, as well as one of pleasing appearance. Unfortunately, over the years a marked difference has developed in the appearance of Beagles bred for field work and those for conformation. Practically never do we see a field Beagle obtaining his conformation championship. The show Beagle in a field trial is almost immediately penalized by the judge and ridiculed by the field-trialers. Some effort toward a return to the original tradition of the dual-purpose Beagle is under way through the gun-dog movement and some of the formal pack Beaglers.

A good head is one which allows for maximum function of the *olfactory system* (sense of smell). Good running gear is important for endurance and speed. Good chest is required for endurance. Pack temperament is necessary, for these hounds must get along when run and kenneled together. Balance is important for efficient running; good strong feet necessary for the rough terrain. Thin coats do not protect the Beagle from brambles, and a too-gay tail cannot be seen over the brush and high grass. There are other points, of course, that are more related to beauty: eye color, length of ear, lack of throatiness, coat color and markings.

The Standard states that the Beagle should be a "miniature Foxhound, solid and big for his inches, with the wear-and-tear look of the hound that can last in the chase and follow his quarry to the death." The proper English Foxhound is a well-proportioned hound, elegant in style, balanced fore and aft, nicely boned and four square.

The Beagle, too, should be balanced fore and aft. A too-heavy, broad-muscled front and a straight, lighter rear will certainly not be as effective a running machine as one with balanced front and rear. The dimensions referred to as four square are those from the tip of the shoulder to the back of the tail and from the tip of the shoulder to the ground. A too short coupled dog cannot run efficiently. The short-legged Beagle will not have the reach in proportion to its weight for speed. But I am hard pressed to explain why the longer-backed dog, if running gear is in order, might not move just as efficiently as the better-balanced dog. So perhaps here it is just the question of aesthetics in respect to profile.

Head

The head counts for 25 percent of the total points in the Standard, an important chunk. Remember that the size of the skull is related to the size of the lobes of the brain, as well as the size of the sinuses. The late Braxton Sawyer, American Foxhound breeder, stated that one-eighth of the scent hound's brain is committed to the olfactory center, and that over 50 percent of the internal space of the scent hound's nose is occupied by olfactory receptor endings. The ethmo-turbinates, the primary location of the olfactory receptors, are situated in the posterior aspect of the nose and extend up into the frontal sinus area. These features necessitate a skull fairly long, slightly domed at the occiput, with the cranium broad and full. The muzzle is of medium length, straight and square-cut. The stop is moderately defined with plenty of room for the frontal sinuses, while the nostrils are wide and open to enable clear and open passage of the scent.

Skull and muzzle account for 10 points. The planes of the head should be parallel with lines drawn on either side of the muzzle. The same should be true for a side view of the head. The line along the top of the skull should parallel that of the muzzle. In addition, the length of the head from occiput to stop should be approximately equal to the length from stop to nose.

I have always been puzzled as to why ears count for another 10 points. They should be set moderately low on a level with the outer corner of the eye; should be long, reaching when drawn out almost to the end of the nose; should be fine in texture, fairly broad and with almost entire absence of erectile tissue, fitting close to the head with the forward edge slightly inturning to the cheek, rounded at the tip. Frankly, I have never seen a Beagle *without* the ability to lift his earset upward to some degree when his attention is caught by something of interest.

One can speculate that a high-set thick ear would not be as effective a protector of the ear canal from foxtails, cockleburs, etc. But really, excessive length of ear could be a handicap in a running dog. Long ears are more apt to be torn on brush. Ears that hang down into feeding dishes will get crusted or moist, aggravating preexisting wounds that may be present. As a matter of fact, the English Foxhound puppies have their ears shortened by the hound master with a hot iron just to prevent such complications.

The expression of the Beagle is important and counts for 5 points. It should be soft and pleading, very appealing. This is produced by a large eye,

VISUALIZATION OF THE BEAGLE STANDARD

Correct Head: Planes of skull and muzzle should be parallel. Length of skull from occiput to stop should be approximately equal to length of muzzle from stop to tip of nose. Ears should be set on at a level with outer corner of eye.

Incorrect Head:

Skull too wide and flat.
Eyes small, with harsh expression.

Incorrect Head:

Muzzle too narrow, ears short.

23

HEAD

Incorrect Head:

Skull domey, stop too exaggerated.

Incorrect Head:

Flat skull, not enough lip.

Incorrect Head:

High ear set.

Incorrect Eye:

Eye too small.

Incorrect Eye:

Eye too prominent.

Color of the beagle's eyes should fit the coloration of the hound, but preferably darker rather than lighter. A yellow eye gives a harsh expression. Darkly pigmented hair around the eye (mascara) adds to the softness of the beagle's look.

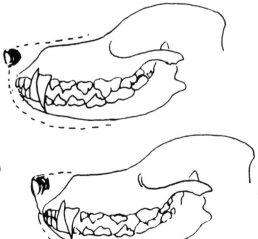

Correct Scissors Bite:

Level bite permissible.

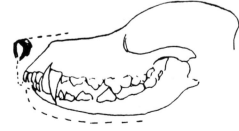

Incorrect Overshot Bite

Incorrect Undershot Bite

24

set well apart from its mate, and of a color that fits the coloration of the dog, preferably darker rather than lighter. The Standard states that the eye should be of a brown or hazel color. Color of the eye is certainly not utilitarian, but a yellow eye that looks out like a headlight produces a hard, mean look.

There is no mention of bite in the Beagle Standard, but the Foxhound Standard calls specifically for teeth that meet squarely, neither overshot nor undershot. An improper bite in the Foxhound calls for disqualification under the Standard, though not so in the Beagle.

A scissors bite is preferred, but level is acceptable. Peter Emily, D.V.M., defines scissors bite as one in which the upper central incisors (two middle teeth) overlap the facial (outside) surfaces of the two lower central incisors and a small portion of the mesial (inside) surfaces of the intermediate lateral incisors. In addition, the first upper premolar, the tooth next to the large canine on the side of the jaw, should lie behind the lower first premolar.

In the overbite the upper jaw lies forward of the lower jaw, resulting in a space between the upper and lower incisors when the jaws are closed and, in addition, a malalignment of the premolars and molars.

In the underbite the lower jaw is forward of the upper jaw, resulting in an overlap of the lower incisors in front of the upper incisors, and a shift forward in alignment of the lower premolars and molars relative to the upper.

Occasionally the position of the incisors may be a correct scissors bite, but the relationship of the remainder of the teeth is improper. This latter condition constitutes an incorrect bite.

Nose pigment should also fit the color of the dog. In a tricolored Beagle, a pink nose should be penalized. In the lemon-and-white or red-and-white, the lighter pigment is acceptable. In general, however, the darker the pigment, the better. Darker pigment is supposed to indicate more olfactory endings present.

Neck

Neck is allocated 5 points.

Common sense requires a neck of adequate length, neither giraffelike nor bull-like, of *moderate* length, strong but not thick, rising free and light from the shoulders, pliable and long enough for the nose to reach the ground for tracking without forcing the dog to crouch. Excess of skin is to be penalized, probably for practical reasons, similar to excessively long ears. The English Foxhound Standard calls for a light convexity to the curve of the neck from the occiput to the shoulder. I prefer that on the Beagle as well, rather than the straight or slightly "ewed" look.

Shoulders and Chest

Together shoulders and chest account for 15 points.

Again the English Foxhound Standard is a bit more specific when it comes to shoulder structure. In addition to the requirement that they shoulders be sloping, clean, muscular, conveying the idea of freedom of action with strength, there is specific reference to the "true arm" or humerus, that it be

NECK

Correct Length and Thickness of Neck:

Note arch below occiput.

Incorrect: Short and thick.

Incorrect:

Too slender neck, absence of slight arch below occiput.

CHEST AND SHOULDERS

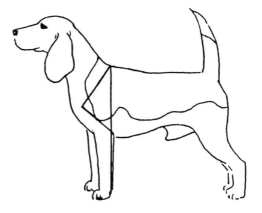

Correct Shoulder Assembly and placement of the foreleg in relation to shoulder. Note depth of chest to elbow and amount of fore-chest visible.

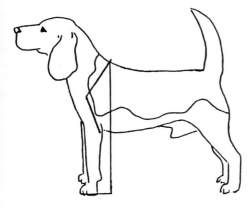

Incorrect: Placement of upper arm (humerus).

Incorrect: Shallow chest.

Correct: Clean shoulder.

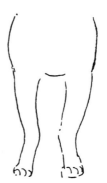

Incorrect: Crooked forelegs, heavy in shoulder.

27

long and muscular. This makes sense, for a longer bone would give a greater arc of movement in forward propulsion of the foreleg and allow for greater length of those muscles which activate the forearm.

Note once again that the shoulders should not be heavy or loaded.

The chest should be broad and deep for good lung and heart space, but not so broad that the free movement of the shoulder is interfered with.

Ribs, Back and Loin

Fifteen points are credited to these structures.

Ribs should be well sprung, again for lung capacity. A flat or slab-sided appearance is not desirable.

The back is short, muscular and strong.

Loin should be broad and slightly arched. This does *not* mean roached, nor does it refer to a low tail set, which can give the illusion of a curve over the loin due to the drop-off in front of the tail base. Muscle development along either side of the spine gives the slightly arched look when viewed from the side. Both the English Foxhound and English Beagle standards specify a *level* topline.

Running Gear

Fore- and hindquarters account for 30 more points.

Forelegs should be straight, with plenty of bone in proportion to the size of the hound, and with short straight pasterns. It stands to reason that a large circumference of bone will allow for a greater area of muscle attachment, adding to the endurance of the runner. Too much bone, as is sometimes seen in a form of dwarfism, is not only unappealing but requires extra work for the dog. Pasterns, though straight, should not "knuckle," or buckle forward.

The requirements for the rear quarters include hips and thighs that are strong and well muscled. McDowell Lyon states that this is a way of ensuring a greater length of femur, the large upper bone of the hind leg, and a hock joint set close to the ground. Moderate angulation at the stifle joint, the knee joint, is needed. Hocks are firm and symmetrical, and the hock joint, equivalent to the human heel, is moderately bent.

Feet alone count for 10 of the 30 points, emphasizing their importance. Catlike in appearance, with hard, full pads, the feet should never be spreading, flat or open at the toes. Occasionally one sees a foot with an exceptionally short toe, usually the outer one, and generally on the forefoot. This does not conform to the required "cat foot" and is generally found on feet that otherwise are nice, short toed and compact. The short toe may represent an exaggerated form in the evolution of the good foot.

Tail

The Beagle tail is a delight, short in proportion to the hound, with a nice brush giving the impression of sturdiness and strength. It should be set moder-

BACK, LOIN AND RIBS

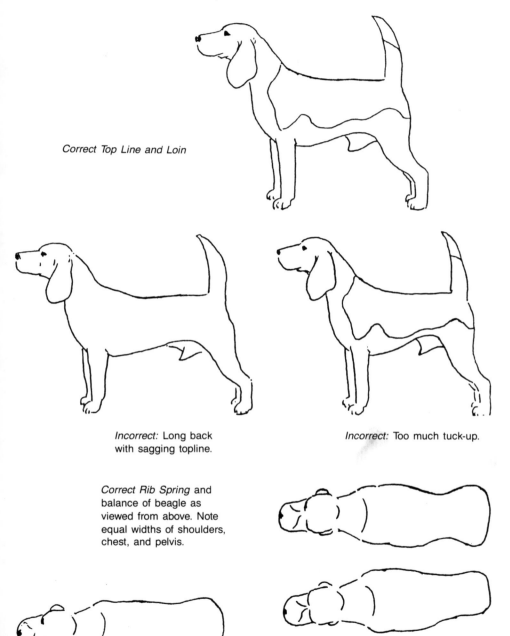

Correct Top Line and Loin

Incorrect: Long back with sagging topline.

Incorrect: Too much tuck-up.

Correct Rib Spring and balance of beagle as viewed from above. Note equal widths of shoulders, chest, and pelvis.

Incorrect: Flat ribs.

Incorrect: Width of pelvis is narrow in relation to width of chest.

FORELEGS AND FEET

Correct: Clean shoulder, straight forelegs.

Incorrect: Out at elbows, toeing in.

Incorrect: Crooked forelegs, heavy in shoulder.

Incorrect: Down at pasterns.

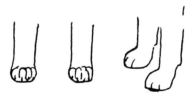

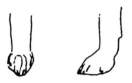

Correct Cat Foot

Incorrect Hare Foot

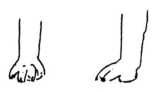

Incorrect Flat Spread Foot

Incorrect Large Foot

REAR RUNNING GEAR

   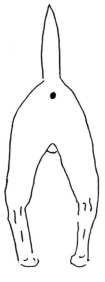

Correct Rear:

Note parallel
position of legs.

Incorrect:

Cow-hocked.

Incorrect:

Narrow rear.

Incorrect:

Bow-legged.

*Correct
Rear Angulation*

Incorrect:

Straight.

Incorrect:

Too angulated.

CORRECT BALANCE

Correct Balance: Note ratio of height to length, approximately square from tip of withers to base of tail to ground. Distance between withers and ground is equally divided by elbow and depth of chest.

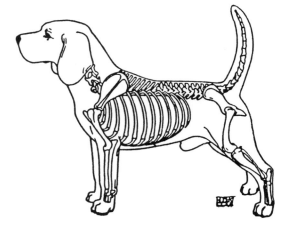

Skeletal Anatomy of the Beagle

INCORRECT BALANCE

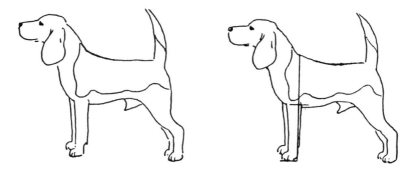

Incorrect Balance: Too high on leg. Distance between point of elbow and ground is greater than from tip of withers to elbow.

Incorrect Balance: Short on leg. Distance between point of elbow and ground is less than distance from point of elbow to tip of withers.

Incorrect: Too-short back.

Incorrect: Too-long back.

TAIL SET

Correct Tail Set and Length of Tail

Incorrect: Low tail set.
Too-long tail;
thin, with no brush.

Incorrect: Low tail set.
Gay tail.

ately high, carried up but not over and should have a very slight curve like a sickle. The tip is white (as should be the four feet of the Beagle), for this is the "flag" by which the Beagle telegraphs his whereabouts.

A too gay tail or one that is carried at half-mast is to be penalized. Five points are allotted for tail. I personally would tolerate a gay tail more happily than a "down" tail, for the Beagle is typically a merry little dog whose tail reflects his attitude toward his surroundings. Low tail sets and gay tails, unfortunately, are common.

Coat and Color

The Beagle coat (5 points) should be close, hard, of medium length, all for obvious protective reasons. A short, fine, soft coat is much easier to care for, but is not proper.

Color can be any hound color. These include black, tan and white (tri); red and white; lemon (a pale tan) and white; and blue (a tri with a bluish cast to the coat associated with a light eye color). The English Beagle Standard excludes the color liver from its acceptable list. Livers and chocolates can be shown in the field, but should be severely penalized in the conformation ring because of the associated yellow eye and pink nose pigment.

Markings can add or detract from the overall appearance of the dog, but the structural quality of the Beagle, not the arrangement of color, is the important factor. Lemon-and-white Beagles are sometimes discriminated against in the show ring, which is unfortunate. If two dogs are of equal quality, then one's personal preference as to color may play a part in the final judgment. But if the lemon-and-white is the better Beagle, he should be the winner.

The points of the Beagle—that is, the tip of the tail and the feet—should be white.

In some regions of the country it is common practice to artificially darken the back of the Beagle to give the appearance of a richly colored tricolor. Beagles that carry the lemon factor recessively will frequently "fade" as they mature, losing the black blanket that is so distinctive. These are the blankets that are sometimes "touched up." Whatever agent is used neither runs in the rain nor comes off on the hands. Until accurate tests for dyeing are available, this practice unfortunately will probably continue. It is not only against the American Kennel Club rules, but is totally unnecessary. A faded tri is an honorable color.

Size

Two varieties of Beagle are recognized: thirteen-inch and fifteen-inch. Those which measure under thirteen inches at the shoulder and those which measure between thirteen and fifteen inches are shown in separate classes. Size is the only disqualification in our Standard. The division into two sizes should be just that: the thirteen-inch should be a smaller replica of the fifteen-inch. And both should be smaller proportionate versions of the English Foxhound.

MOVEMENT

Correct: Note reach and drive.

Incorrect: Restricted reach and drive.

Correct: Note parallel placement of legs at a slow gait. Feet approach center line at fast gait.

One sometimes sees a Beagle that is only under thirteen inches by virtue of shortened legs. If it had more leg under it, in keeping with the size of the body, that Beagle would make a grand fifteen-inch! The true thirteen-inch Beagle should be in proportion.

Measurement

For a measurement with the American Kennel Club official measuring stand or the thirteen- and fifteen-inch wickets, the Beagle should be stacked on a level surface in a normal show pose. Forelegs should be perpendicular to the floor or grooming table, and the head should be held up moderately as when shown. The wicket or measuring stand is brought from *behind* the dog and placed on the *highest point of the shoulders*. Both legs of the wicket or measuring stand must touch the flat surface to indicate that the Beagle is within the acceptable height range for its variety.

Temperament

Temperament is extremely important. A courageous little dog, the Beagle should not be foolhardy. He is happy, easy to get along with. Shy or mean Beagles are problem Beagles. Tail should be up in the show ring. A down tail indicates either an unhappy or frightened Beagle.

Gait

Though not specifically mentioned in the Standard, movement is implied by the description of the running gear, shoulder and rear structure.

The Beagle works in the field at a walk, trot and gallop. While hunting the scent of the rabbit, the dog trots along with nose to the ground, circling, nosing under brush. Once the trail is found, the Beagle signals with his full-voiced cry and off he goes at a gallop in hot pursuit. Hours of hunting may be required.

In the conformation ring the hound should be viewed from the side, front and rear while moving at a *moderate* trot. There should be good reach of the front legs and good drive with the rear when viewed from the side. From the front, the forelegs should move straight toward the observer at a slow trot, with the hind legs following in the footsteps of the front. From the rear, the hocks move perpendicularly to the ground, neither too wide nor too close. As the speed of the Beagle increases to a faster trot, both front and hind feet tend to approach the center line to maintain balance. If the Beagle is moving properly, the topline should remain fairly level when viewed from the side.

Paddling (tight shoulder action that results in the dog moving as though stroking with oars), out at the elbows, high-stepping gait, hock joints turning in or out, pounding and close approximation of the hind feet are all examples of faulty movement and indicate improper structure.

Hounds at full cry.

Monroe Beagle Club, Monroe, Georgia. Cherokee trials.

Hounds & Hunting

3

Field Beagles

A MAN, his Beagle and his gun form a triad that might have well been written into the Constitution of the United States or Bill of Rights.

For the solitary hunter, it was but a natural step to join with others in organized Beagle field activities. The original pack trials based on the English tradition, in which hounds are hunted in three-, four- and eight-couple packs and judged on the merits of the pack as a whole, was and still is, to some extent, a moneyed sport.

The traditional or formal pack huntsman and his whippers-in, or assistants, dress in green jackets, white pants and black caps. Individual piping on the jackets distinguishes one pack from another. This oldest form of Beagle trials in the United States still flourishes today, with subscription packs (supported not by the huntsman alone but by interested Beaglers) joining the private packs at the Spring and Fall Trials at the National Beagle Club running grounds, Institute Farm, Aldie, Virginia.

In the early 1900s it was the individual hunters who owned at the most four Beagles and hunted, not on large estates but in their rural neighborhoods, who organized Beagle Clubs. Trials were held in which the hounds were judged individually while working in pairs by sex and size, known as "Brace Trials"—"small pack," of four to seven hounds usually, and "large pack," with as many as thirty to sixty in a class.

The number of Beagle Clubs holding field trials mushroomed in the United States and Canada, with the kind of trial run determined by the terrain and available game. The small cottontail rabbit, as well as the sand rabbit of Texas, flourishes in land with brush and covert, runs a small swing and goes

Ch. Eberle's Mickey II, fifteen inches, show champion, field winner, hare trial winner and good gun dog. He sired Ch. Thornridge Wrinkles, owned by Sam Granata.

National Beagle Club Brace Trial, 1989: "Starting Off."
Rene Chicoine

National Beagle Club Brace Trial, 1989: "Hunting."
Rene Chicoine

to ground. The swifter varying or snowshoe hare is much larger, quite intelligent, leaves a stronger scent, runs in wide swings, does not go to ground and thrives in mountainous and swampy terrain.

The Beagle that hunted cottontail, and in the trials needed to work only up to forty minutes at a time, was selectively bred over the years for less speed, more meticulous tracking ability and a very keen sense of smell. The hound run on hare required more speed and greater endurance to run for several hours at a time, and less emphasis was placed on keen scenting ability. These Beagles were bred to be larger in size and longer in limb.

The original good field-trial Beagles performed well on both kinds of game, but increasing specialization has led to two quite different-looking hounds.

With the loss of undeveloped land to growing cities and suburban development in this century, the early field trial clubs found it necessary to purchase or lease acreage for their functions. It is a requirement by the American Kennel Club that each member or recognized field trial club have its own running grounds. Fencing of the property became mandatory, to prevent the hounds from crossing heavily trafficked highways in pursuit of game. This, in turn, affected the behavior of the rabbit, requiring even more selective breeding for a slower, more painstaking Beagle.

Serious Beaglers have joined the ranks of conservationists in order to protect the land needed for wild game propagation and survival. Some clubs sponsor rabbit and hare breeding programs in an attempt to replenish the diminishing supply of rabbit and hare.

By the 1970s concern was growing among a large group of rabbit hunters that the brace Beagle was losing its ability to run and hunt. As a result, what is known as the gundog movement grew apace, leading the American Kennel Club in 1977 to license testing for gunshyness in what is known as the Small Pack Option. This system selects the best hounds of a first series of four to seven Beagles to run in a second series, the winners of which compete in the Winners Pack. During the course of the trial, a shot with blank cartridge from a 20-gauge shotgun or a .32 or larger pistol, is fired after all the Beagles are working a trail. The gundog movement now has clubs in twelve states, each with forty to fifty members. The clubs, in turn, have formed regional coalitions called federations.

A significant move in the United Beagle Gundog Federation is the requirement, as of 1987, that any Beagle competing in a qualifying trial and the National Run-off must be a dual entry in both field and conformation. A Grand Final Winner and Grand Final Runner-up awards are presented to those Beagles with the highest and second highest number of points accumulated both in field and conformation judging. Other gundog federations are considering this option as well. This represents the first organized push toward reestablishing the ideal of a proper-looking working Beagle.

ORGANIZATION

The Beagle Advisory Committee (BAC), composed of twelve members and chaired by a member of the American Kennel Club executive staff, oversees the licensing of Beagle field trials. In 1936 the National Beagle Club, inundated by the growing number of field trials, surrendered its responsibility as the parent club to license trials to the BAC. Members of the committee are appointed by the American Kennel Club from the delegates of the Beagle member clubs to the American Kennel Club. The BAC has proven to be an administrative body responsive to the changing needs of the field trial Beaglers.

FIELD TRIALS

There are three kinds of Beagle field trials: those held by member clubs, official members of the American Kennel Club; those held by nonmember clubs licensed to hold field trials; and field trials sanctioned by the American Kennel Club and held by both member and nonmember clubs. Championship points are awarded to winners of only the first two.

FIELD CHAMPIONSHIP

In order to obtain a Field Championship, a "hound of either sex must have won three first places and 120 points in classes with not less than six *starters,* an eligible hound not disqualified or measured out for the second series or winners pack in brace, small, or large pack, at licensed or member field trials" *(American Kennel Club Beagle Field Trial Rules).*

The winner of first place in each class is awarded 1 point, second place 0.5 point, third place 0.33 point and fourth place 0.25 point. An additional award of NBQ is awarded the fifth-place winner, but no points are given.

MEASUREMENT

Basically, a Beagle must be officially eligible for its class by size. Rules for when the measurement is done and by whom vary with the kind of trial procedure: Brace, Small Pack, Large Pack, or Small Pack Option. Official measurement cards attesting to under thirteen-inch or between thirteen-inch and fifteen-inch are also available under American Kennel Club regulations.

Lookout trial for field champions, 2nd series, high brace fifteen-inch champions; March 1988.
Hounds & Hunting

Lookout trial for field champions, 2nd series, high brace fifteen-inch champions; March 1988.
Hounds & Hunting

JUDGING

For Brace, Small Pack and Large Pack field trials, two judges are required. Additional judges may be needed for Large Pack trials if the number of entries is large.

As the *Beagle Field Trial Rules* state, "The Beagle is a trailing hound whose purpose is to find game, to pursue it in an energetic and decisive manner and to show determination to account for it."

Points on which the judges base their decisions are searching ability, pursuing ability, accuracy, proper use of voice, endurance, competitive spirit (only a plus when focused on running game, not beating the other hounds) and intelligence.

From each class, first through fourth place as well as a fifth place, NBQ (Next-Best Qualified), are awarded. Judging is a process of elimination, with the winners of each class competing in a second series and ultimately a Winners Pack, from which the winner in that variety is selected.

PORTRAIT OF A BRACE BEAGLER

(Based on material obtained from Mr. Bushey by Nadine Chicoine.)

Warren A. Bushey, the current National Beagle Club director representing the field membership, has always been a "gunner," hunter of rabbits with dogs. His organized Beagle activities began in 1947 with the purchase of his first purebred Beagle, a win at his first field trial and membership in his first Beagle club. Since 1949 the National Beagle Club has been his home club.

From his first breeding, a bitch, Fd. Ch. Cap Maid Margo, finished in the early 1950s. Since then he has finished nine champions, "several over those alloted to me." Four of these were homebred, five acquired. He presently owns three field champions and is working five promising young hounds.

"Bushey" breeds only his "very best bitch" and feels his most successful results come from purchasing young bitches, seven to eight months old, who have already started to run rabbits. This way he can see their style, realizing that it will change somewhat up to two years of age. New bloodlines are very important.

Recently Fd. Ch. Triple "C" Joyell, winner of the International Federation Trial in 1987 and the Southern All Field Champion Trial in 1988, has joined his kennel. Her dam, Greenfield Joy, has produced two more champions in this litter, with another on the way with one win. Joyell is the "best I have owned. I feel strongly she will be a producer of field trial hounds."

Training of his young Beagles begins at six or seven months of age. The pups are placed in a starting pen, at least an acre of enclosed hunting area stocked with rabbits, where they learn to use their noses and get the feel of hunting. At about fourteen to sixteen months the young Beagles are run individually or in a brace for another six months of training. Bringing the

Fd. Ch. Rock Creek Amy, fifteen-inch winner, Lookout trial, March 1988.

Hounds & Hunting

Fd. Ch. Triple "C" Joyell, thirteen-inch winner, Lookout trial, March 1988. Now owned by Warren Bushey.   Hounds & Hunting

Fd. Ch. Blue Amos, thirteen-inch winner, Honey Bee trial for field champions, Heartland Association, 1988.   Hounds & Hunting

Fd. Ch. Rock Creek Big Mama, fifteen-inch winner, Honey Bee trial for field champions, Heartland Association, 1988.

Hounds & Hunting

young Beagle along slowly gives the "gunner" the opportunity of selecting only his best hounds for the first field trial.

SMALL PACK OPTION BEAGLE

(Information furnished by Herman Pyrkosz, Perky's Beagles. Mr. Pyrkosz, conformation director of the United Beagle Gundog Federation, has finished seventeen field and about thirty-five conformation champions in his forty years of Beagling. His goal is to make a dual champion, not seen for many years.)

Training

The gundog not only must hunt, but cannot shy from a gunshot. Introduction to loud noises starts early for these Beagle pups, with feeding times being accompanied by loud startling sounds. The young Beagle does not go into the field until six months of age, for a younger pup too easily learns mistakes that are difficult to correct. Obedience training prepares the hound for his introduction to field work.

Training takes place in ten-acre, forty-acre and hundred-acre enclosures. The pups start working with the older, experienced pack. Once they have learned the rules, they are then worked with younger, more aggressive Beagles. After three months, both owner and trainer evaluate the Beagles. At eight months it is possible to select the best and place the others as individual hunting dogs.

With the growing emphasis on a good-looking hound, show training is part of this Beagle's early schooling, starting at five or six weeks.

Health Problems

The liver, lemon and blue Beagles seem more prone to skin allergies during the summer months. Blues are predisposed to swelling of the eyelids. The tricolored Beagles with the darker eye have fewer problems.

"Running fits," seizures resulting from low blood sugar after running, appear to run in families. Feeding a high-protein mixture before running helps maintain the needed blood-sugar level and reduces the chances of a seizure.

Skipping, or "hitching," in the rear also appears to run in families. Out of 310 Beagles observed during 1988, only 4, all littermates, hitched. Their dam was spayed when this was discovered.

Abscessed teeth, usually the premolars, can be a problem. Bruised ears and injured tails, especially those without proper brush, can occur if the Beagle is caught on brush.

Brucellosis testing is scrupulously and regularly done on these pack Beagles.

Northern Hare Beagle Club, first licensed hare club.

Fd. Ch. Sammy R, owned by Ike and Anna Carrel, original owners/publishers of *Hounds & Hunting,* was an outstanding hunter and sire during the 1940s. He was the son of Fd. Ch. Yellow Creek Sport, an impressive stud during the late 1930s.

Hounds & Hunting

47

LARGE PACK ON HARE

(Information provided by Clifford and Edna Warren and Herman Pyrkosz.)

No doubt the most exciting form of field work is done by a pack of thirty to sixty Beagles running joyously in pursuit of the large hare. These hounds run so swiftly that even a man on horseback cannot keep up. Hare hunting runs in the blood of its enthusiasts.

Organization

The Northern Hare Beagle Club of New York, established in 1916, was the first to concentrate on holding pack stakes on the snowshoe hare and the first to hold a licensed hare stakes.

Today active clubs exist in all the hare states. The ten hare clubs of Northern Michigan and the lower Michigan peninsula comprise the Northern Michigan Hare Association. This group, plus the Hare Association of the Eastern United States, which includes Maine, Vermont, New Hampshire, New York and Massachusetts, are overseen by the Federation of Large Pack on Hare.

Circuits, a series of trials given by regional clubs at the time of year best for hunting, attract many participants.

Early Bloodlines

Yellow Creek and Shady Lake: L. M. Watson's Yellow Creek line in Missouri and Harvey Low's Shady Lake Beagles in New York were two of the best-producing kennels during the 1920s and 1930s. Mr. Low's Fd. Ch. Flip of Shady Lake, a product of two conformation champions, illustrated the dual use of the Beagle of that day. Fd. Ch. Sammy R, out of Yellow Creek stock, was an outstanding producer of both field and conformation champions. Sammy R was owned by Ike and Anna Carrel, the original owners and publishers of the magazine *Hounds & Hunting.* A grandson of Sammy R's, Fd. Ch. Gray's Linesman, sired fifty field champions in the 1950s.

Both Yellow Creek and Shady Lake were tightly in-bred lines. Harvey Low, with his excellent sense of good quality, introduced new blood occasionally and always with good results. His theory was: "You don't need a special hound for hare trials, just a good hound."

At the time of Sammy R, who completed his championship in 1938, it was not unusual for a good hound to win at both rabbit and hare trials.

Northwood's Beagles: Clifford and Edna Warren of Chassel, Michigan, founders of the Northwood line, have not missed a Federation Hare Hound circuit since its inception. Both are active in the Northern Michigan Hare Association, and Mrs. Warren has served as secretary since 1983. Mr. Warren's field training began in 1938. As a matter of fact, he was present when Sammy R completed his championship.

Their foundation bitch, Fd. Ch. Northwood's Nubian Queen, was bred,

48

Fd. Ch. Flip of Shady Lake, bred by Harvey Low, was a dual-purpose Beagle from the outstanding Shady Lake line; sired over 200 field champions.

The Beagle Yearbook, *1942*

Yellow Creek Ben, a product of the famous Yellow Creek Kennels.

The Beagle Yearbook, *1945*

raised, trained and finished by the Warrens. Both her sire, Nr. Int. Fd. Ch. Northwood's Jungle Jim, and dam, Fd. Ch. Leitza's Daisy II, were outstanding hare hounds, harking back to Int. Fd. Ch. Mt. Zion Pete. Pete's sire, Fd. Ch. Dagwood's Labaan, and dam, Nr. Fd. Ch. Baronet Darkness, were also splendid hare hounds.

"I have always stayed with my original breeding program and have not just bred to every Tom, Dick and Harry willy-nilly, as some new Beaglers are wont to do," states Mr. Warren. When shipping by air was more reasonable, the Warrens shipped bitches to some of the most famous and well-bred males compatible with Northwood's breeding. One near-disastrous episode occurred when two of the Warrens' bitches, Nubian Queen and her daughter, Countess, were returning from breedings in New York. A winter snowstorm required snow-ploughing on the runway where the two bitches, in a by-then-damaged crate, waited for the last leg of the flight home. Frightened by the large, noisy equipment, the younger bitch, Countess, bolted from her crate and disappeared. Queen remained safely inside and arrived home intact. Countess, found after two days' "touring" Milwaukee, returned home none the worse for her adventure.

Fd. Ch. Northwood's Belladonna (by Fd. Ch. Tuttle's Beauchamp ex Fd. Ch. North Bend Mahogany) and Fd. Ch. Northwood's Ballerina (by Fd. Ch. Northwood's Spotty Sam ex Fd. Ch. Corullo's Belle) finished with points acquired in both the thirteen- and fifteen-inch classes. Spotty Sam's excellent pedigree includes Fd. Ch. Lakeside Snowflake and Int. Fd. Ch. Robanit's Spotty Jan.

Fd. Ch. Northwood's Nubian Flakers, a granddaughter of Nubian Queen, completed her championship in three consecutive trials—and she was the only bitch in her class!

Hare Trials

Run very differently from other kinds of field trials, Hare Trials require the Beagles to run for at least eight hours. The judges, spotted about the terrain, allow the dogs two hours of running time to find the hare's trail before beginning to judge. Throughout the day at regular intervals, two or more judges meet to compare notes, eliminating Beagles at each conference. However, all the hounds continue to run until they tire or the trial is over and the winners selected.

Training

Pups start early with training on cottontail rabbit. Once they learn line control, the ability to follow the rabbit's trail, training on hare begins. Enclosures are not used because the hare could be easily caught. A promising hare hunter will be obvious by a year of age. These Beagles' performance peaks at four or five years of age. Such physical endurance is required that the older Beagles cannot perform as well.

4

Starting and Training
a Pack of Beagles

by David B. Sharp, Jr.

(Joint Master of the Nantucket-Treweryn Beagles)

David (Bun) Sharp's Treweryn Pack was formed in 1924. He was widely recognized, in both the United States and England, as an expert huntsman. His Field Ch. Treweryn's Forger, which Bun described as "terrible looking but with a phenomenal nose," won the three-hour stakes in 1931, a win he repeated on three consecutive years. Treweryn's Bugler, a thirteen-inch male, was his most important stud. Sire of ten to twelve litters, when bred to Nantucket's Hoodwink he produced Beagles of great hunting ability and good Beagle type.

Becky Sharp, Bun's wife and Joint Master of the Nantucket-Treweryn Pack, began her pack experience in Nantucket, whipping in with some of the finest huntsmen and packs of the day. In 1926, she founded the Nantucket Pack, using as her foundation bitches two English imports, O'Berkeley Primula and Bolebroke Heiress. After their marriage, Bun and Becky competed with their packs, but then merged them in 1964 to form the remarkable Nantucket-Treweryn Pack.

Becky and Bun died in 1988 within six months of each other, both in their eighties. Their pack continues on as a subscription pack.

J.M.

I ORIGINALLY wrote most of this article over forty years ago for *Hounds & Hunting* and now try to bring it up to 1983.

At the request of the editor, I am writing my thoughts on the organizing, training and management of a pack of Beagles. These suggestions are by no means to be considered a commentary on the sport of beagling, but are merely my conclusions based on our experience over the last fifty-four years, and are given with the hope of being useful to anyone intending to start a pack. Several interesting and thoroughly exhaustive books have been published on this sport,

---

This chapter has been reprinted from *Hounds & Hunting,* November and December 1983.

The Merry Beaglers.

Treweryn Beagles, David B. Sharp, Master. Oil painting by W. West Frazier IV.

Photo by Nancy Stettinius

of which a few are: *The Art of Beagling*, by the late J. Otho Paget; *Hare Hunting and Harriers*, by H. A. Bryden; *Hints on Beagling*, by Peter Wood. I cannot recommend these books too strongly and of the three I consider *The Art of Beagling* to be the best.

Beagling, or the sport of hunting the hare with packs of small hounds or Beagles, is indeed an ancient sport predating that of foxhunting. Suffice it here to say that Nimrod, who lived 2,000 years before the birth of Christ, is credited with having hunted the hare and Xenophon, who lived 350 years B.C., was definitely known to be an enthusiastic and regular hare hunter.

There are today in England eight-four packs of foot Harriers and Beagles as against sixty-eight in 1938. In the United States there are now twenty-nine active packs of Beagles with collars registered with The National Beagle Club of America against twenty packs in 1928. Thus, we can safely say that the sport as practiced by packs is showing a healthy growth in popularity, to say nothing of the terrific increase in the number of field trials held in this country for single hounds and the number of hounds competing in these trials and bench shows. However, twenty-nine active registered packs is still a very small number for America when compared with eighty-four in England. The reason is in part that there are probably hundreds of sportsmen in this country who own and regularly hunt a pack of six or eight couples of Beagles without an organization or the formality of green coats, the color of whose collars is registered with The National Beagle Club. This article is dedicated to those who would like to perpetuate the sport in the traditional English manner as is now being done by the active registered packs in this country.

THE COUNTRY

The first point to be considered by anyone wishing to start a pack of Beagles is, where will we hunt? The type of country to be selected depends largely on the quarry to be hunted. Most sections of the United States abound with cottontail rabbits and if this is the quarry to be hunted almost any type of country will do unless it is so thickly wooded, grown up with undergrowth and filled with such deep swamps that it would be impossible to stay with your hounds when running or see much of their work. The ideal cottontail country to my mind would contain sufficient woods, clumps of undergrowth and briar patches to harbor game in bad weather and protect it from vermin, and at the same time have open fields between coverts so that the rabbits when driven would leave covert and circle, or if driven hard, would run straight away in the open to the next patch. Whether your quarry be hare or rabbit, pasture land is the best as scent always seems to lie better on grass than on plowed or barren land.

If hare, either European or Kansas Jacks, are to be hunted, a more open type of country should be selected. The more grass or pasture land the better, gently rolling but not too hilly. A hill may often be a fine place from which to view a hunt, but if too steep and your pack drives a hare straight away over several crests, you will soon wish for a new pair of legs. Always try to pick a country with as few paved roads as possible. I know of no more heartbreaking sight than to see your pack running straight towards a highway crowded with automobiles traveling at fifty-five miles an hour and not be able to get to your hounds to stop them or to get to the road to stop traffic. It is indeed a miracle that more hounds are not killed by autos considering the number of roads crossed in the average run of a hare.

Snowshoe or varying hare and swamp rabbits may also be hunted in certain sections of the country but the natural habitat of these animals does not lend itself to following your hounds closely on foot or seeing much of their work. Many excellent runs may be had on the Northern hare but not to the satisfaction of those who like to run with their hounds and watch them work closely.

After selecting your country, the next step is to make friends with the farmers and other landowners and get permission to hunt over their land. Never forget that the farmer is and must be your best friend. Without his friendship none of us could get far with our sport and there is no more annoying experience than to have a hare shot ahead of your hounds or to be loudly told to "get the hell off my place!" It is not enough to merely get permission to hunt over a farm. Always stop to see the owner or tenant before you start your day's hunt or if you run onto his land from that of a neighbor do not fail to call a greeting as you pass. If you send out a notice of the time and place of the hunts for the month, as is customary with most packs, be sure that you send one to those whose land you propose to cross and always invite them to hunt with you. You will soon find that the farmers will take a keen interest in the sport, often driving miles and bringing their whole family to see the chase. They are invaluable for protecting hares during the gunning season and I have known farmers who have issued orders that no hares are to be shot on their property as they prefer to see the "Bagles" run them.

An annual puppy show held at your kennels is a most enjoyable event to which all landowners should be asked to come. If you can get your farmers to raise some puppies for you and bring them to the show next year you will have accomplished a great good for the sport and your pack, as farm-raised hounds are far superior to those raised in a kennel. This is called putting puppies out "at walk" and should build up much interest in your pack. While on the subject of the country, it should be mentioned that great care should be exercised not to do damage to crops, fences, etc. when hunting. A field of 100 to 150 people, a frequent occurrence with many of our large packs in the East, may do considerable damage if wheat or new grass is run over when the going is soft. A broken fence or a gate thoughtlessly left open may cause livestock to get out and do terrific damage, to say nothing of the time lost by the farmer in recapturing them. Finally, do not pick a country that is already being hunted by an established pack of Beagles or Foxhounds unless you have their permission and the country is big enough for all.

Nantucket-Treweryn Hostess, by Nantucket Rover (son of Bugler and Hoodwink) ex Bolebrook Heiress (English import), was Grand Champion Beagle at Bryn Mawr Hound Show, 1973, 1975 and 1979, the last at ten years of age. *Daphne Stettinius*

Nantucket Hoodwink, foundation home-bred bitch. *William Brown*

PROBABLE EXPENSES

Having located a suitable country and learned what is necessary to keep it open to hunting, the matter of expenses should be taken up. To properly maintain a pack of Beagles with all attendant expenses such as a kennelman, a hound van, kennels, feed, insurance, veterinary services, license fee, will cost anywhere from $2500 to $5000 a year.* Few men young enough to run after Beagles or hare are so wealthy. It is then necessary to raise the money by forming a club or taking annual subscriptions to meet expenses from those who hunt with the pack. This is a very fair way of sharing expenses and several of the larger packs in the East are now operated on this basis, having over 100 subscribers.

If the kennel work is done by you or your family and/or with the help of your amateur hunt staff, this expense can be cut in half or more. To save the cost of a hound van many packs now use a small trailer.

ACQUIRING A PACK

Here the inevitable argument as to 13-inch or 15-inch hounds is bound to begin and may be carried on far into the night whenever beaglers meet. To my mind it is just as silly to argue for or against 13-inch or 15-inch Beagles as it is to perpetuate the age old argument of the quality of English Foxhounds versus American Foxhounds. Both types of Foxhounds have their good points and each is suited to a particular type of country. And so with the two conventional American sizes of Beagles. Pick hounds to suit your country. Fifteen-inch hounds being naturally faster will probably kill more hares in rough country containing much plowed ground, cornfields and fields over-grown with weeds than the 13-inch hounds. It is by far easier for the big fellows to get over rough ground. However, if your country is very hilly or you and your staff are not good cross country runners—better stick to small hounds or hunt rabbits, not hare. It is indeed poor sport to see your pack disappear over a hilltop and, gasping for breath, struggle on in their wake never seeing anything of their work until they come to a check. On a good scenting day even 13-inch hounds will run away from their field but generally a fair runner in good condition can keep them in sight. I, personally, am an advocate of the 14-inch Beagle for either hare or cottontail hunting. However, small hounds have one distinct disadvantage in that it is a great deal more difficult to obtain good looks in 13-inch hounds than it is in 15-inch hounds. If the looks of a pack is to be a primary consideration, then select the 15-inch variety.

*AUTHOR'S NOTE: The above estimate of annual expense was written years ago. Thanks to inflation it now could be doubled or even tripled, depending on whether a full-time kennelman is employed and the size of the kennel. Fifteen couples of hounds are not necessary for cottontail rabbit hunting; in fact, the National Beagle Club will register a pack of four couples and officially list a pack of five couples as a Recognized Pack.

The delight in beagling to a true hound lover is to watch hounds work and to stay long with beagling one must be a hound lover, therefore pick the size of hound to suit your legs and your country. A good plan would be to hunt with several packs both 13-inch and 15-inch the season before you start your own pack and compare results over country as nearly similar as possible to the one you plan to hunt. This will also enable you to learn how a pack should be handled in the field and to pick out hounds that are good in their work with an idea of buying them after the end of the season. Almost any large pack will sell a draft of old hounds after the season to make room for their incoming young entry. When buying hounds to start a pack, it is by far better to purchase four or five couples from one pack that are broken and used to hunting together than to pick an individual here and there and attempt to combine them into a pack.

Starting with a nucleus of, say, four couples of old steady hounds from two different packs, the balance of the pack can be made up of young hounds purchased here and there who will quickly learn what it is all about from the oldtimers. Buying hounds in the spring has the double advantage of a cheaper price from the packs who want to lighten up and providing time for pack breaking and road work before the start of the hunting season in the fall.

Concentrate on pack hounds that have been bred by a good, recognized pack for many generations—or their bloodlines. Stay away from AKC show hounds or BRACE field trial hounds. Get as much bloodline going back to the English packs as you can. Their hunting is so much better than anything in this country that there is no comparison. Over there, hounds usually meet at 12 noon and hunt hare till dark, covering miles and miles of country. They can't afford to keep a poor hound, so these are quickly eliminated. All our hounds trace to two bitches that Phil Burrows of the Bolebroke gave us years ago and we are going to stick to his line.

KENNELMAN AND KENNELS

Before acquiring a pack it is of course necessary to find someone to take care of them. Most masters of Beagles carry the horn themselves and are assisted in the field by friends who act as non-paid honorary whippers-in. The hunt staff, or those handling hounds in the field, should be good runners if hares are to be hunted. There are, however, many more important qualifications for the kennelman than being fleet of foot. First of these should be a love for hounds. An even temper, a quiet voice, cleanliness, patience and willingness to work without regard to hours are all equally important attributes of a good kennelman. Beagles are naturally rather mild creatures and will easily become shy if yelled at and beaten by a bad-tempered kennelman or one who is afraid of them. A man who has had experience with Foxhounds or another Beagle kennel and who is too old to act as huntsman should make an excellent kennelman if he has the aforesaid qualifications. This type of man would be particularly desirable if the master himself is a beginner. If a man with experience cannot be found then pick a boy or a girl who is keen about hounds and hunting and has these qualifications of character. Take him to a good kennel and let him spend a few days watching how others do things, then talk over the matter of how best to care for your own hounds and set down rules for cleaning kennels, feeding, etc. Everything should be done on a schedule with a fixed time each day for each task. An intelligent person will soon work out his own system based on his equipment and kennels. Don't employ a "grafter"—it has often been said that some stablemen and kennelmen set by a tidy sum from what they get from feed and supply stores. Your kennelman should be thoroughly honest and should be interested in seeing the pack grow and improve. Even so, the master should arrange all purchases and take away this temptation from his kennelman.

Many of the finest packs of Beagles in America are kenneled in adapted barns or chicken houses. I do not mean to say that this is ideal, but often it is perfectly possible to remodel or adapt an old building into a practical kennel at a great saving in cost. The main things to remember when building a kennel are that it should be on high ground, well lighted and ventilated, warm and dry. The kennel should face south and have lodging rooms for dogs and bitches separated by an alleyway or entry where hounds can be drawn out and fed. This will also enable visitors to see hounds in bad weather without discomfort to man or beast and provides an excellent place for brushing, doctoring and otherwise working on hounds under cover. The lodging rooms should provide wooden benches raised above a cement floor for sleeping quarters. Adjoining this would be an ideal place for a room for puppies and on the opposite side separated by a wall from the kennel should be a hospital room which can also be used for bitches while whelping or in season. Many variations of this plan have been used and these suggestions are given to those who contemplate entirely new construction. Hunting Beagles do not need artificial heat except when down with distemper or other illness and in fact they are generally hardier and healthier without it. The hospital pen should therefore adjoin the feed room or if in a separate building should have its own heating.

All lodging rooms should open onto concrete or gravel runs to which hounds should have access at all times. They will learn quickly to use these runs as toilets, which will greatly facilitate cleaning. These runs need not be large but should connect with large grass runs for daytime use.

BREEDING

This is an all important subject. The beginner should refer to some of the books mentioned in the beginning of this article and then seek advice from someone with experience. It has been said that "breeding is, at best, a gamble," which may be true, but if carefully handled the odds against your success may be greatly reduced. Good plus good will not necessarily produce good. The produce largely depends on the ancestors of "good" and "good." Breed first

Nantucket-Treweryn Pistol, thirteen inches (Nantucket-Treweryn Musket ex Nantucket-Treweryn Patsy), fine producer and Champion 13″ Dog at Bryn Mawr hound show for four years and Grand Champion of the show in 1980. Both his sire and dam go back to Bugler, and the dam goes back to Hoodwink as well. *Freudy*

for hunting ability and secondly for looks. Select for your best bitches the best sires available and never breed a hound which has an outstanding fault. A pack that does not keep young blood coming in each year will soon die out.

We practice "line breeding," by which we mean breeding a dog to a bitch that has the greatest number of the *same* hounds in each pedigree that are outstandingly good hounds both in conformation and hunting ability, *PRO-VIDED* that there is at least one outcross of a hound with completely different (unrelated) breeding in three generations. If you follow this practice and use the right stock you should end up with an excellent pack of "look-alikes" that have a stamp of their own and eventually will be known by everyone as *your* pack.

If you are lucky enough to breed the right dog to the right bitch and get a litter that is really good both in looks and work—*stay with it* and keep on breeding that pair as often as you can. Don't change your luck and shop around for a new stud dog. Many people do just this and I can't understand why. Let me give you an example. My good wife and now joint master, when she had her own pack, The Nantucket, bred her good bitch, Hoodwink, to Treweryn Bugler *four* times. The result was a pack that was first place in the eight couples class at the National Field Trials four times out of five years and placed second in the year remaining. They also won the 15-inch pack class repeatedly at the Bryn Mawr Hound Show. They were all brothers and sisters!

We do *not* believe in "inbreeding," that is sire to daughter, son to mother or brother to sister.

From the puppies weed out the babblers and those that run mute, get rid of the skirters and backtrackers. Then when your pack is running "cut off the head and tail"—i.e., cull those that are too fast or too slow for the majority. This sounds like brutal treatment but it is the only way to build up a good pack. Of course, your discarding cannot all be done in the first year or so but it must eventually be done in this manner if you are to succeed. It may break your heart to sell a hound that always leads your pack, but the fact that he always leads shows that he is too fast for his fellows and they are forced to follow him without doing their share of the work. When he is gone you will soon see an improvement in the others. The goal to shoot at is a level hunting pack, evenly sized and beautiful to look at.

Good conformation should be an important consideration in breeding as a hound with a bad shoulder or bad feet cannot run with the ease of his well made brother. Pay strict attention to this. Buy a copy of "The Beagle Standard" and study it well but pay no heed to color or markings. You will find it difficult enough to breed hounds of good conformation and good field ability without breeding for color. True are the words, "a good hound cannot be a bad color."

Your bitches should be bred so as to whelp in the early spring. The period of gestation is generally between 60 and 65 days. There is no doctor as good as "Old Sol," and puppies raised without summer sun are seldom as healthy and require twice the care if whelped in winter. Now that heat (infrared) lamps

60

are available, we usually breed in February or March so that the whelps when they leave their bed can get the full benefits of the spring sun. Be very careful in the use of heat lamps, however. We rig ours with a cord through a pulley so that they can be raised or lowered to a height sufficient to keep the floor of the bed warm, not hot. Each lamp should have a safety chain so that if the cord breaks it cannot fall in the bed. Several kennels have suffered bad fires from this cause, one losing their entire kennel and most of their hounds when a heat lamp fell in the straw.

The bitches should be specially fed on plenty of meat several weeks before due and should of course be separated from the other hounds. When the bitch becomes uneasy or starts to make a nest out of her bed someone should be in frequent attendance. No solid food should then be given, just a little warm soup. It is always best to let nature have her way first, as the majority of the bitches will have their puppies without assistance. But should she labor unduly long, a competent veterinarian should be called in. A pup too large to pass, dead, or one that has turned may well be the cause of the death of a good bitch, and someone should look at her at frequent intervals during her labor and until all the puppies are whelped, to see that all goes well. Instruments may be purchased for the extraction of dead puppies but I would suggest that the novice leave this to a veterinarian.

FEEDING

There are many prepared dog foods on the market and most of them are suitable for feeding to hounds. They require no cooking and need only to have water added, allow to soak, then feed. We purchase meat scraps, mostly bone and fat, from a local slaughterhouse, keep it in a freezer and boil a few handfuls to make a soup to pour over the commercial dog food. In the summer on Nantucket Island we use fish heads and backbone left after filleting instead of meat scraps. They love it and it makes their coats shine, but it is quite a job to pick the bones out.

© Ann Mackenzie '89

5

Breeding Obedience Beagles

by Marie Shuart and Rosalind Hall

Marie Shuart, Teloca, Reg., has been breeding Beagles for over twenty years. Among her dogs are several National Beagle Club Specialty and Sweepstakes winners. Since the 1960s she has put more than twenty-five Companion Dog titles on her dogs. She won High in Trial at the 1983 National Beagle Club Specialty, as well as Obedience Beagle of the Year for the same year.

Rosalind Hall, Sirius Beagles, has been training Beagles in obedience for over ten years. She has put five CDs, three CDXs and two UDs on her Beagles, one CD on a miniature Wirehaired Dachshund and is currently training a standard Schnauzer. She has taught basic and advanced obedience classes for the Dog Obedience Club of Hollywood, Florida, for six years, and is now working a Beagle in tracking. Her dogs have been selected to represent her club in state team competition for seven years, and have been high in Obedience rankings almost every year.

WHEN PLANNING a breeding for Obedience prospects, we would consider the same factors we consider when breeding for Conformation. The two main areas are soundness and temperament. Far too many breedings take place because two dogs have done well in Obedience. Often little consideration is given to the background of the dam and sire or whether their combined backgrounds will produce quality pups. For example, if both parents are minimally overshot, it may not pose a problem for them, but such a breeding could prove disastrous to their offspring.

STRUCTURE

Because soundness is important to the well-being of any dog, anyone who breeds dogs, for whatever purpose, would be well advised to learn as much as possible about canine structure and movement. Why do some horses have a smooth, comfortable trot and others rattle the rider's teeth even at a slow trot? Structure. And it is this structure that enables the horse to cover ground smoothly without tiring or to clear a jump effortlessly.

Why are we discussing horses? Many Obedience exhibitors do not seem to realize that their dogs are working animals just like horses. Structure can make their work easy or impossibly difficult.

Everyone knows about hip dysplasia; often, however, too little consideration is given to other important factors. Consider the dog with improper shoulder layback. In Advanced Obedience on a three-day weekend, this dog could be required to clear a jump fifteen times. Since straight shoulders do not permit it to bend its legs easily and cushion its landing, its shoulders and legs take an unbelievable amount of abuse. Eventually the dog will turn up lame or will refuse the jumps "for no apparent reason." This may explain why a dog with a leg or two in Utility is suddenly retired. Investigation may uncover a dog whose poor structure has finally caught up with it. The pain may have become so intense that it cannot continue to jump. Time and training have been wasted, and that longed-for Utility title is beyond grasp.

In order to breed for proper structure, we must understand what it is and why it is important. Many good books have been written on the subject, such as Rachel Page Elliott's *The New Dogsteps,* and they are of great value to the breeder.

Before choosing to breed, we will want to observe the movement of the potential dam and sire, both on lead at show gait and running free. If possible, we will watch them both jump. Their movement should be strong and free, without restriction. A strong rear with good drive makes the takeoff to the jump easier. A dog that skips or hops may have slipped stifles—not necessarily a crippling problem, but one that may interfere with jumping. Arthritis or spinal problems on either side of the pedigree should be identified.

In many breeds, including Beagles, "More Is Better" is the rule of the day when it comes to bone. This is certainly not true in a dog that is expected to perform athletic feats. Add heavy bone to a dog with moderately straight shoulders, and you have trouble. Instead, for the parents of our future "High in Trial" dog, let's choose a dam and sire with moderate bone, good shoulder layback and proper turn of stifle. Let's watch them move. Look for feet or hocks that turn in or out. Look for sidewinding or crabbing. Any of these factors will weaken a dog and cause it to tire more easily. Continued jumping of an unsound dog with the resultant concussion can cause complete breakdown of the dog's front assembly.

TEMPERAMENT

Now, ideally, we have found parents with proper structure. Next we will consider the other most important factor: temperament. While it is obvious that a dog that is terribly shy or easily spooked will have problems in the

Ch. Teloca Sirius Morningstar, UD, finding the scent articles that had been handled by owner-trainer.
Robin Whitelock

Ch. Teloca Sirius Honor Bright, CDX, nine years old, enjoying her leap over the broad jump.
Robin Whitelock

65

Obedience ring, other personality traits can help or hinder our star. In our opinion, the perfect temperament for an Obedience dog is one that is alert, attentive, willing to please and stout of heart.

It is easy to see how our curious, independent, lounge-lizard hounds have gotten a bad rap in the Obedience world. No, we are not referring to "working dogs," who have been bred for generations to hang on their masters' every word. However, some careful selection can improve the likelihood that our dog will pay attention and get the job done handily.

Again, observation is a key. How do the prospective parents relate to people and other animals? We would choose parents who prefer the company of humans to other canines. Many Obedience experts will not bother with a dog that will not play with people, and we consider this important. After all, aren't we going to expect these pups to play some very complicated games?

Too much submissiveness or dominance presents its own set of problems. The dog that is very submissive is not likely to stand up well to the constant correct-and-praise of Obedience training. It may also have trouble with the stress of new environments and with new people and dogs. While the dominant, and even aggressive, dog can be trained, and may end up being a good worker, getting and keeping its respect may present a real problem.

Is it possible to breed dogs that perform well in Obedience and also approximate the breed standard sufficiently to show in Conformation? We believe that it is not only possible, but highly desirable. The basic structure needed for obedience is the same that produces a dog that moves properly in the Breed ring.

The temperament desired in an Obedience dog makes for a good show dog.

The past record illustrates that it is indeed possible to show the same dogs in both Conformation and Obedience. A prime example is Mr. and Mrs. Mark Schaefer's Ch. Daisyrun Benbrae Dauntless, CDX, who completed her championship requirements and Companion Dog title at the same time. She was then shown as a champion while working on her Companion Dog Excellent title. The result? One weekend this lovely bitch, owner handled, was awarded a Hound Group Third on Saturday and a Second Place in Open A on Sunday.

In fact, training and showing in Obedience can provide the show dog with confidence and stability. We have shown several dogs in both Breed and Obedience at the same time. Ch. Teloca Pruf O' the Puddin', CD, attained his Companion Dog title while being campaigned as a champion. Ch. Teloca Honor Bright, CDX, finished her CD and championship at the same time and achieved her CDX while being specialed. And, to illustrate our position on soundness, at the age of nine, Honor still jumps her required height easily.

Ch. Teloca Sirius Morningstar, UD, TT, matured more slowly, so she got her CD while we waited for her to grow up. Then she completed her championship while we showed in Open. Margie, campaigned in Open and Utility, also scored a very respectable 72 on the American Temperament Society test to earn her TT.

66

The one-minute sit during class at an armory. If the third beagle from the right looks a little bored, it is probably because she is fourteen years old.   *Robin Whitelock*

Ch. Teloca Sirius Rhedd Butler, CD, fifteen inches, Reserve Winners Dog at the National Beagle Club Specialty, 1988. Owned by Rosalind Hall and Marie Shuart.   *Earl Graham*

Recently we have found that the care taken in breeding for stable temperament is beneficial in another field, as two Teloca Beagles have been selected to work for the United States Department of Agriculture. Ch. Teloca Jussie's Girl and Ch. Teloca Sheik Rattle And Roll have the "merry little Beagle" temperament that makes them nonthreatening to travelers as they sniff luggage for contraband food and plants. To do this important work, they must be impervious to the noises and confusion of one of the busiest airports in the United States.

Although heredity is not the only important factor in good temperament, we consider it so important that four pups from the litter of Ch. Teloca Patches Educated Guess, who is now being shown for her Novice title, have been kept or placed as Obedience prospects. The granddam of this litter, Ch. Teloca Upstage Bann'd in Boston, CD, was number-three Beagle in Obedience rankings and number-three thirteen-inch Beagle in Conformation at the same time. The number of CD titles in this pedigree, as well as the temperament of the parents, lead us to expect these pups to have the aptitude for Obedience training.

TRAINING

What will we do with these pups now? We do not begin formal Obedience training with very young puppies. However, there are many games and activities that we can enjoy with them that will enhance their later training. Teaching a pup to fetch a favorite toy or to come to you for a treat or a pat are good starters. Any game that will cause the pup to focus its attention on you will help it to learn to concentrate on your commands later. We feel that the more of this type of human attention that a pup receives at a young age, the easier its training is later.

Playing, however, is definitely for puppies. When we begin our formal training, we do not play or use food as a training method. Basically, we use a correction-and-praise method of training. There are many good Obedience-training books on the market, and many of the authors present seminars in which they explain their methods and work with handlers and their dogs. We have found these seminars very useful in our own work and we are constantly searching for new and better ways to train.

Before adopting any training method, you should understand it thoroughly. For a method to work well, you must adapt it both to your dog and to your philosophy of training. Any method is more likely to be successful if it suits your personality and you feel comfortable with it.

It is, however, extremely important, whatever method is used, that the trainer assume an unquestioned position as "pack leader." Our little hounds are very quick to take advantage of anyone they perceive as an "easy mark." We are patient when teaching a new exercise. But once the dog knows what is being asked of it, a quick collar correction is given if it fails to respond to a command. Every correction is followed with praise so the dog will know we

Ch. Daisyrun Benbrae Dauntless, CDX, fifteen inches, BV, National Beagle Club Specialty, 1987 (Ch. Teloca Patches Littl' Dickens ex Ch. Fairmont On Golden Pond), owned by Mr. and Mrs. Mark Schaefer.   *John Ashbey*

P. J. and handler at work at the San Francisco International Airport for the U.S. Department of Agriculture.

Ch. Jana Malia, CDX, thirteen inches, high-scoring Hound in Trial, Santa Clara Valley Kennel Club, 1978 (Ch. Jet's Gremlin of Starcrest ex Jana Ellie Belle), owned by Mary Powell and Trudi Reveira.   *Bill Francis*

Ch. Teloca Lacoste Color Me Red, CD, fifteen inches, High in Trial at the 1983 National Beagle Club Specialty with owner-trainer Marie Shuart and Judge Judy Brown.

are pleased with it for finally obeying our command. Losing one's temper or using nagging corrections bring out spite and stubbornness in most dogs, especially hounds. Consistency and praise usually produce happy, dependable workers.

WHAT OBEDIENCE OFFERS

Obedience training and exhibiting offer an avenue of accomplishment and companionship with our dogs. The American Kennel Club has structured this activity so it is available to everyone, whether the goal is a Companion Dog title on a retired show dog or a Utility Degree with class wins and High in Trials.

Admittedly, it may be difficult to train a Beagle for the quality of performance that is needed to achieve the high scores required for placements. However, the degree of difficulty is matched only by the feeling of pride and satisfaction when, having placed in a difficult class, you are standing out front with your Beagle among the "obedience" breeds.

Of course, there are pitfalls. Training for excellence can produce an intensity that takes all the fun out of exhibiting. And our little hounds seem to sense this. It leads to severe cases of canine amnesia, during which a UD Beagle forgets what the word "heel" means. Or, being natural clowns, they may resort to comedy and create new and clever ways of performing the exercises. One of our dogs left the ring and climbed into a friendly lap ringside, where she doubtlessly felt she would find sympathy.

We do strive for the best possible performance that each dog is capable of on a particular day, but we try to do that maintaining our sense of humor and our knowledge that whatever our dog might do has probably been done before.

For most of us, the championship title is the end to a dog's conformation career. While we may go on to breed our champion, he is basically retired. Obedience training and exhibiting can add continued years of companionship and enjoyment for both dog and master.

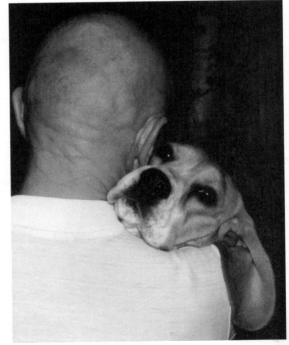

Starcrest's Mr. Tee, fifteen inches (Ch. Fresca's Tab of Starcrest ex Ch. Page Mill Billie J. O'Starcrest), owned by Herman J. Mueller.

72

6

The Beagle as a Pet

BEAGLES are not for everyone—but almost.

Not only the personality, but the packaging of this little scent hound makes it an ideal breed as a house companion. The only thing better than one Beagle is two!

PERSONALITY

Friendly, outgoing and into everything as a young dog, the Beagle matures into an affectionate and active adult. The combination of the gentle, pleading expression with an enormous curiosity is comical. Beagles are natural clowns. It is hard to be downhearted with a Beagle around.

Unfortunately, many of the qualities that make the Beagle an ideal companion also make it an ideal experimental animal. Beagle colonies in veterinary research centers abound. The hound's general docility, eagerness to please, lack of aggressive response to handling, adaptability to people and other dogs and sturdiness of health are characteristics of the breed.

Unlike some breeds that bond to one family member, Beagles bond to all, especially children. Kids smell good, play and run, all aspects a Beagle loves. Friendly almost to a fault, the Beagle is not a dependent dog. There is always "important business" that the Beagle must attend to—checking the yard to see what interesting smells may have developed overnight, inspecting the kitchen refrigerator when the door is open to determine what good things there might be there, finding out who that *is* on the other side of the fence.

73

Herman Mueller's "pack," all house dogs, fifteen inches. *Left to right:* Colegren's Great Expectations (Ch. Hickorynut's Hangman ex Dutchamity's Corry Craigwood); Ch. Starcrest's Duke of Castile (Ch. Starcrest's Apollo ex Petite Sarah of Sun Valley); Colegren's Royal Destiny (Ch. Colegren's Duke Devil ex Ch. Pickadilly Pin-Up of Colegren, TD); and Starcrest's Gold Doubloon (Ch. Page Mill on the Road Again ex Ch. Starcrest Pirate Treasure).

Am./Can. Ch. Foyscroft Wild Goose, Am./Can./Bda. CDX, Am./Can./Bda. TD (Ch. King's Creek Triple Threat ex Ch. Pixshire's One and Only), owned by Linda A. Forrest.

Linda Forrest

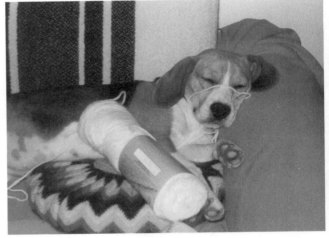

"Who gets the lap?"

Some Beagles dig and climb. Some bark. They may appear stubborn. Their sense of smell is so keen that when it is focused in on an interesting trail, repeated attempts to get their attention may be necessary. They will roam if not properly fenced.

PHYSICAL CHARACTERISTICS

The Beagle is a short-haired, small- to medium-sized scent hound. Adult thirteen-inchers weigh between thirteen and twenty pounds, fifteens up to twenty-eight pounds. Shedding does occur, particularly in the spring.

Its gentle look with the face framed by long ears gives it a very appealing demeanor and a perpetual puppy expression. People are always asking about your white-faced, dark-eyed fourteen-year-old: "How old is your puppy?"

A BAD HABIT

Probably the most unpleasant habit a Beagle has is the result of its ability to eat anything and everything. Stool-eating occurs commonly, particularly with several Beagles in a household. Occasionally a single Beagle will recycle its own droppings.

There are more hypotheses regarding possible causes than there are cures. Reasons listed range from boredom through nutritional deficiencies. My guess is that they simply like it. Not all Beagles recycle, but a significant number do.

Bad breath, ingestion of parasites and weight gain can result.

Efforts to combat coprophagia, a fancy term for stool-eating, include picking up immediately after defecation; placing an unpleasant-tasting additive, such as Adolph's Meat Tenderizer, on the stool prior to attempted ingestion; adding a multivitamin, garlic or enzyme obtained from your veterinarian to the daily ration that makes the stool unpalatable.

Good luck!

Trailer, Beagle belonging to General Rowett, 1880.
Prentice, The Beagle in America and England

Frank Forest, an important early American stud.

Windholme's Robino II, a famous early American Beagle.

7

The Conformation Beagle

IN THE LATE 1870s American shows included classes for Beagles. The breed grew in popularity, and with the importation of stock from English packs, quality improved.

The import of Warrior and Sam by Charles Turner, Dolly by J. M. Dodge and Ringwood by Norman Elmore added the much-needed new blood to produce the outstanding Rowett line. These Beagles have been described as black, tan and white in color with good bone and cobby balance. When General Rowett died, his dogs were incorporated into the breeding programs of Pottinger Dorsey of New Market, Maryland, and C. Staley Doub of Frederick, Maryland. Both men were highly respected for their knowledge and integrity. It was said that Mr. Doub never charged a stud fee, never sold a dog and never killed a rabbit!

The Rowett strain was incorporated into the breeding stock of many other lines during the 1880s and 1890s. Hiram Card's Blue Cap strain (descended from Captain William Assheton's imported utility stock) combined with the Rowett type of Beagle to produce hounds noted for their excellence in the field, having particularly keen noses and good voices. Mr. Card's preference was for the blue ticked or mottled color, feeling this was the proper hound color.

Edward Marshall of Dowagiac, Michigan, used his Rowett strain to produce his Middletown hounds, known for their clean necks and shoulders.

Mr. Dodge's Rattler (by Mr. Turner's imported Warrior ex General Rowett's Rosey) had an impressive show record, never failing to take first place. Belle (by Darwin ex Millay), his kennel companion, had three firsts to her credit.

In 1884, the same year the American-English Beagle Club established the first Beagle Standard, Dr. L. H. Twaddell imported Bannerman for Lewis Sloan of Philadelphia. A small hound, Bannerman came from a pack of smaller Beagles and was used by many to reduce size. Unfortunately, he had a "defective" head and tended to produce puppies with a preponderance of white, so he was not used as much as some of the other top studs of the day.

Chimer, an import of Mr. Diffendoeffer of Pennsylvania, was used extensively with bitches of the Rowett line, along with Mr. Elmore's hounds. Two of the top show winners of that time, Fashion and Ch. Robino II, were grandsons of this dog.

Heated debate over what constituted a proper Beagle flourished in the press of the 1880s. *Forest and Stream* and *American Field* published letters (most authors signing themselves as "Zim," "Briar," "Rusticus," etc.) in which size, dwarfism, long backs, cobby backs, bench versus field Beagle, pedigrees, color, the quality of American Beagles over the English, styles of hunting, etc., were discussed endlessly. And good heavens, there was even a reference to the famous imported Ch. Ringwood that described him as a caricature of a Bloodhound!

As you can readily see, heated debate has long been a part of the Beagle world.

The ongoing derogation of the "bench" type Beagle by the field men led James Kernochan, owner of Hempstead Beagles, to import hounds from English hunting packs in 1896, Beagles that conformed in type to the American standard. This was another effort to produce a Beagle that was excellent in both field and bench. It proved highly successful with progeny performing well in both.

With the establishment of the National Beagle Club of America, it became a tradition "that bench show is held during the fortnight of the trials, generally on a Sunday, to which the countryside is invited and entertained at lunch" (Eugene Lentilhon, *Forty Years Beagling in the United States,* [New York: E. P. Dutton and Company, 1921]). The first National Beagle Club Specialty show was held in 1891 in conjunction with the club's second meeting. This event continued for several years thereafter.

In 1898 Mr. Kernochan held a puppy show for Beagles in his neighborhood. An English custom, this endeavor failed to continue after the first match.

Portions of a wonderful letter from George Reed (breeder of Frank Forest, an outstanding sire of his day) to Staley Doub after the New York show of 1897 follow:

> Now Post asked for dogs for Special No. 1. In comes Thornwood, Truman, Hector, Florist, Ring Leader, Roy K and Frank Forest. Ringleader had already

Western Beagle Club Specialty show, 1919.

beat Frank and Roy K, Lonely II, Oronsay Matron and old Champion Lonely, and the fun went on. Now, boys, I was ready for this procession. I was with Harker five minutes before they were called, and Old Bill (William Saxby) was to come to the bench when they wanted him and let me know.

I had the rough hair on his shoulder flat the rest of the body and coat I let alone. I took off his collar and put on a small but firm fish line, as I have noticed a collar presses the skin back, making his shoulders look loaded. You could not see the cord. It was under the hair, and I snapped a chain on the cord; so here we all go around the ring for ten minutes. Lonely II bothered Harker, as he could smell her as she was in heat.

The first ones to go into the corner were Hector, Frank, Roy K, Truman, then old Lonely, then Thornwood and Robino, then Matron. This left Ringleader, Florist and Harker. Then dear old Pard, I needed all my nerve, for I could hear and feel my heart beat. Post ordered us to the bench in the middle of the ring. First Harker on the left, then Florist and Ringleader, then I reached down and unsnapped the chain from the cord and dear old Harker stood like a statue, legs well under him, brush carried gaily.

First Post looked Ringleader over, then Florist, then he told the great Joe Lewis with his great Ringleader to take Ringleader to the corner with the rest. Staley, I did not dare look up or away from Harker for fear I would smile. Now he takes Harker and the dear old boy stood up like a major. I snapped the chain on the collar and gave him a run across the ring to show his motion and back on the bench, and boys, I done my level best. I drew my hand down over the fore leg to the feet, for I knew if Post looked at his feet I could beat Florist there. I had a small piece of Vermont horse (hoof) in my hand and Harker knew it was there.

At last Mr. Post awarded me the ribbon enclosed in this letter, and it was over. My hand trembles now to think of it. The feat had been accomplished. Harker had won over the four cracks, Ringleader, Lonely, Frank Forest and Roy K. All the boys clapped their hands; the first to congratulate me by shaking hands was Mr. Kernochan, and on leaving the ring, I raised my hat to the bunch. It took me some time to put on his collar for tears were running like the devil, boys, and I felt good. Staley, you say you boys felt good. Do you think you can imagine my feelings? No, I know you can't half. Think what I had been through since I saw Harker was in the wrong class. I had made this victory for my dear Maryland friends, not for myself, and dear old Maryland friends, if it has given you boys any pleasure I am glad, for first among my heart friends are you boys.*

George B. Post, Jr., the judge of the day, was one of the early and successful exhibitors of Beagles. His stock, too, was of Rowett breeding.

Initially classes were divided by varieties, but first-place class winners, both fifteen-inch and thirteen-inch, competed for Winners awards and points toward championship. The entries in thirteen-inch were small, for generally the larger Beagle was awarded the points. It was not until 1928 that Beagles were shown in two totally separate varieties and points awarded to both.

From the early 1900s to the 1920s shows were dominated by entries from

*H. W. Prentice, *The Beagle in America and England* (1920).

80

Ch. Meadowlark Draftsman, sire of both field and show champions.
Hounds & Hunting, *July 1938*

Four generations of Kinsman Beagles. *Left to right:* Ch. Kinsman Little Merryman, Int. Ch. Kinsman Jimmy Valentine, Int. Ch. Travis Court Terwillegar and Int. Ch. Kinsman High Jinks.

Ch. Craftsman of Walnut Hall, fifteen inches, owned by Mrs. Harkness Edwards.
The Beagle Yearbook, *1942*

81

outstanding packs of the day: Windholme, Rockridge, Sir Sister, Waldingfield, Wolver, Somerset and Wheatley. Ch. Windholme's Bangle, a fifteen-inch bitch, captured the first Beagle Best in Show at the Ladies Kennel Association of America, held at Madison Square Garden, New York, in December 1901.

The 1940/1950s saw the rise of Kinsman (Lee Wade); Sogo (Clinton Callahan); Liseter (Mrs. A. du Pont); C.S. (Charles Schultze); Johnson's (Ed Johnson); Forest (Ed Jenner); Johjean (Mr. and Mrs. John Refieuna); Validay (Mr. and Mrs. Val Davies); Jacobi; White Acres (Margaret White); Meado-Glo (Elsie Johnson); and Ralph's (Donald Ralph). Pedigrees of the dogs of that day contain names of pack and field dogs, and many were dual-purpose hounds. Ch. Duke Sinatra and Ch. Thornridge Wrinkles are two of the most widely known dogs of that period. Meado-Glo, Ralph's, Validay and White Acres are kennels that continue to breed and exhibit at present.

The years since the early 1960s have seen a veritable explosion in the number of conformation Beagle breeders throughout the United States and Canada as interest in the breed has increased. Based on some of the lines that were prominent during earlier decades, breeders who have carried out more extensive breeding programs include Alpha-Centauri, Buglair, Busch's, Chardon, Colegren, Elsy's, Felty's, Foyscroft, Fulmont, Junior's, Kings Creek, Lanbur, Meadowcrest, Merry Song, Navan's, Page Mill, Pickadilly, Pine Lane, Pin Oaks, Pixshire, Plain & Fancy, Starbuck, Starcrest, Sun Valley, Sure Luv, Swan Lake, Tarr Hill, Teloca, The Whim's, Wagon Wheels, Wilkeep, Wright-Eager and Yaupon Row. Many of these breeders are active today.

Other breeders, although with limited breeding programs, have had an influence on the breed. These include Beagle Chase, Birchwood, Brantwood, Buttonwood, Chrisette, Daf-i-Dale, Daisyrun, Densom, Dismal Creek, Downey, Englandale, Gar-Rene, Graadtre, Hare Hollow, Hayday, Hemlock, Hollypines, Jabrwoki, Jam's, Jo-Lee, Just-Wright, Kamelot, Lacoste, Lee's, Lohenbru, Nieland, Pacific, Perky's, Powviera, O'Boy, Rancho Glen, R.D.'s, Rowdy's, Saga, Shaw's, Southspring, Stonebridge, Tanbark, Terwillegar, The Tavern's, Whiskey Creek, Whisper, Windy-roc and Yarra-belle.

Four of the registered Beagle packs—Bedlam, Glenbarr, Sandilly and Sir Sister—have performed both in the field and in the show ring with success.

In the last twenty years many Beagles have achieved recognition in the all-breed Best in Show ring. Some of them are Ch. Starbuck's Hang 'Em High (David and Linda Hiltz); Ch. Kings Creek Triple Threat (Marcia and Tom Foy); Ch. The Whim's Buckeye (Dr. and Mrs. A. C. Musladin); Ch. Busch's Nuts to You of Brendons (Mr. and Mrs. Bill Busch); Ch. Teloca Patches Littl' Dickens (Wade Burns, Jon Woodring and Marie Shuart); and Ch. Navan's Triple Trouble Rick (Virginia Flowers). All were multiple Best in Show winners. More recently, during the late 1980s, Ch. Keith's Wilkeep Nicodemus (Barbara Cosgrove) and Ch. Page Mill Upset the Applecart (Greta Haag) have been garnering Bests in Show in various parts of the country. The number of shows has proliferated markedly, and combined with the ease of air transportation, it is is quite probable that previous records for winning Beagles will continue to be broken.

Head study of Ch. Duke Sinatra, fifteen inches, BIS beagle of the late 1940s, owned by Mrs. R. G. Hess.

Ch. Validay Artist, thirteen-inch winner of the 1940s (Ch. Jubilee Gay Cinder ex Ch. Validay First Lady), owned by Validay Beagles.

Ch. Wandering Wind, fifteen-inch BIS Beagle in the 1960s (Ch. Page Mill Whirlwind ex Ch. Wandering Sue), owned variously by Arthur and Carroll Gordon and A. C. Musladin.

As you can see by the number of conformation Beagle kennel names, there has been a definite shift away from large, wealthy kennels dominating the shows to a myriad of small breeding programs. From the 1880s to the 1940s, and even into the early 1950s, Beagles competed in the field and in the Conformation ring concurrently. Now, in the 1980s, most conformation Beagles have never even seen a rabbit, much less run one. Many of the current breeders live in or close to metropolitan areas. Kennel facilities range from separate small buildings equipped with runs through basement housing for the dogs and even to the small operation handled within the main residence itself. Breeding for nose, voice and tracking skills has been replaced by breeding for looks and disposition.

With limited space, selection of stock retained has to be made early. Breedings, perforce, are limited. But it does mean test breeding takes a back seat to breedings for good show prospects. Reliable information about genetic and temperament problems has never been more important.

Conditioning your Beagle takes place, not in the field, but in the backyard, school grounds after hours, city parks or behind a bicycle or jogger.

Beagle clubs sponsoring specialties come and go. Though licensed field trial clubs number in the hundreds, AKC-licensed clubs holding annual conformation specialties now number seven: Blossom Valley Beagle Club, San Jose, California; National Beagle Club, the parent club; Phoenix Arizona Beagle Club, Phoenix, Arizona; San Jacinto Beagle Club, Pasadena, Texas; Southern California Beagle Club, Los Angeles area, California; Wisconsin Beagle Club, Ft. Atkinson, Wisconsin; and the Southern New York Beagle Club, held with the Westchester Kennel Club show. In the last ten years four long-existing clubs—Bay State, Chicago, Northern California and San Joaquin Beaglers—have either disbanded or dropped their annual specialties.

All of the above clubs, with the exception of the Blossom Valley Beagle Club, hold licensed field trials. With many, the annual specialty show has been a long-established tradition. With others, Southern New York and San Jacinto, a small nucleus of conformation Beaglers joined receptive field trial clubs to hold licensed Plan B and A Matches required by the AKC before permission was granted to hold an annual specialty show. Several attempts have been made by groups in New Mexico, Georgia and Ohio to form clubs, but AKC policy encourages collaboration with already-existing field trial clubs. Not every field trial club wants to be bothered. Fortunately, there are some. Great Lakes Beagle Club, with running grounds and clubhouse near Flint, Michigan, enthusiastically sponsored a successful Plan B Match in 1987 and a Plan A Match in 1988. Next comes its first Beagle specialty show.

It can be done!

CONFORMATION SHOWS

Each year hundreds of AKC-licensed all-breed shows are held throughout the country. Conformation classes are offered for each of the breeds. To

Ch. Page Mill Trademark, thirteen-inch BIS beagle during the 1960s (Ch. Page Mill Whirlwind ex Ch. White Acres Lady Slipper), owned by Arthur and Carroll Gordon. *Ludwig*

Ch. O'Boy's The Barrister, fifteen inches, Specialty winner and BV, American Kennel Club Centennial dog show (Ch. Kamelot's Playboy ex Ch. Validay Diamond Lil), owned by Janet E. Wolfley. *Fox/Cook*

obtain a Conformation Championship Certificate, a dog must win a total of fifteen points, including two major wins (three to five points each) under two different judges. The point scale is determined regionally by the number of dogs defeated, a number that varies in different parts of the country, based on the previous year's entry for the breed in that region.

Classes at the shows are divided by sex, age and special categories, with six months being the age of eligibility. In Beagles there is also a division into two varieties, under thirteen inches at the shoulder and between thirteen and fifteen inches. Currently the Winners Dog and Winners Bitch (best of the class entry for sex) compete in the Specials Class, along with champions, for Best of Variety. The two variety winners then are eligible to compete in the Hound Group. Winner of the Hound Group competes against the other six Group winners for Best in Show.

A Specialty show is a Conformation show for one breed only. The same AKC rules apply here as well. Here the two variety winners compete against each other for Best of Breed award (unless the Specialty is held as regular classes at an all-breed show).

WHERE DO YOU START?

Most of us began with just an "ordinary" Beagle. Each breed has its own particular characteristics and appeal. Beagles are not everyone's dish of tea. For those, however, who come to love the breed, it is a natural step to look at other Beagles. Local dog shows provide an opportunity to see Beagles from different lines and to meet various breeders.

Once the decision is made to obtain a good Conformation prospect, here are some tips:

What to Look For

For me, the most important quality to look for is temperament. A good conformation Beagle will be outgoing, friendly and will have a "look at me" attitude. In addition, you will want a nonaggressive hound that will get along with other dogs as well as people. Usually, the dominant Beagle of the pack makes the best showman. Attitude in the show ring makes all the difference in the world. However, long after the show and breeding days are over, you will want a Beagle with which you can enjoy living.

Second in importance is type. The hound must *look like a Beagle.* Many lines present good Beagle type and yet may have slight differences. Within good Beagle type, there are many "looks" from which to choose. This is a strictly personal choice. A good linebred or inbred breeding generally gives you more predictable get than an outcross.

How to Find Your Beagle

Read. Read the Beagle Standard (chapter 2) and as many books about the breed as are readily available. What you need is good general information

Am./Can. Ch. Merry Song's Uppity Ms, fifteen-inch multiple BIS, Group and Specialty winner, as well as winner of the National Beagle Club Specialty, 1982; a top producing dam, 1983 (Am./Can. Ch. Starbuck's Hang 'Em High ex Ch. Sun Valley's Honey Bear). *Ludwig*

Ch. Validay Merry Monarch, fifteen inches, National Beagle Club Specialty Best of Breed, 1971, and top producer (Ch. Johnson's Fancy Boots ex Ch. Validay Queen of Hearts), owned by Validay Beagles. *Ludwig*

about Beagles. Look at as many pictures of Beagles, old and current, as you can get your hands on. Your local kennel club has a list of Beagle breeders within your area, and the National Beagle Club has a list of Beagle breeders by region that it provides upon request. (For names and addresses of current club secretaries write to the American Kennel Club, 51 Madison Avenue, New York, NY 10010.) Visit as many breeders as possible, and write to those out of your area. Ask questions! Look at pedigrees. Somewhere in all this, one or two lines will appeal to you more than the others.

You need to inquire about the whelping history, health and genetics of the Beagle families you are considering. Whelping histories are important. Usually fifteen-inch bitches have a greater percentage of normal deliveries than do the 13-inch bitches, but not always. It is not the overall size of the bitch, but the size of the bony pelvic outlet that is the critical factor. So ask about the frequency of Caesarean sections in the line.

Ask how long you can expect the dog to live; what health problems are encountered as the dog grows older; what is the incidence of epilepsy, dry eye, hypothyroidism.

Should you choose a dog or a bitch? Obviously no breeding program is launched without a good foundation bitch. The purchase of a good dog as your first conformation Beagle, however, can provide you with much-needed experi-ence in training, grooming and handling. A novice Beagle with a novice owner will likely require more time to complete its championship. But this time in the show ring provides opportunities to watch and learn.

If you are limited in the number of Beagles you have room for in the first few years, a bitch would be the better choice with which to begin. Either way, dog or bitch, most likely you will acquire a second within two to three years.

Once the decision is made to breed a line of your own, a plan is essential. Revisions in that plan will most likely occur as circumstances dictate. An eagerly awaited outcross litter uncovers a new genetic problem or that special stud dog suddenly becomes sterile. But the goal of a good breeding program (the production of good-natured, sound Beagles of good type) does not change, only the route to that goal.

KENNEL FACILITIES

Home sweet home—most of us begin with a house built for people. The Beagles come later. It certainly is possible to operate a small breeding program within your home, but local animal regulations, proximity and type of neigh-bors and your own ability to care for and supervise your Beagles are important considerations.

A Beagle raised in the house makes for the best temperament develop-ment and training. Though eager to please its human friends, the hound can't learn the house rules by being relegated to the "back forty." Adjustable gates for doorways or pass-throughs save many a repainting job and provide the

Ch. Page Mill Upset the Applecart, fifteen inches, multiple BIS and Specialty winner, and winner of the National Beagle Club specialty, 1988 (Ch. Page Mill On the Road Again ex Tarr Hill Love Me Tender), owned by Greta Haag.

Cott/Daigle

Ch. Meadow Crest's Fireside Chap, fifteen inches, multiple BIS and winner (Am./Can. Ch. Teloca Patches Littl' Dickens ex Am./Can. Ch. Starbuck's Meadow Song), owned by Annette M. Didier.

Booth

Beagle puppy with a view of the household without risk of accident. Crate training, a safe, enclosed indoor area (kitchen, laundry room, etc.) and an adequate outdoor exercise yard are essentials.

Gardens do not make good exercise yards for Beagles. Easy access to pesticides, snail bait and toxic plants leads to dangerously ill animals. Not to mention what the Beagle does to your garden! Excavating to China is marvelous fun for the puppy but not for the hardworking gardener. A fenced run with access to an enclosed area within the garage works beautifully. Beagles can be climbers and diggers, so fences need to be at least six feet high and buried deep into the ground. Laying chicken wire, bent to a right angle, with the vertical portion attached to the bottom of the fence and the horizontal section extending below the ground into the exercise area for three or four feet should defeat even the most enterprising of excavators. The surface of the yard needs to be of material that can be easily cleaned and disinfected. Concrete or certain types of flat rock work well. Unfortunately, some Beagles are inveterate gravel-grazers, so a footing of pea gravel should be avoided.

Of course, provisions for shade, shelter and plenty of cool water are mandatory.

Whatever system you work out, the climate and kind of house will determine what works best. Some homes have large basements that serve well in cold winter weather. But remember, Beagles who live in basements are deprived of sunlight, fresh air and opportunities to learn about new sights, smells, sounds and people. Also, the logistics of disinfecting and cleaning basement kennels can be difficult.

When whelping a litter, an additional, different kind of space is needed. The best setup I've seen was built by Louise and Bob Merrill of Starcrest Beagles. Just off the family room and kitchen is a large room with vinyl flooring, two separate whelping areas, one enclosed area for small pups just weaned, an adjoining bath and sink, shelves, cupboards and access to a covered screen porch with a concrete floor. This latter area is perfect for the eight- to twenty-week-olders who require constant cleanup in the context of house living. The pups visit in the family room and kitchen, but are easily returned to their own quarters for safekeeping.

Seldom mentioned is the fact that the people living in your home need to have some living space without dogs if they so wish. Not all of your friends love to sit down to dinner with either one or several hungry hounds.

If I only had a kennel. . . . Kennel facilities certainly make life easier. There is one problem. Because Beagles are pack dogs and get along well with one another, it is far too easy to keep more hounds than is sensible. The population seems to expand to fill the available space. How many breeding kennels have you visited with an empty run or two?

What works best in respect to kennels will depend upon where you live and the climate.

Neighbors close enough to be disturbed by Beagles barking at night

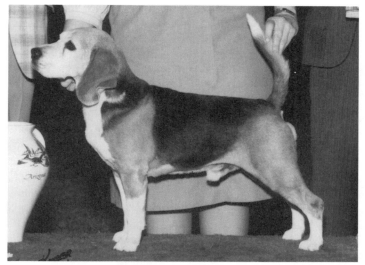

Ch. Dismal Creek's Damon, CDX, fifteen inches, is a Specialty winner from the Veterans class (Ch. Buglair Super Star, CD, ex Ch. Jingle Belle of Jamar, CDX). His show career spanned a decade in both Conformation and Obedience with ranking in the Top Ten Beagles. He is owned by Patricia Seifried.

Ch. Pin Oak's Ruffles N' Ridges, fifteen inches, BIS winner (Ch. Kurilko's JoJo's Jason ex Ch. Hearthside Lovely Talisman), owned by J. Ralph Alderfer.

Pierre Wibaut

means the construction of a relatively soundproof kennel. Ideally, there should be plenty of light, air, exposure to everyday noises and lots of human activity. Concrete floors make for easy cleanup. Pass-throughs between inside and outside runs can be equipped with flap doors or guillotine doors.

Runs should be separated by one-and-one-half-foot concrete walls topped by fencing. Some Beagles, bosom buddies when together, do fence-fight when separated. The concrete base wall protects feet and ears from being snagged and torn at such times. In addition, one run's occupants are not able to urinate on their neighbors' homes. Another nicety is the presence of a similar wall along the kennel hallway. Though it does mean stepping over it to get in and out of the runs, it eliminates "watering" the hall.

When it comes to fencing materials, we prefer a good grade of wire fencing where the wires run vertically and horizontally. Though chain link is wonderfully durable, its diagonal pattern produces a narrow angle where beagle toenails can easily get caught and torn off.

The outside runs should be partially roofed for shelter and shade, and a raised sleeping pad of wood or heavy plastic provided. At least one or two completely covered runs are useful for bitches in season or to prevent the occasional climber from visiting adjacent runs.

Sleeping quarters pose somewhat of a problem. Many Beagles mark their sleeping areas by urinating on them. Some breeders use a box containing cedar shavings or hay, which can be replaced. Sleeping areas should be raised from the concrete flooring, facilitating cleaning. We and our Beagles are great enthusiasts for double-strength cardboard banana boxes, which are placed on wooden platforms. The Beagles love the enclosed feeling of the boxes, three or four frequently cramming into one box. When bored, they can always dig in and chew on them without deleterious effect.

Ideally, a kennel room containing a sink (large enough for Beagle bathing), a small refrigerator, cupboards, storage space for food, shelves and space for grooming table and crates polishes off the structure.

Your kennel should have a heating and cooling system.

A large dirt or grassy exercise area into which the kennel opens provides the Beagles with plenty of room to run. Whether or not your hounds will utilize all that space depends upon its shape and what stimulation for activity exists. Many are the breeders who have invested in large fencing expenditures only to find all their Beagles heaped up around the entrance closest to the house, just waiting for their next meal. Rectangular yards don't seem to work as well as U-shaped or irregularly shaped ones. At least with a U-shaped yard surrounding the kennel building, the Beagles have to run from one side to the other to check on the action.

Of course, plenty of fresh water and shade should be available in the exercise area.

Perimeter fencing has to be high enough to discourage climbing and imbedded deep enough to prevent digging out. Sleeping or sitting pads off the ground add to the attraction for the dogs. The large wooden spools used for wrapping telephone cables make ideal platforms for rest or play or as observation posts.

Make your kennel setup as practical and convenient for you and your dogs as possible. Clean completely daily, pick up as often as necessary and disinfect regularly with a rotating schedule of disinfectants. Not all bacteria, viruses and fungi are susceptible to the same chemicals. Therefore, rotating Clorox, Weladol, Roccal and Nolvasan will cover your needs nicely.

YOUR BREEDING PLAN

Luck plays an important part in any successful breeding program. A fortunate combination of genes enables an exceptional stud or brood bitch to produce consistently excellent get. Consider yourself blessed to have one of these producers.

What *is* within a breeder's control is the selection of stock to be used. A bitch puppy from a line with consistently good bitches is a better choice than one from a line weak in bitches, and a male Beagle whose get from a variety of bitches shows his consistent excellence is the best bet as a stud.

The pedigree and appearance of your foundation Beagle determine the next step. Cementing the virtues within a good line while weeding out the faults is everyone's goal, and while this can be done over several generations, there comes a time when new blood is needed to restore vigor and bone and increase fertility.

Not infrequently, however, new problems arise from these outcrosses. Sometime a genetic dead end results. Such was the case with one of our better show bitches. With a little luck, however, the Beagles from this first-generation outcross, when bred back into either line, will reproduce well.

The choice of which line and Beagle to use may not be easy. Some breeders opt for the top winner of the day. If the Beagle happens to be a fine producer, as was Ch. Starbuck's Hang 'Em High, the choice is excellent. But not all top-winning conformation Beagles reproduce in kind. Here a stud of proven ability but with a lesser win record might serve your bitch far better.

There really is no single right way to breed good Beagles. Many routes to the same end exist. One breeder did get consistently good conformation Beagles while breeding to successive top-winning males. Others outcross frequently but to Beagles of the same general appearance with successful results. We linebred very closely as well as inbred a time or two and had a good run for our money for several years.

Conventional wisdom dictates that new gene pools are necessary after three or four generations. A look at a cross-section of current Beagle pedigrees indicates a shrinking of our conformation pool. This is probably why we are seeing an increase in certain genetic problems.

Frankness among breeders about particular unwanted recessives can make for better-informed breedings.

AN IMPORTANT AFTERTHOUGHT

You must leave instructions re feeding, medications and cleaning, plus name, address and phone number of your veterinarian whenever you are away from home for an extended period of time, or in case of sudden illness. Also, be sure you make provisions in your will for financing care and disposition of your dogs, with a particular person responsible for administering these provisions.

8

A Breeder's Notebook

MANAGEMENT OF THE BROOD BITCH

Good reproductive care of your potential brood bitch begins long before her first breeding. Priscilla Stockner, D.V.M., recommends that between seven and ten months of age, prior to her first season, your puppy bitch should have a good physical examination, including as well a blood panel, urinalysis, brucellosis blood titre and thyroid function tests. The vaginal examination, both digital and visual, with smear and culture will uncover any physical obstacles to breeding and potential for infection. It is a bit disconcerting to discover at the time of breeding that your eager Beagles are unable to consummate their "marriage." Persistent hymens do occur.

Vaginal Cultures

Thirty to forty percent of vaginal cultures from healthy bitches, taken midcycle, will grow out no organisms. With the onset of a season, bacterial growth will flourish. Therefore a repeat smear and culture need to be done during early proestrus. Certain bacteria are disease producing, and if found, must be treated. Heavy growth of *E. coli,* if untreated, will lead to pyometria (infection of the uterus) by four years of age. Eighty percent of bitches so infected are infertile. Beta-hemolytic streptococcus flourishing in the vagina reduces the chance of pregnancy, slows sperm motility and leads to 80 percent of neonatal deaths.

So one can see how important it is to recognize such problems early.

Am./Can. Ch. Starbuck's Meadow Song, fifteen inches, Best Puppy in Sweepstakes, National Beagle Club Specialty, 1978; H.I.S. Silver Certificate of Distinction holder, June 1984; top producer in 1980, 1982 and 1985; dam of twelve champions (Ch. The Whim's Buckeye ex Ch. Elsy's Shooting Star). She is owned by Annette Didier.
Ritter

Ch. SureLuv's Sumer Mist of Harnett, fifteen inches, National Beagle Club Dam of the years 1985, 1986, 1987 and 1988, with eighteen champions as of 1988 (Ch. Swan Lake Luke of Craigwood ex Ch. SureLuv's Heather Mist), owned by Helen L. Daley.
Ashbey

Ch. Topono's Juliet, fifteen inches (Elvee's Brandy Alexander ex Topono's Independence Hall), dam of twelve champions from two litters. She is owned by Irene Norman.
Leistner

Douching once daily with the appropriate antibiotic solution for varying lengths of time can control these organisms. If there is not a reproductive veterinarian in your area, your veterinarian can work in consultation with one in order to give you the best help.

After a series of newborn deaths in our Beagle population, our veterinarian recommended vaginal smears and cultures on all bitches prior to breeding. In addition, the appropriate oral antibiotic was to be given during the bitch's season, as well as four days before and ten days after delivery of the puppies.

From 1981 through 1987 a total of nine different bitches in our kennel were tested with each season. At the same time, a rotating disinfectant program for the kennel was begun. Cultures of three of the bitches produced heavy growth of *E. coli;* two of beta-hemolytic streptococcus; two of Pseudomonas; and four of *P. multicita.* Organisms cultured could vary from season to season in a single bitch.

Chloromycetin was the only antibiotic to which *E. coli* was sensitive; previous use of Ampicillin had not been successful in preventing infection in some of the newborns. With this earlier regimen of oral administration of antibiotics we lost no more puppies to infection.

However, the technique of vaginal douching offers the advantage of directly applying the antibiotic to the affected tissues as well as eliminating the possible toxic effects on the developing fetus from systemic antibiotics.

Brucellosis

Repeat brucellosis titres are essential prior to each breeding. *Brucella canis,* the organism causing brucellosis, is spread by both oral and genital contact. Sterility in the male and spontaneous abortion in the female are consequences of this infection. Highly contagious, the organism can be picked up on contaminated ground. Until recently, the diagnosis of brucellosis meant castration and spaying, if not euthanasia, for the affected dogs. However, treatment with a combination of antibiotics over a long period of time has been effective in some experimental programs.

Thyroid Function

Repeat blood tests for thyroid function should be done prior to each season. The section on genetics (pages 179–94) gives further details.

Parasite Control

An ongoing parasite control program is essential with your Beagles. Fleas, hookworms and whipworms thrive in hot, humid climates. Coccidia abound, and Giardia is becoming more common. And, of course, heartworm is now nation- if not worldwide. Stool checks and specific medications for each of the above, plus specific instructions for disinfecting the environment, may

Ch. Starbuck's Hang 'Em High, fifteen inches, top winning and producing Beagle of all time (Ch. The Whim's Buckeye ex Ch. Elsy's Shooting Star), owned by David and Linda Hiltz.
Booth

Ch. White Acres Second to None, fifteen inches, multiple Specialty and Group winner (Ch. Whisper's Inflation Fighter ex Daf-I-Dale's Peaches N' Cream), owned by Delores Dills and White Acres Kennels (Carol and Ed Tyte).
Bill Francis

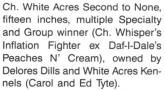

Ch. Starbuck's Fair Warning, fifteen inches, is a multiple BIS and Group winner, and National Beagle Club Beagle of the Year, 1983 (Ch. Meadow Crest Grand Slam ex Ch. Starbuck's Carry Nation). Owned by Robin Zieske and David Hiltz, at present by Annette Didier. *Olson*

be obtained from your veterinarian. The alternative to routine use of a heart-worm preventative is a twice-yearly blood test. If the test is positive, then the dog is treated.

Once your bitch is bred, it is too late to launch an extensive extermination effort. Whatever goes in or on her for treatment can adversely affect the developing fetus.

Encysted roundworm larvae in the dam may be released at about forty-five days of the pregnancy into the placenta, thus infecting the puppies. Hookworm infestation of young puppies can be very dangerous.

Feeding

Contrary to popular opinion, dieting your bitch prior to her season and breeding is not the best route to a successful pregnancy. On the other hand, a grossly overweight Beagle is not a good candidate for motherhood.

Experiments suggest that increasing food intake by 10 percent with the beginning of her season until breeding, then dropping back to normal food intake after breeding increases the chances of conception. There is some evidence that overfeeding after breeding leads to a drop in fertility.

Meat, chicken, cottage cheese, egg yolk and fish added in small amounts to a good basic dog food provide an excellent source of animal protein. Raw liver, one tablespoon three times a week, ensures an adequate amount of zinc, which is necessary for healthy, vigorous newborns. Total fat content of the diet for a pregnant bitch should not exceed 15 percent.

The dam's intake will need to be increased gradually, beginning with the fifth week after breeding. The amount required will be determined by the size of the litter. Maintaining about one-half inch of subcutaneous fat over the ribcage is ideal in a Beagle. The pregnant bitch will be more comfortable if she is fed twice daily, dividing the daily portion during the last two to three weeks, particularly if she is carrying a large number of puppies. A few bitches will lose their appetites a few days before whelping, but most continue to be absolutely ravenous until labor commences!

Once nursing begins, your bitch will require extra food, the amount once again determined by the number of puppies. Adequate nutrition is absolutely essential to good milk production. Phyllis Holst, D.V.M., recommends one-and-a-half times the normal intake for the first week, two times for the second, and three times from the third to sixth week. Animal protein, added in small amounts daily, and vitamin-mineral supplement continue for the duration of nursing. Bitches fed adequately need not suffer weight loss.

Vitamin-Mineral Supplementation

A general vitamin-mineral supplement, begun at about four weeks after breeding and continued through lactation, is a good idea unless the bitch is on a dry dog food especially designed for pregnant bitches.

Some years ago a calcium-phosphorus-vitamin D additive during preg-

Ch. Swan Lake's Ginger Snap, thirteen inches, BB, National Beagle Club Specialty, 1981 (Craigwood's TicTac ex Ch. Swan Lake's Big Bad Mama), owned by Pam and Betsy Powell. *Rene*

Ch. Teloca Lacosta Judith Anne, thirteen inches (Ch. Teloca Navan Pruf O' the Puddin, CD, ex Ch. Teloca Good as Gold), BV, National Beagle Club Specialty, 1987, under A. C. Musladin. She is owned by A. Gil Del Real, J. M. dePoo III and Marie Shuart. *John Ashbey*

nancy was considered essential to prevent eclampsia in the lactating dam. Current veterinary practice, however, is to give small amounts daily beginning the last week of pregnancy. Too much dietary calcium can prevent the bitch from being prepared to deal with the calcium requirements of milk production. Too-high levels of calcium can interfere with blood levels of zinc, known to be important in good uterine contractability as well as normal-sized healthy offspring.

Boosters

No medication (with the exception of medication for heartworm control) should be given during pregnancy. If, for some reason, antibiotics are required, only those safe for pregnant bitches and developing puppies are to be used, on the advice of your veterinarian.

MANAGEMENT OF THE STUD DOG

As with the care of the brood bitch, an ounce of prevention is worth a ton of cure.

There have been a number of good conformation Beagle males in the past twenty years that have become infertile after siring one to three litters. Diagnostic studies done after the fact indicate that some, if properly treated early, may not have become permanently sterile.

A good general physical and genital examination of the young males, nine to twelve months old, is a must. This workup should include a blood panel, thyroid level and a brucellosis titre. Examination of the genitals, observation of breeding behavior and a semen check complete the picture.

Semen should *always* be collected in the presence of a "teaser" bitch;* without her presence, false negatives sometimes occur. The three portions of the semen (first and third portions are prostatic fluid, normally clear, the second containing sperm, milky in color) are examined microscopically. Number, shape and motility of the sperm provide a baseline with which future counts can be compared. Semen examination should be repeated yearly.

Prior to each breeding a blood brucellosis titre should be obtained.

Normal thyroid function is necessary for sperm production. Early diagnosis and treatment of hypothyroidism (indequate thyroid hormone production) can make a difference between a temporary and a permanent infertility.

Chronic prostatitis, usually bacterial in origin, also affects sperm production. Copious urination (in contrast to the usual or normal marking pattern) and smaller, flatter stools may indicate enlargement of the infected prostate gland. Again, the earlier the treatment, the better the chance that the infertility is reversible.

*In lieu of a teaser bitch when you need a sperm specimen, saturate cotton balls with vaginal discharge of a bitch in season, place in a freezer bag and freeze immediately. When needed, remove one of the balls and let the male smell it as the specimen is obtained.

Ch. Fairmont Sound of Music, fifteen inches, multiple BIS and multiple Group winner; Beagle of the Year, National Beagle Club, 1986 (Ch. Hickorynut's Hangman ex Ch. Pickadilly Pin-Up of Colegren), owned by J. and B. Ware, Wade Burns and Ed Jenner. *Missy Yuhl*

Ch. Teloca Patches Littl' Dickens, thirteen inches, a multiple BIS, BIS Group and Specialty winner; sire of three BIS winners and many Group winners; Beagle of the Year, National Beagle Club, 1984 and 1985; 13″ Beagle of the Year, National Beagle Club, 1986 (Ch. Teloca Patches On Target ex Ch. Teloca Upstage Bann'd in Boston), owned by Wade Burns and Jon Woodring. *Graham*

```
STUD CONTRACT

This is to certify that stud: _____
was bred to bitch: _____
on the following dates: _____
Stud Fee: _____
Due to whelp: _____
There are no conditions binding upon this breeding except the
following: _____
_____



Owner of Stud:                    Owner of Bitch:
_____              _____
Signature                         Signature
Address: _____           Address: _____
_____              _____


Please sign and return.
```

THOSE FEMALE SEX HORMONES AT WORK

Poor timing in a breeding accounts for 25 percent of missed conceptions. The remainder are due to problems with low fertility or infertility. Early diagnosis and treatment of the latter may reverse the situation.

If, like me, you are forgetful, a quick review of the reproductive physiology of the bitch is always in order.

Ovarian Cycle

There are four phases of hormonal changes and associated behavior in the bitch:

1. Anestrus, the resting phase, is characterized by absence of reproductive activity. Vaginal smears show only a few nonsuperficial cells, white blood cells and occasionally a few old superficial cells. Progesterone levels are low. Duration of this phase can vary from one month to twelve months.
2. Proestrus, the beginning of reproductive activity, is accompanied by gradual swelling of the vulva, a serosanguineous discharge (a combination of a thin clear fluid colored with blood) and increasing blood level of estradiol. Average length is about nine days, but can vary from zero to seventeen days.

Ch. Lanbur Love Notes, thirteen inches, a Specialty Best of Variety winner (Ch. Teloca Patches Littl' Dickens ex Ch. Lanbur Bonus Baby O' Swan Lake), owned by Patty Keenan. *Cott/Daigle*

Am./Can. Ch. Wishing Well's One Step Ahead, winner of three Canadian all-breed BIS and Top Beagle in Canada, 1988 (Ch. Jams Arnold Schwarzennege ex Ch. Wishing Well's Wild Woman), owned by Bar bara Keenan and Mr. and Mrs. Fred Baxstrome. *Denni*

3. Estrus is that period during which the bitch is receptive to the male. The color of the vaginal discharge may or not change and is *not* a reliable indicator of the onset of estrus. During this time, the bitch's vulva is full and she will present her perineum (bottom) to the male, flagging her tail. Hormonally, this behavior occurs when blood levels of estradiol decrease and levels of progesterone increase. Luteinizing hormone ("a pituitary hormone with action on target cells in ovaries and teats," Phyllis Holst, D.V.M.) is released in a surge over a period of twenty-four to forty-eight hours and leads to ovulation. Ovulation, the release of eggs, occurs most usually in three days.
4. Diestrus lasts approximately sixty days and is the stage during which progesterone is the primary circulating hormone. This hormone leads to enlargement of breast tissue and activity of the lining of the uterus.

All primary oocytes, the female reproductive cells, are produced over a twenty-four-hour period (Priscilla Stockner, D.V.M.) and begin to descend through the oviducts, the tubes connecting the ovaries with the uterus. Three days are required for these eggs to be ready for fertilization. The egg's life span at that point is from twenty-four to forty-eight hours. Actual conception takes place three days after ovulation, when fertilization occurs in the lower end of the oviduct.

Vaginal smears reveal that maximum cornification is attained during late proestrus and early estrus. These large sheets of superficial cells persist until the end of estrus, the fertile period. Smears will not tell you when ovulation occurs except in retrospect. The length of time of full cornification varies from bitch to bitch, lasting from ten to fourteen days. For each individual bitch, however, the length of complete cornification remains constant from season to season. A complete tracking of your bitch's estrus with serial vaginal smears can give a reliable blueprint for future breedings.

Bitches bred two days after ovulation have the highest conception rates. However, successful breeding can occur in bitches bred from four days before to three days after ovulation. The best program is to breed six days, four days and two days before onset of diestrus. Since sperm can live as long as eleven days in the female reproductive tract, fertilization can occur even when the breedings may not be as ideally timed. One can assume, however, that the fresher the sperm, the greater likelihood of conception.

Not everyone will wish to take the time and trouble of daily visits to the veterinarian for serial slides or even to learn the technique of "doing it yourself." Therefore, a good rule of thumb is to breed first when the bitch is receptive and then every other day until the bitch declines. The bitch will make it amply apparent when she no longer wishes to be bred.

No one need worry about different degrees of maturity of the newborns, for all eggs are fertilized within a twenty-four-hour period.

With the above information you will be able to time the matings to maximize chances of conception.

Ch. The Whim's Skyrocket, fifteen inches (Ch. Wandering Wind ex The Whim's Firecracker), and his champion get, under judge Herman Cox, Ladies of British Columbia Kennel Club, 1978. Skyrocket is owned by Gwen Marotta. *Don Hodges*

GETTING THE JOB DONE

Many Beagle bitches are as enthusiastic about being bred as they are about everything else. Occasionally the level of enthusiasm is so great that the actual mating can become a wrestling match involving Beagles and humans. Since the hounds are relatively small and agile, breeding them fortunately does not require an army of assistants, as do Bloodhounds and Bassets.

For the safety of the male and in the interest of saving time, two people, one small piece of carpet (large enough to accommodate two Beagles and two sets of knees) and perhaps some sterile packets of K-Y Jelly are all that is needed.

Giving the two a few minutes of "foreplay" enables you to note the bitch's willingness to be bred and also provides the hounds, who may be strangers, an opportunity to get acquainted. Leads on each provide control in the event the bitch is not quite ready and defends her chastity by attempting to savage the dog.

Normal breeding behavior is characterized in a receptive bitch by enthusiastic play, sniffing of the stud's penis, curling the tail to one side and presenting her vulva to him. Normal male behavior also includes play, licking the bitch's vulva and mounting her from the rear, clasping her "waist" with his forelegs and thrusting with his pelvis.

When ready, one person holds the bitch's head. I prefer to do this from the right side of the bitch, so that if she attempts to turn, I have more control. The second manages the male.

Some studs prefer to do it themselves and are put off by human help. Others, in their enthusiasm, may miss the mark by miles, hurling themselves with abandon completely over the bitch. We have found that the person at the working end can be of assistance by placing the left hand under the bitch from the left side with palm up and the index and middle fingers on either side of the vulva to serve as a support and guide for the penis. When penetration has occurred and active thrusting is taking place, the other hand can push the male gently into the bitch until a tie occurs.

Once a tie has been secured, the male can be turned.

Not all Beagle bitches are delighted with breeding. A strange environment, an unknown stud, presence of a doting and talkative owner can disrupt the process. If the rear end of the bitch is obviously willing, as evidenced by flagging and tilting up the pelvis, but the front is vociferously protesting, a soft cloth belt or old pantyhose make an excellent muzzle. Tie either over the top of the bitch's muzzle, bring it back under the jaw, tie again, and then loop over the neck and tie in a bow. The belt or pantyhose should be loose enough to enable her to open her mouth slightly to pant but tight enough to prevent snapping.

If all else fails, artificial insemination is an easy remedy. Since the AKC has approved the use of artificial insemination by breeders in their own homes or kennels, it is a simple matter to obtain the proper equipment. The technique is not difficult to master. There are excellent descriptions in both Phyllis Holst's book and Priscilla Stockner's articles.

The use of frozen semen and now cooled fresh semen allows for a greater choice of stud and eliminates shipping of the bitch. With the increasing concern over contagious canine venereal diseases, artificial impregnation, as has been done with cattle for many years, can be an added protection for the stud.

Remember that whenever we humans intercede in the process of canine reproduction, there is the risk that we may unwittingly perpetuate the continuance of certain behavioral problems.

THERE'S A BEAGLE IN THE OVEN

Diagnosis of Pregnancy

Eggs are fertilized about two days after ovulation as they reach the distal end of the oviduct. Division of cells begins and implantation of the embryo in the uterine wall takes place about eighteen days post breeding (about seventeen days after ovulation). Whelping is most likely to occur fifty-six to fifty-eight days after onset of diestrus, or sixty-three days after breeding. Larger litters tend to deliver earlier.

Tiny embryos can be felt as early as nineteen days after the onset of diestrus, but are best felt at twenty to twenty-eight days. Sonograms, used routinely by many veterinarians, provide a reliable and safe diagnostic confirmation. The visit to the veterinarian at this time enables him/her to check for any potential problems.

Proper care of your pregnant bitch, as discussed earlier, also includes a checkup a week before her due date. Sonograms at this time may tell you the number and size of the puppies, information helpful in the management of the actual delivery. Arrangements for emergency coverage should be discussed with the veterinarian, for most bitches seem to deliver either late at night or very early in the morning. Unplanned visits to a strange emergency room in the middle of the night are not ideal ways to deliver a litter of puppies if assistance is required.

Preparing for Delivery

Whelping area: The first requirement is a quiet, warm room, free from too much activity. We have found that the removable metal pan of a commercial whelping bin, lined with abundant paper, works well as the delivery site. We surround this pan with a large exercise pen so that, during the early stages of labor, the bitch can move about the exercise area when not resting in the delivery pan and yet will be confined to some extent. One can move in and out of the exercise pen to check the bitch's progress and to clean up as necessary.

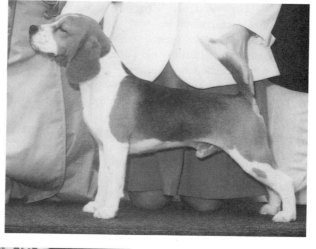

Ch. Whisper's Inflation Fighter, fifteen inches (Ch. Whisper's Call Me Mister ex Ch. Suntree's Pucker Pellet), owned by White Acres Kennels (Carol and Ed Tyte). He is the sire of thirty-two champions, including one BIS, two Group winners and three Specialty winners.
Carl Lindemaier

Ch. Page Mill On the Road Again, fifteen inches (Ch. Fulmont's Flash Cube ex Ch. Page Mill Winnie the Pooh), owned by Carroll Diaz, is the sire of twenty-two champions, including multiple BIS and Specialty BOB Ch. Page Mill Upset the Applecart. *Graham*

Ch. Fulmont's Flash Cube, thirteen inches, BIS winner (Ch. Fulmont's Pub Crawler ex Ch. Fulmont's Fable), owned by William and Julie Fulkerson. *Twomey*

Nursery setup: What has worked best in our kennel is the three-foot square metal whelping pen within its fencing. The level of the pan can be adjusted so you can reach the puppies easily while sitting down next to the pen. We place two of these pens side by side, with the doorways open between the two. One is used as the nursery area, the other is an easily cleaned exercise area for the bitch.

When the litter is old enough to start traveling around the pens, a small cardboard bridge can be placed between the two pens to prevent the puppies from catching a foot or slipping through the small gap between the two pens.

Clean cardboard panels attached to all sides of the pens provide a well-insulated nursery, so important in maintaining proper ambient temperature for the newborns.

In one corner of the nursery pen, the one most accessible for the breeder, place a heating pad that is *covered* with a piece of plywood. To afford traction for the puppies, a densely woven cloth can be applied to the plywood, and soft padding or newspaper can be used to cover the rest of the pad. The padding tends to cradle the developing bony parts. Pups and mother can move on or off the heated area as comfort dictates.

The nursery should be in a draft-free room, separate from the rest of the household.

To aid in maintaining a warm environment, a heat lamp that can be adjusted as to height is placed over the whelping pen.

Equipment to have on hand:

Lots of clean towels.

Two small hemostats (serrated-edge clamps).

Scale calibrated in ounces as well as pounds.

Cardboard box lined with a soft towel and placed half on a heating pad. Newborns are placed in the box as they are delivered.

Soft rubber bulb syringe for aspirating mouth and nose of newborns, if necessary.

Sterile hypodermic needles and syringes plus a vial of oxytocin, the latter to be used *only as your veterinarian advises.*

A small cylinder of oxygen, if you can obtain one.

A total of two heating pads and a heat lamp.

Feeding tubes.

Baby bottle with preemie nipple.

Esbilac (bitch's milk substitute).

A bottle of Ringer's lactate reconstituted with 5 percent glucose.

Nail clipper.

Kaopectate.

Eyedropper.

Supply of distilled or purified water for the nursing bitch and very young puppies.

Sterile surgical gloves.

K-Y Jelly.

110

Ch. RD's Rhinestone Cowboy, thirteen inches, Group winner and Best Veteran, National Beagle Club specialty, 1985 and 1987 (Ch. The Whim's Buckeye ex Ch. RD's Highland Heather), owned by Ardie Haydon.

Ch. Wilkeep Peggy Sue, fifteen inches (Ch. Yaupon Row Sailor Boy, CDX, ex Ch. Wilkeep Tutsy of Starcrest), owned by Caroline Dowell.

Labor

Introduce your bitch to her new quarters several days before her due date. If she has been in the kennel, bring her into the house and allow her to sleep in her "nursery."

Prediction of delivery: Most puppies deliver between the fifty-ninth and seventieth day following breeding, sixty-three days being the average. Larger litters tend to deliver earlier than smaller litters. In actuality, gestation lasts sixty days from fertilization. The actual day of fertilization is not easy to determine unless one has previously determined the onset of diestrus from serial vaginal smears.

The simplest predictor of imminent delivery is a significant drop in the bitch's rectal temperature. Bitches in the late stages of pregnancy normally run temperatures between 99 and 100.2°F. With the sudden drop in blood level of progesterone about twenty-four hours before delivery, the temperature drops to below 99°F and stays down until labor commences. Unless rectal temperatures are taken every eight hours, this drop can be missed.

A simple graph on each pregnant bitch records her rectal temperature every eight hours beginning six days prior to the expected due date (sixty-three days from the first breeding). Other pertinent data regarding labor and delivery can also be noted on the form. These charts serve as useful references in subsequent pregnancies. On the reverse side, puppy records can be charted. In this way you have a simple summary of each litter.

The pattern established in our closely inbred and linebred bitches is one of a drop in temperature to below 98°F twenty-four hours prior to onset of labor. During that twenty-four-hour period, the first stage of labor occurs as the cervix begins to dilate. The bitch may either pick at or refuse food and urinate frequently. If there is no sign of impending labor after twenty-four hours from time of the temperature drop, immediate consultation with your veterinarian is in order. A blackish-green vaginal discharge indicates placental separation and requires immediate examination by your veterinarian.

The next phase of this first stage of labor is manifested by periods of resting alternating with periods of restlessness, during which the bitch is in obvious discomfort. She will pant. A mucous discharge from her vagina is normal. If, after two to three hours, good hard labor has not begun, notify your veterinarian immediately.

Once the cervix is completely dilated, the second stage of labor begins during which the puppies are delivered. Obvious uterine contractions are palpable and the bitch begins to bear down, groaning as she does. Vomiting usually occurs as well as frequent urination.

Delivery

The bitch's perineum bulges as the puppy makes its way through the pelvic outlet into the vaginal canal. A sac of amniotic fluid usually precedes

112

the puppy in appearing at the vulva. If this sac ruptures too early, a dry birth may result. Once the puppy has made its way into the vaginal canal, pup and placenta usually deliver within three to five good hard contractions. If progress is slow, "feathering," stroking the anterior wall of the vagina with your gloved forefinger, may facilitate better contractions. Placentas don't always arrive with the puppy, so make sure all are accounted for.

Puppies present about equally as head first or hindfeet first. The head being more compact and firmer in consistency acts as a better dilator of the cervix and vaginal canal than do the feet in a footling presentation.

If no puppy delivers within thirty minutes, an obstetrical emergency is declared and Caesarean section should be considered. Time lost in transit to the veterinary hospital lessens chances of that puppy's survival. This is especially true if the first puppy is a footling.

The intervals between deliveries vary from minutes to several hours. If six hours elapse without any sign of labor between puppies, notify your veterinarian.

Most Beagle bitches will immediately clean off the sac that surrounds the puppy at birth and bite the umbilical cord through. Watch that the cord is not bitten off too close to the pup's abdominal wall. The dam's enthusiastic and vigorous licking and shoving around of the pup stimulate the newborn, forcing liquid from its lungs and helping clear the airway.

If the bitch does not begin to take care of the puppy immediately or appears too rough, remove the puppy and placenta from the whelping box, place in a clean towel and quickly wipe away membranes from the mouth and nose. Rub the pup briskly, holding it with head angled downward. Gentle aspiration of fluid from nose and mouth with a soft rubber bulb syringe helps clear the airway. Don't worry about separating pup from placenta until the airway is clear and the pup is breathing well and is pink. Crying facilitates lung expansion; snapping toes and feet stimulates crying. Holding the head and body firmly with both hands so that the head and neck are splinted, bring your hands with the puppy from above your head to down in front of you quickly. This sudden movement also helps clear fluid from the airway.

Once the pup is breathing and its tummy is pink, clamp the umbilical cord with a hemostat about three-quarters inch from the abdomen and tear the cord with your fingernails on the placental side of the clamp. Clamping and tearing aid in sealing of the cord, whereas cutting with scissors allows seepage of blood from the puppy and may allow infection in.

Check each puppy for any abnormalities, such as cleft palate or defects in the abdominal wall. Record weight and description of the puppy.

At this point, return puppy to mother for more stimulation and licking, unless she is already engaged in delivering her next offspring. The additional attention from the bitch helps to clear the airway further, but also aids in evacuation of the sticky meconium, that first stool passed by the newborn. Vigorous puppies gravitate quickly to the nipple for suckling, which in turn stimulates the onset of labor again.

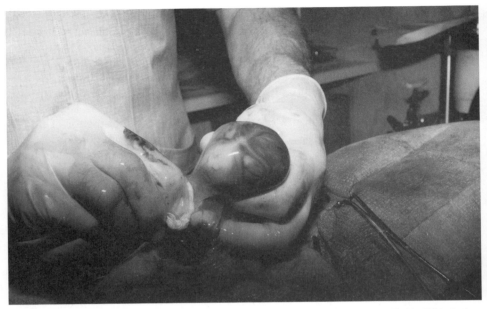

Newborn Beagle being delivered by Caesarean section.   *Robin Whitelock*

Ch. Jim-Mar's Call Me Just Wright with her day-old pups.   *Julie Wright*

All placentas should be accounted for. Bitches, if allowed, will eat them, and vomiting may then follow. Certainly it is Nature's way of cleaning up the birthing area and giving nourishment to the bitch. It is the breeder's choice to make as to how many are consumed. Probably one is enough!

If delivery is a long process, water and/or warm chicken or beef broth can be offered the bitch.

When the last of the pups has arrived, wash the blood and fluid off the dam and dry her. The simplest way is to put her in a bathtub and wash her hindquarters under running warm water. Rinse all soap off and dry her thoroughly. She and her pups are then moved into the permanent nursery. Adjust the heat lamp as needed to provide a warm environment. A relaxed bitch settles down with her brood and ultimately sleeps.

At this point, you can, too!

Unfortunately, some Beagle dams, especially with their first litters, are nervous, and need to be watched carefully initially. Some are uncaring as to where they lie down, and newborns may have to be moved quickly to avoid suffocation under the dam. This is especially a worry with bitches that have had a Caesarean section. Often they are still sedated and disoriented from the anesthetic, even though awake and on their feet. These bitches are better off crated, separated from their litters, except when the breeder is present and supervising nursing every hour or two.

Once the bitch recovers totally from her anesthetic, she usually needs a day or two before her milk is adequate and before she is comfortable with her puppies. These pups need supplemental feeding and even more careful supervision. Some dams will nurse their puppies happily but, most fastidiously, will absolutely refuse to clean up after them. These pups will need regular stimulation following nursing or feeding in order to induce defecation and urination for the first week or ten days.

After the dam and puppies are settled into their nursery area, the pups will gradually dry off and crowd around the bitch's mammary glands to seek out the teats. Make sure each pup knows how to "latch on" and has a good sucking reflex. A vigorous sucking reflex will be obvious if you insert your little finger into the pup's mouth. If the puppy rejects the finger or simply gums it, it may need to be warmed more and require special observation. The suction produced by a vigorous puppy is unmistakable.

Many veterinarians recommend an injection of oxytocin following completion of delivery. This stimulates contraction of the uterus, which aids in evacuating any remaining fluid and tissues within the uterus as well stimulating milk production. *Follow your veterinarian's advice on this.*

Caesarean Section

Caesarean sections are not uncommon with Beagle bitches, especially with the thirteen-inch variety. When done either as an emergency intervention during labor or by plan, it is important that the veterinarian be experienced.

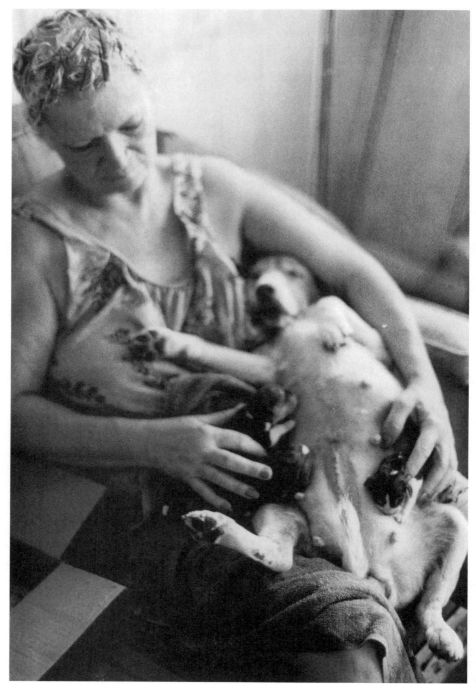

Post-Caesarean section dam getting some help with her new pups. *Robin Whitelock*

116

It may take some looking to find one who enjoys working with breeders and fits your needs.

Our experience with planned Caesarean sections dictates that the procedure be done *after* the bitch's temperature drops. When done arbitrarily on the first expected due date before the bitch has shown any signs of incipient labor, the newborns are likely to be somewhat premature and have more difficulty surviving. Sometimes proper timing requires a weekend or holiday section; hence, the necessity for a flexible and obliging obstetrician.

SUMMARY OF WHELPINGS IN OUR KENNEL, 1965–1988

Number of litters bred: 47
Number of puppies whelped: 202
Number of puppies surviving: 167
Stillborns or dead fetuses: 21
Pups put down or died before four weeks: 14
Size of litters: 1 pup to 7; average number: 4.3 pups per litter
Normal (non-Caesarean section) deliveries: 25
    Presentation of puppies: Cephalic: 44
                                  Footlings: 45
                                  Remainder not recorded
    Presentation of first puppy: Cephalic: 18 with 1 dead at birth
                                      Footling: 9 with 3 dead at birth
Planned Caesarean sections: 15
Unplanned Caesarean sections: 7
    Total: 22
Sex of puppies: Female: 101
                    Male: 94
                    Unrecorded: 7
Mortality rate overall: 16+ percent
    Stillborn: 10 percent
    Died or put down under four weeks: 7 percent

Two-day-old Beagle pup.

George Eaton

9

Beagle Puppies

NORMAL BEAGLE PUPPIES

At birth, Beagle pups are black and white or pale tan and white in color. A puppy may appear to be white at birth, but the adult color will be a pale tan and white. Those pups which carry the lemon factor frequently have a brownish cast to the black portions of the coat, a cast that fades out as the puppy grows older.

As in other breeds, the Beagle puppy is blind, the lids being sealed, and has poor hearing. Ears are mere tabs. There is some reaction by puppies to odors, pain and touch. The puppy crawls, searching for the dam, a heat source, with head swinging from side to side. It can right itself and sleeps with frequent muscle twitches or involuntary contractions.

Crying occurs when it is separated from its mother, if hungry, chilled or in pain. Ninety percent of its time is spent sleeping. Normal urination and defecation occur only with stimulation. Umbilical cords drop off at two or three days.

Normal Development

Eyes open: 10 to 14 days. Can be as late as 21 days, however.
Ears open: 13 to 17 days.
Begins to walk: About 18 days.
Urinates and defecates without assistance: At 3 to 4 weeks.
First teeth: Usually about 3 weeks.

Primary socialization: 3 to 10 weeks is the most crucial time.

Permanent teeth: Beginning at about 16 weeks, completed by six months.

Sexual maturity: From 8 months to 18 months. Some bitches do not have the first season until 24 months.

The period from ten weeks to six to eight months (about puberty) sees continuing growth, independence and roaming. Mounting behavior in both male and female occurs, and the male begins to lift his hind leg to urinate rather than squatting.

In Beagles, "adolescence" lasts from about six months to twenty-four months and is marked by playfulness, chewing, digging and greater exercise requirement.

Adulthood: By two years, the Beagle will spend much of the midday sleeping, with periods of activity in the morning and late afternoon.

Weaning

At about three weeks of age, normal Beagle puppies may be started on a warm, mushy gruel of Esbilac, strained chicken and rice or Hi-Pro baby cereal. Orphan pups can be started earlier with baby cereal and Esbilac. We have found that puppies do not gain as well on a diet consisting only of Esbilac and that they are always hungry.

Offer the meal in a raised pan, encouraging each pup to lap or lick food from your fingers to begin with. Gradually increase the number of meals offered per day to four or five over a period of the following three or four weeks. Offer the meals after the dam has been separated from the babies for a while.

Bottled water should be available from about three weeks on, making sure the container is not so large that the puppies may fall into it and be unable to get out.

Often the pups will flock about the dam's food dish as she eats. And, of course, she is more than happy to polish off any of their leavings.

Puppies' food mixture should be gradually changed to include a good grade of commercial dry puppy food, reduced to a fine granule in a food processor initially, plus cooked egg yolks, cottage cheese, yogurt and fresh cooked beef or chicken. Add each new ingredient separately, and do not add another for two or three days to see how the puppies tolerate the diet change. Vitamins can be added to the food as soon as the puppies are eating. Careful dosage is required, for commercial dog foods contain added minerals and vitamins.

Between six and eight weeks, most Beagle dams will begin to discourage nursing, becoming restless and irritable as the pups' sharp teeth hurt. Separating the bitch from the pups during the day and returning her to them for the night for the final few days before total separation make for a gradual, rather than abrupt, break.

120

Ten-day-old puppy. *Lynn Heltne*

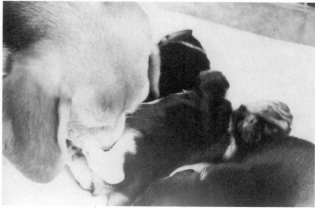

Clean-up time for eighteen-day-old pup.   *Lynn Heltne*

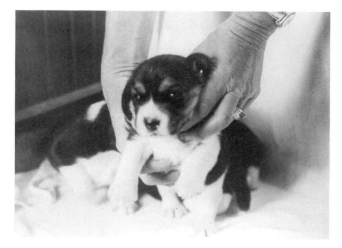

Eighteen days: eyes fully open.
Lynn Heltne

Occasionally, especially with a singleton puppy, the bitch is content to remain forever. Actually this works well for the solitary puppy, who then has companionship, a playmate and a teacher.

Once the pups are taking solid food, heartworm preventative can be given.

Don't be surprised if the pups prefer nursing to "dining out" at first. Ultimately they will learn. After all, have you ever seen an adult Beagle that won't wolf down whatever is placed in front of it?

The singleton puppy, without the competitive pushing and shoving of siblings "at the trough," may be slower to learn to eat. Placing the food pan on the floor and sticking your own head down to it, making slurping noises as though you are enjoying this marvelous treat, encourages the puppy to imitate.

Feeding Schedule

As the puppies get older, it is a good idea to begin feeding them individually so you will know exactly how much each is eating. Placing each puppy in a crate, either adjacent to or facing each other, provides the competition factor while ensuring that each gets the proper amount.

Eight to twelve weeks: Four or five small meals a day works well.

Morning: A good grade of commercial dry puppy food mixed with cooked beef or chicken or a good brand of canned dog food. Add vitamins and the heartworm medication.

Afternoon: Dry puppy chow mixed with a small amount of cottage cheese, yogurt and chopped egg.

Evening: Dry food plus meat as in the morning.

Bedtime: Bowl of canned milk diluted one-to-one with water plus a bowl of dry puppy chow.

Fresh bottled water should be available at *all* times.

Twelve to sixteen weeks: Reduce meals to three per day, continuing all the previous ingredients.

Sixteen to twenty weeks: Number of meals per day can be decreased to two as weight and appetite of the pup or pups dictate. Bedtime milk can be eliminated.

Twenty weeks to five months: Two meals per day of puppy chow plus small amounts of meat, cottage cheese and yogurt. Of course, vitamins should continue, as well as heartworm medication. During the teething period appetite may wan due to sore gums.

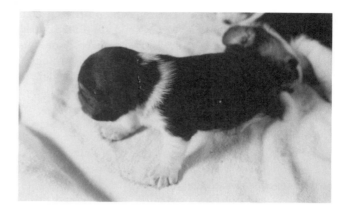

Eighteen days: up on her feet.
Lynn Heltne

Eighteen days: normal sleeping position.   *Lynn Heltne*

Litter of eight Starcrest pups, age four weeks.

123

Full growth: Occurs somewhere between eight and twelve months. At this point, a maintenance dry food should be substituted for the growth formula and one meal a day is offered. Small amounts of meat, cottage cheese, yogurt or acidophilus milk will add animal protein. One meal a day works well until the Beagle begins to age, when two smaller meals per day place a lesser demand on the heart and circulatory system.

Dewclaws

All Beagle pups are born with anterior dewclaws and some with rear ones as well. If the condition of the newborn warrants, the dewclaws can be removed at three days of age.

Rear dewclaws generally are large and unsightly; anterior are smaller and easier to remove. It is a painful procedure for the puppy, unfortunately, and not every breeder has the stomach for this home surgery. Either you or your veterinarian can do it. Sometimes the trip to the veterinarian and the separation from the dam add further stress to the pups.

If the puppy has been slow to gain or seems not to be thriving, delay the dewclaw removal. Later removal when the puppy is older, however, is not as simple a matter, for the bones are larger and the risk of infection is greater. In these cases surgical removal by your veterinarian is required, usually necessitating stitches and a bandage. Sometimes we have opted to leave the anterior dewclaws. If the Beagle is running in the field, the dewclaw can catch on brush and tear. But around the house or kennel, as well as in the show ring, there is little danger. Removal does give a cleaner line to the front pastern, but we have found leaving them on does not handicap the dog in the ring.

The procedure we followed in the past included the puppy, the operating surgeon and an assistant. The assistant held the puppy tummy up, cradled in the palms of both hands. The pup's feet can be restrained at the same time so that the surgeon won't be interfered with while performing the operation. Since the puppy generally cried during the operation, I, as assistant, would slip one of my fingers in the pup's mouth for it to suckle. The dewclaw and the surrounding area were cleansed with an iodine solution.

The surgeon would then grasp the dewclaw—either with fingers or a hemostat—and with small, sharp curved scissors amputate it at its base, ensuring that all the cartilaginous or bony matter was completely excised. Silver nitrate sticks, obtainable at the pharmacy or from a veterinarian, or other cauterizing substance stopped the bleeding.

The site of amputation must be watched over the next several days for any signs of infection. Usually the little crust or scab that forms drops off after two or three days and the area heals quickly.

In our line the Beagle pups invariably suffered from colic, painful bowel contractions, several hours after dewclaw removal. This condition lasted for several hours and contributed to our decision to discontinue removal.

124

Ch. The Whim's Stemwinder, fifteen inches, Specialty BOB and multiple Group placer (Ch. The Whim's Buckeye ex Ch. The Whim's Ten Ton Tessie), shown with son, Ch. Lohenbru's Close Encounter, fifteen inches, also a Specialty BOB and Group placer, ex Ch. Lohenbru's Pride 'N' Prejudice. Both hounds are owned by Judy and Neil Holloran.   *Ralph Karlen*

Ch. Buglair Petty Larceny, fifteen inches (Ch. Brantwood Buglair Bandit ex Ch. Buglair Ruffian), Best in Sweepstakes, National Beagle Club Specialty, 1986. Owned by Janet Wolfley and Larry Poindexter.

Kohler

ENSURING PUPPY SURVIVAL

The three most important factors in newborn survival are air, heat and hydration. *Never forget these.*

In our newborn population, from delivery to six weeks of age, the mortality rate overall has been about 16 percent. Ten percent of our total puppies were stillborn, and an additional 6 percent of deaths occurred prior to six weeks of age. In retrospect, I think some of these deaths could have been avoided by more informed obstetrical management and by better understanding and management of early bowel symptoms. Unfortunately, we learn by mistakes—often fatal ones.

Normal Beagle newborns range in weight from eight ounces to as much as fifteen. The average is probably about ten ounces. In our kennel, any puppy under eight ounces is considered to be more at risk, and at the first sign of any problem, treatment is immediate. Normal Beagle newborns are active and suckle well and have pink tummies and pads. A footling at birth may have a dusky tinge to its hindfeet for the first twenty-four hours. Sleep is active, with twitching and contracture of skeletal muscles. Evacuation of bowel and bladder occurs only with stimulation, either by the dam's licking or by your gentle stroking or massage of the anal and genital area with moistened cotton or facial tissue. We place two pieces of tissue over the area, and with rapid tapping motions of the first two fingers, reflex evacuation occurs. Rubbing, which can be irritating, should be avoided.

It is important to recognize normal newborn behavior. Any alteration, however slight, can be critical in early institution of proper remedies.

Air

Fully expanded lungs and a clear airway are essential to a puppy's survival. After you have done everything you can to ensure this, the newborns should be watched for respiratory difficulties and a less than pink color. Pads and tummies in normal puppies are pink, not bluish pink or bright red.

Listen to puppies' chests twenty-four hours after delivery. A stethoscope, reasonable in price, is a worthwhile investment under any circumstances. But by simply placing the puppy up to your ear you can hear any rattles during respiration. Normal respiratory rate varies from fifteen to thirty-five breaths per minute. If the puppy is wet sounding, an incubator with an oxygen supply can be lifesaving. Strapping the puppy to a small board with its head tilted down about 30 degrees stimulates crying and drainage, both essential to clearing the lungs.

Remember, pneumonia in a newborn is usually a lethal disease.

Heat

A puppy's rectal temperature just following delivery is 101°F. This quickly drops with an ambient temperature of 70°F. Since that is the average

Ch. Brantwood's Bounty Hunter, fifteen inches (Ch. Brantwood's Desperado ex Ch. Craigwood's Shannon), owned by Judy Formisano. Winner of 134 Bests of Variety and two Group Firsts; listed in Top Ten Beagles, 1985–1987; sire of four champions.

Alverson

Ch. Fulmont's Face In The Crowd, fifteen inches (Ch. Jana Nassau of Page Mill ex Fulmont's Face Card), owned by Dr. and Mrs. William Fulkerson. *Joe C*

room temperature comfortable for humans, it is essential that additional heat sources are supplied the newborns.

Heating pads that are set up not to burn under the litter, adjustable heat lamps above, plus—most essential—a maternal bitch with well-developed mammary tissue provide the external temperature that will maintain a normal 96°F rectal temperature in the newborns.

Temperature-control mechanisms are poorly developed in newborns, so minor alterations in any of the above will adversely affect the smaller and weaker pups especially.

After a week of age, normal puppy temperature is 99°F in response to more efficient development of the normal temperature regulating system. The well-known phenomenon of a bitch rejecting a puppy is most likely due to that puppy's being cooler than normal. And, of course, that is the puppy which most needs to be close to its siblings and its mother's belly. Sometimes warming that puppy may reverse the bitch's rejection.

Routine check of rectal temperature of the older newborns need not be done unless a problem exists.

Signs of chilling are crying, increased restlessness and movement of the head from side to side as the pup seeks a heat source. Poor mammary development leads to easy chilling, as there is less than optimal breast tissue to act as a radiator. Attempts to feed a puppy when it is chilled are useless, for the milk substitute simply pools in the stomach and is not moved on into the intestine. *A puppy must be warmed before it is fed.* Eventually, if the pup's temperature drops below 94°F, paralysis of the bowel occurs; the respiratory rate drops and there is a decrease in immunity. These pups are much more susceptible to infection.

The best way of warming a chilled puppy is a gradual one that combines an outside heat source with stimulation of the newborn. Place the puppy in your coat pocket or in your blouse or bra so that your body heat warms it slowly. Your activity will passively keep the puppy moving. Placing a chilled puppy directly under a hot heat lamp simply dehydrates it, adding to your problems.

A warm hot-water bottle is easily fixed by filling either a plastic ziploc bag or a plastic glove with warm water (not too hot). Place the chilled pup in a separate small toweled box with the heat source.

Once the puppy is warm and active again, other measures can be taken as needed, such as supplemental feeding.

Gradually, as the puppy matures, its ability to regulate its own temperature develops. But outside sources of heat should be available as indicated.

Hydration

Newborns are 82 percent water at birth, dropping to 68 percent after five months of age. Water is the essential requirement in the first few hours of life. Though one commonly hears that newborns can go twelve hours without nourishment, our experience differs. Beagle pups that are slow to suckle during the first six to eight hours need supplementation. Dehydration can occur far too quickly.

A dehydrated puppy Beagle is limp, less active, losing its sucking reflex and rapidly losing body heat. Pinch the skin on the puppy's neck. A hydrated puppy's skin will return to normal position almost immediately, while the dried-out pup's will remain tented. Immediate hydration is required.

Dehydration is usually accompanied by hypothermia, drop in body temperature, and hypoglycemia, low blood sugar, so the total symptom complex must be treated. The gastrointestinal tract will not be able to process a milk substitute by mouth and the formula will simply pool in the stomach, causing further problems.

The puppy should be warmed and given initially a subcutaneous (under the skin) injection of a warmed solution of one part Ringer's lactate to one part 5 percent glucose. Your veterinarian can provide you with a 250-cc plastic bottle of the solution. It is a simple matter to withdraw a few cc at a time for use.

Clean the skin over the shoulder on one side with alcohol and insert a sterile needle, size 24 or 25, on a syringe just below the skin, draw back on the syringe's plunger slightly to make sure the needle is not in a blood vessel, then inject the solution slowly. Pinch the site of injection gently after withdrawing the needle to prevent the solution from leaking out. Jacob Mosier, D.V.M., recommends one cubic centimeter per ounce of body weight of 5 to 10 percent dextrose, which can be obtained from your veterinarian, followed by tube feeding, once the puppy is warmed and better hydrated. His formula is 0.25 cc/ounce body weight at fifteen- to thirty-minute intervals until the puppy is well hydrated and urinating.

We have found in the moderately dehydrated pup that two to three cc subcutaneously of the Ringer's lactate with 5 percent glucose, repeated in an hour on the other side of the shoulder, results in an almost miraculous return of vigor, activity, hunger and a good sucking reflex. At this point, the puppy is ready to nurse.

Some Beagle pups, the ones less than seven ounces at birth, are slower to come along. If not encouraged and supplemented promptly so that normal weight gain occurs, these pups are more susceptible to dehydration and infection.

Weighing

The best monitor of puppy health is a gradual and steady weight gain. Because newborns can fade so quickly, it is important not only to observe and feel pups frequently, but to weigh them twice daily for the first three weeks. Once daily is sufficient from three to six weeks. Weekly weights from then until sixteen weeks can give you a good guideline for estimating adult size.

Healthy pups double their birth weight in seven to ten days, and triple

Normal nursing behavior.

it in two weeks. A very slight weight loss in the first twenty-four hours, less than 10 percent total body weight, may occur in some pups, followed by a steady gain. A weight loss more than 10 percent requires immediate supplementation. In practice, we supplement if the pup has not gained twenty-four hours after birth.

Nursing

Sucking skill varies in Beagle babies. Most "latch on" immediately, pumping away with front feet, and are able to withstand some competition for teats from siblings. There are some, however, who are inefficient sucklers. These make a great to-do over the nipple, smacking and nuzzling and appearing to be nursing well. Not so. Tummies may feel and look full, but it is just swallowed saliva, not milk. Check the sucking reflex by inserting your little finger in the pup's mouth to see how tightly it wraps its tongue around it and how strongly it pulls. When latched on to the nipple, a good nurser will have strong contractions of the jaw muscles, which can be easily felt by placing thumb and forefinger on either side of the pup's muzzle.

The size and shape of the dam's nipples play an important part in the efficiency of nursing. Some Beagle lines have small flattened nipples. Pups from these bitches may need extra help in getting latched on initially until the nipples are stretched. The two breasts closest to the hindlegs have a tendency to enlarge more than the others, and if not nursed regularly may become impacted with milk. Thus it is important that the puppies utilize all the nipples. Individual pups vary in their preferences, and occasionally one pup may nurse only from a favorite nipple. Small puppies can be easily pushed aside by larger, stronger ones. So it is important to observe pups and dam frequently, giving what assistance is needed.

Supplementation

Newborns require ten to seventy calories per pound per day for the first week of life. Caloric requirements increase to seventy to eighty calories per pound per day the second week, eighty to ninety calories per pound per day the third, and by the fourth week, ninety to one hundred calories per pound per day is needed. Frequent small feedings every two hours enable the pup to handle the volume required without overloading the digestive tract.

A bitch's milk substitute, Esbilac, is easily obtained, either in powdered or the more expensive liquid form. We prefer the liquid, as the powdered is often difficult to mix thoroughly. Directions for the amount of formula to be given per weight of the puppy are clearly marked on the container. However, the every-two-hour schedule is easier on the puppy than the three to four times a day recommended by the manufacturer. Remember, the digestive tract in the newborn is a very fragile system. It is far better to dilute the formula by two parts distilled water to one part formula for the the first twenty-four to forty-

Ten-day-old puppies nursing vigorously. *Lynn Heltne*

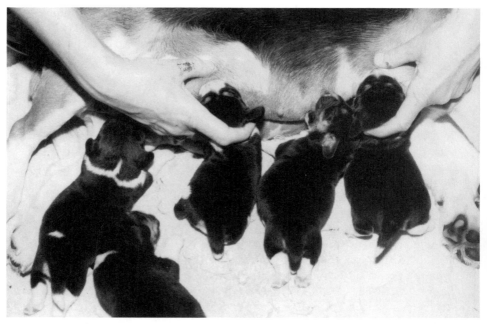

One-week-old litter. How to assist weaker pups by supporting them at the nipple and expressing milk with fingers to increase milk flow. *George Eaton*

eight hours of life, only gradually increasing the formula to full strength by the fourth day of life. Overloading the digestive tract can be fatal, as we have sadly discovered.

Newborns do not develop a gag reflex until about nine days of life. Therefore, one has to be careful how the puppy is fed.

If its sucking reflex is strong, and the reason for supplementing is a bitch whose milk is inadequate in quantity, bottle feeding works well. A pet nurser or a baby bottle with a preemie nipple does the trick. Using a 21-gauge needle that has been sterilized by being burned with a match, poke two holes in the nipple to permit an adequate flow.

With a weakened puppy, tube feeding provides the safest route. For an eight-ounce Beagle puppy a #8 French catheter/feeding tube of soft flexible material fitted on a 10 cc syringe will be appropriate for the size of the esophagus. For a one-pound puppy (sometimes you do get one!) a #16 French catheter is the correct size.

While holding the puppy upright, measure the distance from mouth to the end of the last rib and mark the feeding tube. Slide the tube to the back of the pup's mouth and it will start to swallow the tube. If the newborn coughs, remove the tube and begin again. *Always* check to make sure the tube is in the stomach, not the trachea (windpipe). Pinching the puppy's toes resulting in crying confirms that the airway is clear. Slowly syringe the warmed formula through the tube after pushing out any air. While feeding, always hold the puppy upright; I support the body on my lap in an upright position.

Always burp the puppy following each feeding by either rubbing the tummy or gently stroking the sides of the abdomen downward. Frequently burping occurs while you are stimulating the ano-genital area to induce urination and defecation.

Colostrum

The first milk of the dam, colostrum, is rich in antibodies, which are absorbed through the intestinal tract of the newborn in the first twenty-four to thirty-six hours of life. Those pups which do not get any colostrum are much more susceptible to infection. Plasma infusion (see page 143) may be used if necessary to supply these important antibodies.

COMMON PROBLEMS IN NEWBORNS

Fading Puppy Syndrome

Characteristically, the puppy with this condition is in the smaller range of birth weight. Though vigorous and seemingly normal immediately after birth, it is slower to gain, if at all, during the first twenty-four to forty-eight hours. It may begin to sleep more, miss a nursing or two and have semiliquid or liquid stools. This syndrome may be present in a number of potentially serious problems, but usually it is simply a matter of a small, less-prepared puppy who has to be helped along.

Warming, subcutaneous fluids, if necessary, and one to two cubic centimeters of 5 percent glucose or dextrose by mouth every twenty minutes initially, increased to five to six cubic centimeters at a time about thirty to sixty minutes apart, will usually restore the puppy almost magically.

Diarrhea or liquid stools in the newborn simply means the pH of the digestive tract is acidic. A half-dropperful of milk of magnesia will alkalinize the intestinal tract.

Once the puppy is pink, vigorous and its sucking reflex is present, it can be placed back with its mother. Most likely supplemental feedings of diluted Esbilac several times plus frequent assists at the nipple will be needed. Usually with this help over the first four days, the tiny puppy is over the worst of it.

Diarrhea

Because the digestive tract of the newborn is such a fragile system, diarrhea is a common phenomenon. Normal puppy stools, after the initial dark sticky meconium is passed, are yellow, soft but formed.

Diarrhea can range from simply a softer, more frequent stool with small curds of undigested milk to a profuse yellow liquid.

The former is most common and fortunately poses no danger to the puppy. Causes include too hearty nursing, mixture of formula fed (as when supplementation is given along with nursing) or simply acidification of the digestive tract for whatever reason. Symptomatic treatment consists of one-half dropperful of Kaopectate four times a day for an eight-ounce puppy, one dropperful for a fourteen to sixteen-ouncer. If the stools are very frequent, Kaopectate can be given after each bowel movement until frequency decreases. Antibiotics are seldom needed. Most of these puppies continue to suckle well and gain weight despite the diarrhea.

If the diarrhea is profuse, dehydration can occur rapidly. In this instance, placing the puppy on subcutaneous fluids, as described earlier, and resting the intestinal tract for twenty-four hours will often handle the situation. Alternatively, dextrose and water or Pedialyte (an over-the-counter pediatric preparation for babies with diarrhea) will keep the puppy hydrated. Of course, your veterinarian should be consulted.

It seems to me that once we began using bottled water for the dam, rather than tap water, our incidence of diarrhea in newborns dropped significantly. Some breeders report that a mild continuing diarrhea resists all effort at treatment and subsides only when soft solid foods are begun.

Swollen Eyes

In spite of your best efforts to maintain a clean environment for the puppies, the possibility of contamination is always there. If an infective agent enters the closed eyelids of the newborn, a swollen-appearing eye results. Pus accumulates between the lid and the eyeball. The puppy then looks like the head of a fly with a bulge behind the sealed lids.

Prompt treatment is required, for a generalized infection of the eyeball can result.

Treatment consists of hot compresses, gently prying the eyelid open and expressing pus several times a day and inserting an antibiotic ophthalmic ointment four times a day into the eye.

These puppies, on rare occasion, will develop a dry-eye syndrome. So watch these eyes carefully once the eyes are open. Check to see that the eye is glistening and lubricated. Any discharge or squinting developing later requires immediate veterinarian evaluation. It is my guess that the eventual onset of dry eye indicates a preexisting vulnerability, which resulted in the early infection.

Slow to Walk

It is not uncommon for one puppy in a Beagle litter to be slower than its siblings to stand and walk. The rear legs are weaker, usually extended in position and the puppy lies on its tummy. It scoots itself along primarily by pulling with the forelegs. When this condition is associated with a flat chest and extended front legs as well, the puppy is called a "swimmer."

Once it is clear that the pup cannot get its hind legs under itself, you can support the puppy with your hand and encourage the use of its limbs. Some breeders report excellent results with injections of vitamin E. Bob and Louise Merrill of Starcrest Beagles built a clever U-shaped "walking trough," just wide enough to support the sides of the puppy. The afflicted pup walks from one end to the other at regular intervals throughout the day. The pups love it.

"Supported swimming" in a small tub of water also provides exercise for the limbs without requiring the puppy to support itself by standing.

For the "swimmer" whose front legs are also extended, hobbling them with a figure-of-eight bandage brings the legs under the body with enough room for walking.

Optimal protection for soft chests and sliding feet is afforded by well-padded bedding with a surface that provides good traction. Frequent turning of the pup that lies on its tummy all the time helps distribute the weight evenly over the chest.

Worm Infestation

Roundworm infestation is very common. Encysted larvae in the dam are activated by pregnancy and pass through the placenta to the puppies. Early worming at three to four weeks is indicated. Safe preparations, such as Piperazine or Nemex, are given at weekly intervals until the stools are clear. Reworming four weeks later should suffice, unless reinfestation occurs.

In parts of the country where hookworm is common, an infested dam passes larvae through both the placenta and her milk. Hookworm infestation is particularly dangerous to newborns and must be treated as early as two to four weeks, if necessary. Your veterinarian must supervise treatment.

UNCOMMON PROBLEMS IN NEWBORNS

Septicemia

This generalized blood-borne infection occurs anywhere from one to forty days of age. Most common infectious organisms are *E. coli,* beta-hemolytic streptococcus and staphylococcus. The source of the infection is either an infected breast or, most commonly, an undiagnosed chronic metritis (infection of the uterus) in the dam.

In addition to the typical fading puppy syndrome, these pups will deteriorate rapidly. They will evidence crying, increased rate of respiration, bloating and, finally, shock and death. One after another of the pups in the litter dies.

Good prenatal management of the bitch, as described earlier, is mandatory. Treatment of the affected pups includes removal from the bitch, fluids, warming and antibiotics. Many of the antibiotics effective in adults are not useful in newborns, so careful selection must be made.

All puppies that die should be autopsied, with histological studies made. A blood culture drawn from the heart shortly after death is essential.

Reports from our current conformation population indicate an occasional outbreak in a few kennels. During the 1970s, however, the incidence was much higher, with some breeders losing litter after litter until appropriate antibiotic treatment of the bitches was initiated. With the current veterinary knowledge and practice, the incidence has dropped dramatically.

Canine Herpes Virus

Infection by a herpeslike virus (CHV) occurs in pups *under three weeks of age only.* A soft, greenish-yellow stool is the first sign, followed by persistent, painful crying. Death can occur within twelve to twenty-four hours.

Puppies acquire the virus via the infected genital tract of the bitch.

Treatment consists of fluids to relieve dehydration and low blood sugar, antibiotics and raising the ambient temperature to 100°F for three hours, then dropping it to 93 to 95°F for the rest of a twenty-four-hour period. Rectal temperature of the puppy must be maintained above 96.8°F, for the virus cannot multiply above that temperature. Serum from a bitch who has previously lost litters to CHV given to the afflicted puppies provides antibodies to the virus. Persistently crying puppies have suffered profound liver damage and should be put down. Those pups who are not yet crying can be saved with immediate treatment.

136

Those carrier bitches which develop antibodies to CHV pass those antibodies on to puppies in subsequent litters, but not all bitches develop antibodies. Therefore, repeat breedings of these bitches must be carefully weighed.

Fortunately, reports of CHV in our current conformation population have been rare.

Toxic Milk Syndrome

Characterized by diarrhea, bloating and a red, swollen anus, toxic milk syndrome affects the entire litter.

Though the bitch appears perfectly healthy, her uterus has not involuted (shrunken down) properly following delivery. Toxic protein breakdown in the accumulated fluid is passed in the milk to the puppies.

Treatment is twofold. Remove the pups from the dam for twenty-four to forty-eight hours and treat with oral glucose and water only. Treatment of the dam consists of ergotamine, to flush out the uterus, and antibiotics plus some steroid. After twenty-four to forty-eight hours the pups may be returned to the dam.

Hydrocephalus

Excessive accumulation of fluid in the ventricles (cavities) of the brain produces puppies that fail to thrive and have difficulty with coordination, and is frequently accompanied by a persistently open fontanelle, the central "soft spot" on the anterior skull.

One form is certainly genetic, but other possible causes include nutritional deficiencies in the dam during pregnancy and a high concentration of nitrates in the bitch's drinking water. Some rural communities have a high concentration of nitrates in well water.

Scattered reports of an occasional hydrocephalic Beagle puppy in a litter have been made over the past twenty years. Pedigrees of three beagle litters, each with two hydrocephalic puppies, suggest strongly a genetic basis.

Kidney Disease

Though deaths from kidney disease in Beagle puppies have been reported from time to time in our current population, the causes of the kidney problems have varied.

Symptoms generally include failure to thrive and excessive urination and water ingestion.

The information available to date suggests that these problems are more likely due to some congenital malformation, produced during fetal development in the uterus, rather than genetic.

SOCIALIZATION OF PUPPIES

Once puppies begin to see and hear at about three weeks of age, that next week is the most critical for their social development. From three to ten weeks the pups learn about people, noises and new environmental experiences, with the peak of socialization occurring between five and seven weeks.

Regular playtime with the pups, gradual extension of their space from whelping box to pen to small room, with occasional visits to other parts of the house and outdoors as weather permits, provide pups with optimal exposure. Supervised visits from friends, neighbors and children introduce new human smells and contacts. Toothproof toys—chewsticks, knotted socks (no nylon stockings)—and sturdy stuffed toys entertain both Beagles and owners and encourage chewing on designated objects, not fingers. A radio or TV, tuned to "talk" shows, in the puppy room adds another important exposure.

At six weeks of age, the Campbell Puppy Behavior Test gives an objective evaluation of each pup's personality. Five simple tasks, performed in a test area, will confirm your initial impression of the degrees of dominance/submission patterns.

Tasks consist of (1) attracting the pup to you by clapping hands; (2) walking away from the pup to check its desire to follow; (3) holding the pup down on its back gently for thirty seconds to observe struggling or docility; (4) petting the puppy from top of head downward along the neck and back and (5) cradling the pup in the palm of the hands with the fingers interlaced and elevating it. Responses are graded as shown.

This information makes the decision of what kind of family with which to place a particular puppy much easier.

The dominant dominance pup (two or more *dd* and *d* in remainder) will react in a dominant, aggressive way, and with proper training will fit best with a calm adult family.

The dominant pup (three or more *d* responses) will be an outgoing, quick learner.

Those with three or more *s* responses are more submissive and work well with small children and older folks.

The highly submissive pup (three or more *ss* responses, especially with an *i*) needs consistent and gentle handling to adjust nicely with a family.

Those pups with two or more *i* responses, when associated with some *dd* and *d* responses, may attack if stressed by traditional punishment; whereas those associated with some *i*, accompanied by some *ss* or *s* responses, will tend to be shy under pressure.

I have yet to see a Beagle puppy that falls into the latter category. The vast majority of Beagles fall somewhere between moderately dominant and mildly submissive. Those highly dominant and moderately dominant make the best show prospects. Those with some tail-down responses can be brought along in the show ring with careful, gentle handling.

Remember, the best training system is one that rewards acceptable behavior and ignores that which is unacceptable.

138

Daisyrun puppy, at six weeks.
George Eaton

Seven-week-old pups with their
favorite toy.   *Lynn Heltne*

Ch. O'Boy The Barrister at eight
weeks, owned by Janet Wolfley.

Busch's Razzle Dazzle (Ch. Busch's Ranch Hand ex Ch. Busch's Windyroc Libra), owned by William and Cecile Busch.

Ch. Daisyrun's Flower Power with friend, Jason Eaton.   *George Eaton*

PUPPY BEHAVIOR TEST *(Campbell)*

Section Number and Pup Behavior

1. **Social Attraction**
   Came readily—tail up—jumped—bit at hands   *dd*
   Came readily—tail up—pawed at hands   *d*
   Came readily—tail down   *s*
   Came, hesitant—tail down   *ss*
   Did not come at all   *i*

2. **Following**
   Followed readily—tail up—underfoot—bit at feet   *dd*
   Followed readily—tail up—underfoot   *d*
   Followed readily—tail down   *s*
   Followed, hesitant—tail down   *ss*
   Did not follow or went away   *i*

3. **Restraint Dominance (30 seconds)**
   Struggled fiercely—flailed—bit   *dd*
   Struggled fiercely—flailed   *d*
   Struggled, then settled   *s*
   No struggle—licked hands   *ss*

4. **Social Dominance (30 seconds)**
   Jumped—pawed—bit—growled   *dd*
   Jumped—pawed   *d*
   Squirmed—licked at hands   *s*
   Rolled over—licked at hands   *ss*
   Went and stayed away   *i*

5. **Elevation Dominance (30 seconds)**
   Struggled fiercely—bit—growled   *dd*
   Struggled fiercely   *d*
   Struggled—settled—licked   *s*
   No struggle—licked at hands   *ss*

dd–dominant dominance
d–dominant
s–submissive
ss–strongly submissive
i–inhibited

Fd. Ch. Benbrae Bobolink with owner, Martha Benson.

10

Immunizations

$\mathbf{B}$Y THE TIME this book is published, new information about the safest and best schedule of immunization is likely to be available. At the moment, however, the veterinary consensus is as outlined here.

IMMUNITY

There are many infectious diseases to which dogs are susceptible. These are spread by contact with an infected dog's urine, feces, saliva, respiratory droplets, blood, milk and genital secretions. Protection against infectious disease can be achieved by stimulating the production of antibodies, substances in the blood and other fluids that counteract the invading agent, or antigen. Accidental or planned exposure to the natural infection or a measured amount of a non-disease-producing (attenuated) form of the organism will mobilize the defense system of the dog's body to produce antibodies. However, protection lasts for only a limited period of time. This process is known as active immunity and needs to be renewed or recalled periodically by natural exposure or booster vaccinations.

Passive immunity, the transfer of antibodies from one animal to another, provides protection for the newborn puppy via the ingestion of colostrum, which is the first milk of the dam, or by oral or intraperitoneal (into the abdominal cavity) treatment with dog plasma. These antibodies are absorbed from the colostrum in the newborn's intestinal tract during the first twenty-four to thirty-six hours of life.

Because the amount of circulating antibody in the dam varies, it is difficult to be sure when the passive immunity of the pup begins to drop. Since the presence of circulating antibodies in the puppy can block the development of active immunity with too-early vaccination, most immunization programs rely upon a series of injections. This increases the chances that one or more of them will be of optimal timing.

The major infectious diseases encountered today for which vaccines are available and recommended are: distemper, hepatitis, leptospirosis, para-influenza (kennel cough), Bordetella, parvoviral and corona-viral enteritis and rabies. This is an impressive list. When you consider that multiple vaccinations of each are required to ensure protection, your puppy must begin to feel like a canine pincushion!

Each injection of these foreign proteins requires mobilization of the puppy's immune (defense) system. Hence, each is a stressful occasion. Weaning, separation from its dam and siblings, moving from home to new owners, exposure to an ever-expanding environment are additional developmental stresses inherent in any puppy's growth. When you add up all these stresses, which occur in the first few months of life, you have to wonder about long-term effects on the dog's immune system.

KINDS OF IMMUNIZATION

There are two basic kinds of vaccination materials, those containing modified live infectious agents and those containing an inactivated or killed agent. The modified live preparations are believed to produce longer-lasting immunity, while the killed may need to be repeated more often in order to maintain adequate protection. The advantage of administering the killed preparation is that a lesser assault on the immune system occurs. Also, killed vaccines do not shed virus that can become altered and reinfect other dogs. With a particularly virulent or highly infectious virus such as parvovirus, the assault on a young puppy's immune system may be too great with the modified live vaccine, which in itself is immunosuppressive.

VACCINATION SCHEDULE

The rationale for the following vaccination schedule is based on minimizing the challenge to the immune system at any one time and maximizing the chances of developing active immunity. W. Jean Dodds, D.V.M., who has had extensive experience in immune system problems, recommends this program.

When needed, worming should be done three days prior to vaccination.

| 5½ to 6 weeks: | Canine distemper-measles, adenovirus$_2$, parainfluenza |
| 7 to 8 weeks: | Killed canine parvovirus |

Ch. Pin Oak's Mello Maverick, fifteen inches, Top 15″ Beagle, 1984; National Beagle Club Specialty Best of Breed, 1984 (Ch. Rockaplenty's Wild Oats ex Ch. Hearthside Lovely Talisman), owned by J. Ralph Alderfer.

William Gilbert

Ch. Wilkeep Point of View, fifteen inches, Best of Opposite Sex to Best of Breed, National Beagle Club Specialty, 1987 (Ch. Starbuck's Full Count ex Ch. Wilkeep Hayday Playmate), owned by Alene and Hugh Peek.   *John Ashbey*

10 to 11 weeks:	Killed canine parvovirus
11½ to 13 weeks:	Canine distemper, hepatitis, leptospirosis, adenovirus$_2$, parainfluenza (DHL, PI, adenovirus$_2$) *without* parvovirus
13 to 15 weeks:	Killed canine parvovirus
15 to 17 weeks:	DHL, PI, adenovirus$_2$
18 to 20 weeks:	Killed canine parvovirus
6 months:	Killed parvovirus

An annual booster of DHL, PI, adenovirus$_2$, CPV (modified live parvovirus) should be administered unless the dog or its family have a history of immune-mediated disease in which case only killed parvovirus vaccine is advised.

Those kennels with a history of recurring parvovirus infections are known as "at risk" kennels. Here, vaccination with killed parvovirus should begin at four weeks and repeated every two weeks until the pups are six months of age.

Rabies

While current practices recommend giving rabies vaccine at four months or later, it is advisable to have an interval of at least two weeks between other vaccines and rabies vaccine and to avoid giving rabies vaccine with any other form of immunization whenever possible. Of course, local ordinances and the risk of exposure to rabies in an area may dictate otherwise.

The most widely used rabies vaccines are inactivated viral preparations that are of either one year's or three years' duration and provide effective, safe protection. Modified live rabies vaccines, while still available, are not recommended and are rarely used today.

Bordetella

In some parts of the country Bordetella infection is a major problem. This bacteria-caused upper respiratory infection resembles kennel cough but is more severe. For young puppies it can be a killer, with its quick progression to pneumonia. Vaccination under these circumstances is important to break the cycle of infection.

Two preparations are available, one injectable, the other administered intranasally. The latter appears to be more effective. Two applications of the Bordetella vaccine at two-week intervals are necessary, with yearly boosters. The timing of administration depends on how severe the problem is in your area.

For some breeders, it will be the first vaccination given at five and a half to six weeks of age and timed with the remainder of the inoculations so that there is a week between each. In severely affected kennels, where flareups of Bordetella occur with each litter of puppies, injection of dog plasma from healthy adults in the locale is a safe way to convey immunoglobulins to the "at risk" puppy. It may be given intraperitoneally within the first three days after birth with good results.

Coronavirus Enteritis

Vaccination against coronavirus can be fitted into the above schedule, remembering the general rule of separating each inoculation from the next by a week or more.

HAND-RAISED OR ORPHANED PUPPIES

If newborns do not receive the dam's colostrum within the first twenty-four to thirty-six hours of life, for whatever reasons, transfusion of dog plasma from healthy dogs in the locale can be a useful adjunct to early protection. Your vaccination schedule should begin one to two weeks earlier, provided the pups are vigorous and growing normally. Your veterinarian will help in determining what is necessary.

Many breeders prefer to give their own vaccinations. This is certainly a money-saver, particularly if one has a large number of dogs. Use of reputable vaccine companies and shipping in well-insulated cold packs protects the breeder from the risk of flawed materials; vaccines heated in transit lose their effectiveness and may be unsafe. Puppies vaccinated at home avoid the chance of exposure to contagious diseases sometimes encountered at animal hospitals. However, your puppies will need to be examined by your veterinarian at some point in the first few months of life.

Breakthroughs in vaccination programs can and do occur. Some Beagle kennels have had recurring problems with parvovirus, some with Bordetella. We had a breakthrough of distemper some years ago. Even with the best of immunization programs, however, the occasional puppy will not develop the protective level of immunity it needs. For those kennels so afflicted, tailor-made vaccination schedules may be required. Your veterinarian in consultation with those specialists working in the vaccine field can help work out an effective program.

Future champion The Tavern's One for the Road (The Tavern's Christmas Grogg ex Am./Can. Ch. Foyscroft Wild Goose, Am./Can./Bda. CDX, Am./Can./Bda. TD), owned by Rev. and Mrs. R. Shires.

Linda Forrest

11

Sorting Your Puppies

SORTING your Beagle pups into show and nonshow prospects is generally not difficult in a tightly linebred litter. What is difficult, however, is evaluating a first-time outcross or distant linebred litter. Unfortunately, early decisions must be made, in most cases, to ensure the best timing of placement in the new home.

HOW DO MY PUPPIES GROW?

Most Beagle puppies look just great at six weeks of age, but by eight weeks changes begin to occur. Muzzles may narrow, front legs may curve and rears look narrow. Obviously these pups fall into the nonshow category. By twelve weeks, the puppy is virtually a miniature of the adult dog. This is the time to finalize your sorting.

Judge each pup in a show stack and on a lead in motion, grading against the Standard. Arthur and Carroll Gordon (Page Mill Beagles) evaluated each pup by the Beagle point scale. Those pups scoring over 90 were the show-prospect group.

A soft topline at twelve weeks is a soft topline forever. Adult balance depends upon the particular Beagle line. In ours, a short-on-leg twelve-week-older will be a short-on-leg adult. I have watched pups from other lines producing good-sized fifteen-inch dogs that appear short-legged at 12 weeks, but grow to be well-balanced adults. So you must know how various lines of Beagles develop.

From twelve weeks to six months of age, the Beagle puppy grows in "fits and starts." Heads change from proper to narrow "shoeboxes." Rears may grow faster than fronts in height. Pups lengthen before gaining height. Spindly tails gain brush.

Some pups grow proportionately. In our experience, the pup that does so, always maintaining its balance, usually falls into the thirteen-inch variety.

Basic skeletal structure does not change; a good shoulder is a good shoulder regardless of age. But movement may vary because of erratic growth until adulthood or maturity is reached.

Most thirteen-inch bitches reach full growth at about eight months of age. Thirteen-inch males may grow for a bit longer. Fifteens keep on growing until about twelve months of age.

Average Weight for a 13-inch Dog			Average Weight for a 13-inch Bitch	
Week	Min. Wgt.	Max. Wgt.	Week	Weight
5	3.1618	3.9966	5	3.6267
6	3.6474	4.4597	6	4.0145
7	4.1604	4.9534	7	4.5597
8	4.6996	5.4843	8	5.2227
9	5.2638	6.059	9	5.9639
10	5.8518	6.6841	10	6.7437
11	6.4624	7.3662	11	7.5225
12	7.0944	8.1119	12	8.2607
13	7.7466	8.9278	13	8.9187
14	8.4178	9.8205	14	9.4569
15	9.1068	10.7966	15	9.8357
16	9.8124	11.8627	16	10.0155

Average Weight for a 15-inch Dog			Average Weight for a 15-inch Bitch	
Week	Min. Wgt.	Max. Wgt.	Week	Weight
5	3.2957	5.0943	5	3.7514
6	3.7201	5.5819	6	4.1817
7	4.3071	6.3797	7	4.7788
8	5.0225	7.4055	8	5.5073
9	5.8321	8.5771	9	6.3318
10	6.7017	9.8123	10	7.2169
11	7.5971	11.0289	11	8.1272
12	8.4841	12.1447	12	9.0273
13	9.3285	13.0775	13	9.8818
14	10.0961	13.7451	14	10.6553
15	10.7527	14.0653	15	11.3124
16	11.2641	13.9559	16	11.8177

PREDICTION OF SIZE

Accurate prediction of adult height at the shoulders is impossible! Accepting that fact, there are some general factors that can help you

150

Future champion littermates, Ch. Just-Wright Bedazzler and Ch. Just-Wright Jazz Dancer, at play at four and one half weeks. They are by Ch. Hollypines Star of Jim-Mar ex Ch. Whisper's Jazz Happy, CD.   *Julie Wright*

Dazzler at eight weeks of age. *Julie Wright*

Dancer at three months of age.
Julie Wright

151

make an "educated" guess about which variety is more likely. Each closely bred Beagle line has its own growth patterns. Jean Dills (Pickadilly Beagles) uses multiple measurements, including height, hock length and circumference of legs, at six weeks of age, as indicators. Others use the puppy's weight at four weeks by which to project adult variety.

In our closely linebred stock, weights of all puppies were recorded at four, six, eight, twelve, sixteen weeks and at five and six months. George Eaton correlated the data, producing a graph for each variety and sex within each variety. As can be seen from these charts, there is a borderline region where either thirteen-inch or small fifteen-inch varieties can lie. The weight at twelve weeks is suggestive of adult size, but not certain. When the data are graphed, an obvious zone of overlap occurs. Additional weights at later ages may make more accurate prediction possible.

Obviously, figures from one kennel cannot be directly applied to another. But perhaps the general principle can be used. Remember that weights must be taken on the *same* scale. Even then, it is impossible to obtain totally accurate figures, as puppies wiggle along with the weight indicator!

Parents of either variety can and do produce get of either variety.

It is wise to alert prospective buyers that final size cannot be guaranteed!

BITES

Evaluating bites in your young Beagle puppies can be a tricky business. What you see today may change over a period of months.

Overshot Bite

A severely overshot mouth may be obvious shortly after birth, or, for that matter, at birth. The puppy appears chinless. When viewed from underneath, a small portion of the roof of the mouth (the hard palate) may be seen, even with the mouth closed. These pups may have difficulty nursing.

The less severely overshot mouth may not be obvious until the baby teeth appear. There has been one instance of an overshot bite showing up as late as seven or eight months of age. Whether this condition will correct with full growth is uncertain.

I have never yet seen an overbite that is apparent early in life correct as the Beagle grows.

Undershot Bite

Like overshot mouths, undershot bites vary in degree. Severe distortion shows up early in life, less severe later. In one of the Beagle lines, a mild undershot position can be a transient phase between four to six months of age, correcting with full growth. In one known instance, a minimal undershot bite appeared at about one year of age and became permanent.

It is important to know the history of the Beagle lines in your pedigrees.

I understand that the ever-inventive exhibitor has resorted to various

Monarch's Solo Performance at ten weeks (Ch. Merry Song's High Performance ex Monarch's Royal Debut), owned by Cathy deStout. *Cathy deStout*

Monarch's Solo Performance at seven months. *Fox/Cook*

153

devices to achieve the appearance of a good bite. Surgical realignment of the front teeth, grinding of the upper or lower teeth, use of orthodontic appliances and rubber bands have apparently all been used. Apart from the fact that it is a violation of AKC rules to physically alter the appearance of a dog, remember that bad bites are most likely an inherited trait. So what have you really accomplished?

WHICH DO I KEEP?

Usually there is one pup, or if you are lucky two, in a litter that catches your eye from birth on. And often these pups at twelve weeks stand out.

If you are exceptionally lucky, all pups may appear to be good show prospects. What you keep for future breeding depends upon what improvements you wish to make in your line.

For example, in our tightly bred line, the Beagles tended toward a "short," heavy neck and higher ear set, and the thirteen-inch bitches had some trouble whelping. Therefore, the choice to keep a fifteen-inch, leggy, nicely necked and long-eared bitch was easy. The two smaller, but better overall, bitches went to new homes.

Nothing can match the fun of showing your home-bred Beagle to its championship and beyond. It is every breeder's dream to breed an outstanding Beagle that makes its mark in the ring and on its progeny. With luck, you may get both in one package.

Good bitches are the mainstay of any breeding program. If space limitations prevent you from keeping a good bitch from each carefully planned breeding, then the bitch can be placed with breeding rights. This system has worked well for many breeders, who then whelp and raise the litter before returning the bitch to her home. Our practice was to keep both a bitch and a dog from a particularly good litter. Unless you plan to keep one of the offspring of a particular mating, or unless you have specific requests for pups from that breeding, *do not breed.* The world is full of wonderful Beagles—so many that some end up in Beagle rescue programs.

"I Want a Group and Best in Show Puppy"

Don't we all! Let's face it, the only way you can be assured of a Best in Show Beagle is to buy one—the Beagle, that is.

Group and Best in Show wins depend upon a number of factors, not the least of which are luck and timing. All a responsible breeder can guarantee a prospective buyer is a healthy, good-temperamented, promising puppy when the purchase is made at twelve or thirteen weeks of age.

If the puppy is the product of a repeat breeding where the previous litter has reached adulthood, more accurate predictions of adult conformation and show-worthiness can be made.

12

Seller's and Buyer's Rights

WHAT TO LOOK FOR IN A BUYER

First, you want a household in which the Beagle will be a member of the family and its particular needs respected.

You owe your puppy a home where he will be loved, be trained gently and consistently and receive the physical care necessary. This includes time in the house, a safely fenced yard, protection from weather, good diet, proper vaccinations and veterinary care as needed.

Consider the family makeup. Some young children, even under five years of age, have been taught by their parents to have a real feel for relating to a puppy. Others are not ready until older. A Beagle puppy of twelve weeks is quite small and needs careful handling.

Buyers who want first a good potential show Beagle, and only second a good Beagle friend, may not prove to be the best selection. Enthusiasm for dog shows can fade. But commitment to the dog should remain constant. Always ask what the history of previous animals in the home has been. Some breeders successfully place their show prospects in fine pet homes with the understanding that the puppy may be shown to its championship by the breeder.

In instances where the Beagle will not be shown or used for breeding, spay/neuter contracts *are a must*. Children do not need a reproductive experience in their dogs to provide sex education. And, goodness knows, the world doesn't need any more unwanted dogs.

Ch. Teloca Sirius Rhedd Butler and Ch. Scarlett O'Haira, fifteen inches, littermates (Ch. Teloca Kaja Boo Boo, CD, ex Ch. Teloca Patches Educat'd Guess), owned by Rosalind Hall and Marie Shuart.

Paulette

Registration papers can be withheld pending receipt of a veterinarian's certificate of spaying or neutering. With the AKC plan to issue two kinds of dog registrations, now under consideration, one for those to be used for breeding and the other for dogs that will not be bred, this matter may be handled quite simply.

Your obligation does not end when the puppy is placed. Changes can occur in families. Unfortunately, divorce, aging, death, job transfers may require finding the Beagle a new home. Each buyer should notify the breeder if unable to keep the Beagle. Either the Beagle should be returned to you, the breeder, or you and the owner can agree upon a new home.

A written contract, spelling out all the conditions of sale, saves a lot of worry and potential trouble.

WHAT A PUPPY BUYER SHOULD GET

Always there are choices among various litters, and whenever possible a potential buyer should have some choice within a given litter. Guidance from the breeder as to which puppy would better serve a particular family's requirements is important. No Beagle puppy should ever go to an unsuitable home. Certain pups fit certain styles of living better than others (refer to the Campbell Puppy Behavior Test, page 141).

The buyer deserves a healthy, outgoing, friendly Beagle with some crate experience.

In addition, a "dowry" of the following should accompany the puppy to its new home: health history, record of vaccination and worming, AKC registration paper (unless a spay/neuter contract requires delay in transfer of ownership), pedigree, written instructions for feeding and vaccination schedule and grooming care. These are obvious items; suggestions regarding a veterinary referral, if the owner has none, are helpful. A supply of food for the first few days, some favorite toys and some item with the familiar odor of home, such as a sleeping pad or blanket, will ease the transition for the puppy.

An airline crate for sleeping, transportation and training can be purchased by the buyer. An inexpensive initial investment, this crate will more than pay for itself.

The simple contract between seller and buyer should spell out any conditions of sale, including a requirement by the seller or the buyer to have the puppy examined by a veterinarian within forty-eight hours. Occasionally, a puppy who is healthy on departure from its original home may develop some infection within the first several weeks in its new home. Unfortunately, if a young puppy has not developed active immunity from its parvovirus vaccinations, it may be susceptible to infection with exposure to a new environment and the stress of the change. Let's hope you never have to deal with this tragic situation. Each breeder needs to have some idea of what to do in this case.

For the lifetime of any Beagle that is placed, the breeder should maintain periodic contact with the new family. Certainly in the first few weeks of adoption many questions arise where the breeder can be helpful.

A breeder needs to be prepared either to take the Beagle back at any point during the dog's lifetime or to help place him in a new home if circumstances require.

13

Puppy and Conformation Training

PUPPY TRAINING

Getting off on the right foot with a new puppy requires some clear idea on proper training methods.

Beagle puppies want to please their human friends. Dogs learn best by rewarding appropriate behavior with praise and rewards (treats); punishment is cruel and abusive. Dogs can learn easily what certain words mean. For example, "outside" is the signal for where to go for urination and defecation; "no," on the other hand, gives the puppy no clear signal as to what *is* expected.

There are an enormous number of tasks a new puppy must learn: where to relieve itself; what areas of the house are off limits; when not to bark and when to bark; which items are chewable; how to walk on a leash; as well as a number of specific commands. "Come," "sit," "stay," "outside," "down," "stand" can all be life saving.

No wonder there are occasional mistakes.

Teaching your puppy early to feel at home with handling of its mouth, head, ears and feet makes grooming chores and veterinary visits much easier for all concerned.

Many communities offer puppy training classes, giving puppy and owner a chance to learn.

Ch. The Whim's Cock of the Walk, thirteen inches, owned by Mrs. A. C. Musladin. *Ludwig*

CONFORMATION TRAINING

In the Conformation ring, the Beagle must stand for the judge's examination, trot on a lead with head and tail up and "free-stack," or stand in a stack position on its own with head and tail up. The same training principles apply here that work for general training. Reward your Beagle's desired behavior with praise and treats. Ignore his undesirable behavior.

Stacking experience can begin as early as four weeks of age. Simply set up your puppy in proper stance for a couple of seconds several times a day on whatever elevation is handy. Beds, countertops, washing machines—anything will do. Praise the puppy extravagantly when he stands still for even a moment. As time goes by, he will stand for longer periods of time. Always make each stacking session brief and quit while you are ahead!

When your Beagle can stand for half a minute or so, other household members can play "judge," handling its head, examining its bite, feeling for shoulder layback and presence of testicles.

Collar training begins at three weeks of age with the use of a small, soft puppy collar. By the time the litter has learned to chew the collars off, the lesson has been painlessly learned.

Six weeks of age is the best time to start lead training. Let the pups run around a bit with a soft leather show lead on each, ends dragging on the floor or ground. The baby Beagles love it.

When they appear comfortable with the leads, enlist the aid of family members or friends as auxiliary handlers. Tug gently on the lead, coaxing the puppy along, praising him as he follows correctly. Don't worry if the nose is to the ground. After all, that's what Beagles are supposed to do. Small bits of puppy chow work well as treats for tasks well done. Having the puppies follow their dam on a lead works well, too.

Brief daily training periods initially fix the pattern so the puppy knows what is expected when show-training begins in earnest. These practice sessions should be fun for you and the puppy. Recruit neighbors and children to accustom the pups to being handled by strangers.

As the puppy progresses, follow the standard Conformation ring routine: stack; gait around a large circle, as well as down and back; "make a triangle"; and stop in a show stack pose. This latter step is impressive when seen in the ring.

Initially offer treats while each task is being mastered. Later, with your Beagle in the ring, Dr. Dunbar suggests that treats be offered intermittently for successful performance. This keeps the dog guessing and eager, not sure just when its treat will magically appear. Unbroken repetition becomes boring for your dog, too.

Familiarize your Beagle with measuring procedures as well.

Puppy matches accustom a young Beagle to travel and sights and sounds of the dog-show scene. But make sure these excursions are not too exhausting.

Owners busy with jobs, family responsibilities and several dogs don't

Ch. Kamelot's Queen Bee, thirteen inches, number one thirteen-inch bitch in Beagle history, with three Bests in Show and National Beagle Club Specialty, 1982 (Ch. Rockaplenty's Wild Oats ex Ch. Plain & Fancy's Bumble Bee), owned by Ray Scott. *Klein*

Ch. Jo Mar's Repeat Performance, thirteen inches (Ch. Carwood Capasa Amigo, CD, ex Ch. Lokavi's Sure Shot of Jo-Mar), owned by Marcia Foy, multiple Group winner, sire of twenty champions, including thirteen-inch Ch. Green Mtn Irish Mist. His wins include Best Variety, thirteen inches, and Best of Opposite Sex to Best of Breed, National Beagle Club Specialty, 1980; Best of Breed, Bay State Beagle Club Specialty, 1980; and Best of Variety, thirteen inches, Southern New York Beagle Club Specialty on several occasions.
Charles Tatha

always have time for a daily practice session. If the puppy has had a good basic training experience, brief refresher courses prior to the onset of the pup's show career work well.

Unfortunately, experiences that are startling or frightening to a dog occur at dog shows. Heavy ring stands fall with horrendous clanging. Onlookers scream, shout and applaud suddenly and loudly. Two dogs suddenly begin a fight to the death right behind you and your dog in the ring. Give the puppy a chance to collect himself. Beagles are pretty resilient, but some are of softer temperament than others.

Rewarding spooky behavior, tail down, cringing or flattening itself on the ground, by fussing or coddling teaches the young dog the wrong lesson. Ignore the "nervous Nellie" act and go about your business of signaling that the unexpected furor is no big deal.

Ch. Buglair Brantwood Intrigue, fifteen inches (by Ch. Brantwood Buglair Bandit ex Ch. Buglair Ruffian), owned by Anita and Arnold Tillman. *Sally Anne Thompson*

14

Good Care of Your Beagle

GOOD PREVENTIVE veterinarian care includes a current vaccination program, annual checkups and visits as needed for problems as they arise.

At home, some simple health care tasks should be done regularly.

GROOMING

Ear cleaning, toenail trimming, brushing or stripping out dead coat and anal gland expression should be done monthly. Baths are given as often as necessary.

Because of the Beagle's pendulous ears, ear-mite infestation is common. Cleaning the inside of the ears—the ear canal—gently with Q-tips and alcohol removes dust, superficial wax and debris. One-half eyedropperful of a 1:3 mixture of Canex or Canolene to mineral oil in each ear, followed by gentle massage, once monthly seems to prevent the development of ear-mite infestation. A bad odor or discharge from the ear requires a trip to your veterinarian. Ear infections can be difficult to clear.

An active Beagle running on a hard surface wears his toenails down naturally; The more indolent older Beagle requires more frequent trimming. Short nails enable the foot to maintain a tight compactness; long nails can get caught and torn. Toenails can be kept short either by cutting with a nail clipper or by grinding with an electric grinder. Never cut or grind beyond the tip of the pink nail bed visible within the nail.

Anal gland expression is not the pleasantest of tasks. These glands, located on either side of the anus, secrete a foul-smelling substance. If they should get plugged or impacted, infection can set in, resulting in a painful abscess. Using several thicknesses of facial tissue, you can squeeze firmly on both sides of the anus to express the secretions.

Bathing need not be an ordeal. Beagles, like people, prefer their water warm and don't like soap in their eyes, ears or mouth. Flea and tick shampoos contain various insecticides. Follow your veterinarian's recommendations as to which product can be used safely with your particular flea-prevention program. A good sudsing, followed by a thorough rinsing, brisk toweling and complete drying in a warm, dry room leaves your Beagle "squeaky clean."

CARE OF THE TEETH

Care of your Beagle's teeth requires brushing with a soft toothbrush and a veterinary toothpaste or gel at least twice a week, preferably daily. Use of a salt-and-soda paste also works to slow tartar accumulation, but may not be as tasty to the dog. Tooth scalers for heavier tartar removal are helpful but need some skill to master the technique.

Reward your Beagle with a treat after the above procedures. He'll love it. Ours even line up eagerly to have their teeth brushed and squabble over who will be first!

EXERCISE

Beagle puppies and young adults romp and play with great enthusiasm. A good run or play session in the morning, afternoon and before bedtime keeps your dog happy and well exercised.

As the Beagle grows older, a good walk twice a day ensures better health for both of you. Beagles with chronic disc disease or chronic heart problems will tolerate much less exercise. Follow your veterinarian's advice with these old fellows.

FLEA CONTROL

No doubt the most discouraging problem you will have to deal with is the tiny flea. A scourge to man and beast, the flea is a real survivor. It will drive both you and your Beagle crazy.

Regular spraying of your yard and house most likely will be required, as well as regular flea dips for your Beagle during the "flea season." Insecti-

Ch. Tarr Hill Classical Jazz, fifteen inches, Group winner and Best Veteran, National Beagle Club Specialty, 1988 (Ch. Pixshire's The Entertainer ex Ch. Tarr Hill Triple Tina), owned by Julie Fulkerson and Sharon L. Clark. *Alverson*

Poppy and Boomer, age fourteen and a half years (Ch. The Whim's Buckeye ex Ch. The Whim's Chatterbox), owned by Sandi and Michael Groeschel.

cides change as the flea adapts or becomes resistant, so current recommendation from your veterinarian will hopefully keep you a step ahead.

Because of the additive effect of sprays, dips, flea baths and flea collars, *always* read the directions on each product carefully before using. Don't give your Beagle insecticide poisoning in your enthusiasm to banish the flea.

Tapeworm infestation can be a direct consequence of flea infestation.

WEIGHT CONTROL

If given the opportunity, any healthy, usually ravenous, Beagle will literally eat itself to death.

Obesity complicates any existing illness, predisposes your dog to disc and joint problems, and is absolutely within your control. It is much easier to keep your Beagle at proper weight than it is to try and diet it down from a five- to ten-pound excess. That can take months. A subcutaneous fat layer of about one-half inch over the rib cage is as much as your Beagle needs. When in doubt, weigh.

THE GERIATRIC BEAGLE

Beagles live longer than many of the large breeds of dogs. The average life span is about fourteen years, with some hardy souls making it to seventeen years. Beagle owners are lucky in that respect.

Most Beagles begin to slow down around twelve years of age. Annual checkups, increased to twice yearly at about ten years of age, reveal any developing physical problems.

Failing hearing and vision are inevitable. Old Beagles who by accident wander from home may not hear or see oncoming cars. So extra attention is required when workmen or servicemen open gates or doors.

Changes in routine are more upsetting to the old-timers, and they may become cranky with younger dogs. They tend to sleep a great deal and require fewer calories, and arthritic stiffness and muscle wasting prevent comfortable exercise. Many old Beagles show signs of intervertebral disc disease (degeneration and/or extrusion of the cushion between the vertebrae).

The onset of graying around the eyes and muzzle depends upon the Beagle line. Some show graying as early as two or three years, others not until eight or nine.

Little skin tumors become evident at about ten years, growing in all sorts of places in all sizes and shapes. Fast-developing growths should be removed. Most lumps are perfectly benign, but, unfortunately, not all. Black tumors, especially on the mucous membrane of the mouth, should always be removed and histological sections done. Malignant melanoma, a rapidly growing and spreading tumor, is a not-uncommon cause of death in older Beagles.

Early treatment for any developing physical problem, such as heart, kidney or liver disease, can add years to your Beagle's life. For the deteriorating heart valve, identified by development of a murmur, a change to a low-salt diet, such as Hill's Heart Diet, and medications to reduce the work load on the heart can delay the onset of heart failure.

Proper dietary protein regulation aids ailing kidneys, and thyroid supplementation will be required for hypothyroidism, a common occurrence in middle-aged Beagles.

In those Beagles with epilepsy that have averaged one to three seizures per year, the frequency of seizures may *decrease* markedly.

Two kinds of transient neurological episodes have occurred in some of our old-timers. The first is the sudden onset of a drooping lower eyelid in combination with a constricted pupil. This condition, called Horner's syndrome, usually clears completely within several weeks without any treatment. The second looks like a small stroke, and probably is. The Beagle may appear to be unsteady and confused and have difficulty getting up. Initially, you may think you are seeing an epileptic seizure, but the symptoms persist for several hours. Usually all symptoms clear by eight to ten hours, and your Beagle is himself again. Your veterinarian should be notified, however, when one of these episodes occurs.

When old organs fail or malignancy is winning the battle, the decision to euthanize your old friend must be made. It is so difficult to know exactly when. Sadly, most of us wait too long. Pain, failure of appetite and "no joy in life" mark the time.

Euthanasia in the Beagle's home is ideal, but not always possible. I need to hold my old-timers when my veterinarian gives the last injection.

Remember that this is a difficult task, as well, for the veterinarian who has cared for your Beagle over many years. Sometimes an associate in the same office is a kinder choice.

The following table lists known causes of death from one Beagle kennel over a fifteen-year period; all Beagles involved were euthanized.

Causes of Death

Cancer of the head/neck	4
Malignant melanoma	4
Adrenal insufficiency	1
Heart failure	9
Disc disease	1
Ruptured urethra	1
Pneumonia & heart disease	2
Pancreatitis	1
Cancer of the prostate	1
Histoplasmosis	2
Immune deficiency related	2
Eye-related problems	2

Ch. Swan Lake's Luke of Craigwood, fifteen inches (Ch. Swan Lake's Spirit O'Craigwood ex Ch. Craigwood's Shannon), owned by Sharon L. Clark.
Sabrina

Ch. Validay Columbine, fifteen inches (Ch. Validay King Cole ex Ch. Validay Lorelei), owned by Validay Beagles. *Gilbert*

15

Grooming for Show—An Illustrated Guide

THOUGH the Beagle is a short-coated dog, proper trimming can enhance the outline and present a cleaner line to the animal. Personally, we prefer the more natural look that a scissors trim can give to the "clippered" look. So the following is offered as instructions to achieve the former approach.

EQUIPMENT NEEDED

Grooming table or stacked crates with a nonskid surface and grooming arm
Good source of light, either daylight or artificial
Comb (combination fine and coarse toothed)
Regular barber scissors
Thinning shears (44-20 Taper Fine)
Nail clippers
Terrier stripping knife (fine-toothed)
Small curved blunt-ended scissors
Hound glove

You will also need certain items for emergencies: Eye ointments or drops (for infection), coagulants (for bleeding toenails), oral antibiotics, antidiarrhea medication and cortisone cream (for "hot spots" or foot irritations).

(*How to make pill-giving easy:* Put the pill in a small ball of cold cream cheese and offer to the Beagle as a treat.)

THE GROOMING PROCESS

Depending upon the thickness and length of your Beagle's coat, trimming should begin at least four weeks before show time, and sometimes as early as three months if the coat is particularly thick and heavy ("winter coat" syndrome). The fine touches, such as ears, pasterns and feet, of course, can wait until the day before the show. The major tasks in respect to the coat should begin early, for they will need to be repeated weekly. The stripping process may need to be done every other day or even daily to remove the heavy undercoat on some Beagles.

Head

Eyes: Remove "fuzz" at the inner corner of the eyes with thinning shears.

Ears: Smooth the edge of the ears with scissors and blend the trimmed area with the rest of the ear as shown in figure 1A.

Whiskers: Although we no longer trim whiskers, since they are tactile organs that the dog should have, they can be removed with scissors.

Lips: Smooth the edge of the upper lip with scissors.

Neck

Start trimming the neck on either side with a good, sharp pair of thinning shears, beginning just below the ear, about on line with the back edge of attachment to the skull. Cut the hair away from the surface gradually. Do *not* stick the thinning shears upward under the coat and cut hunks of hair out because in time this will produce an irregular, lumpy, chopped look (see figures 1B and 2).

Gradually trim the coat downward toward the shoulder and, if necessary, over the shoulder and down onto the chest. Your goal is to clean up the lines of the neck and chest.

Many dogs have a "ruff" part way down from the neck onto the shoulder, and this should be trimmed neatly and blended in.

The entire process is repeated on the opposite side.

A very important part in properly grooming a Beagle is stripping out the

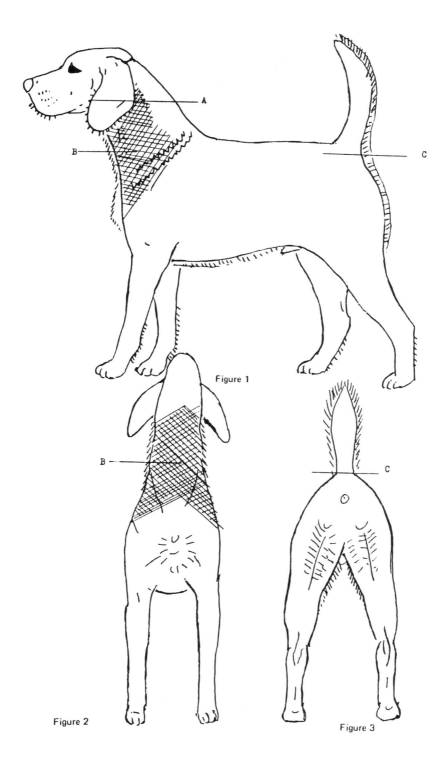

Figure 1

Figure 2

Figure 3

undercoat, as well as all the dead hair. Removal of this unsightly hair will enhance the glossiness of the coat. After the neck has been trimmed, it will appear as though all the color in a dark-coated dog has been removed. However, if you are diligent and keep up the trimming on a regular basis, along with judicious stripping out of the undercoat, you'll be surprised how the color will return. Obviously, this work can't be done a day or so before the show, but should be done well in advance, with maintenance done in the interval.

Blend your trimming of the neck into the chest in a smooth manner. Crosshatched areas on the drawings are the areas to be trimmed.

Chest

Using scissors, smooth the centerline over the front of the chest.

Abdomen and (for Males) Penis

Smooth closely with scissors to develop a smooth arch line in front of the thigh. Trim long hairs over the penis and pelvic area.

Hindquarters

Develop a nice outward arch to the buttocks from the base of the tail downward toward the stifle. Using thinning shears, gradually trim the coat in this area to get a clean line from both side and rear. The buttocks should show a smooth, convex line. Get all the excess hair off, as illustrated in figures 1 and 3.

Next develop a concave or inward curve over the stifle area. Color, both over the buttocks and stifles, can be of help in determining how much to trim. You don't want to trim the buttocks, for example, so much they appear narrow when viewed from the side.

Also trim the fuzzy hair from the inside of the thighs for a clean, trim look (figure 3).

Tail

With a combination of thinning shears and scissors, start an upward line from just above the anus (figures 1C and 3C) and carry it up in a smooth curve to about one-third the tail length. Make this line a smooth transition into the brush. *Do not square off the tail tip;* leave it pointed smoothly, as in the natural state. The tail should be smooth, not irregular.

Feet

Trim around the outside of the feet and between the pads. Toenails should be clipped back.

Ch. Lacoste Simply Red, thirteen inches, BIS and Group winner (Ch. Teloca Littl' Red Corvette ex Ch. Teloca Fairfax Lady Susan), owned by Jose dePoo III. *Earl Graham*

Ch. Lynbrooke Give 'Em the Dickens, thirteen inches, BIS and Specialty winner (Ch. Teloca Patches Littl' Dickens ex Ch. Chardon Woodstone Olympian), owned by Bill and Susan Hayes.

Olson

Ch. Daisyrun's Prunedale Paddy, fifteen inches, Group winner (Ch. The Whim's Spirit O' Seventy Six ex Am./Can. Ch. Ravenswood Cinnamon O' Emania), owned by Nadine Chicoine. *Bonnie*

175

Pasterns

Trimming with scissors should be done so that, when observed from the side, the pastern is straight up and down from the fetlock to the pad. Some of the irregular hair along the back of the front leg can also be trimmed.

Teeth

Teeth should be clean. This can be achieved by regular brushing at home, using a canine dentifrice or a paste of salt and soda along with a soft toothbrush. If necessary, more recalcitrant tartar can be scraped or chipped away with a dental scraper.

Ears

Regular attention to ears to prevent ear-mite infestation or accumulation of cerumen will assure clean ears. A cleanup prior to being shown will generally prevent the dog from shaking his head when the show lead is in place.

Removal of Urine Stains

You may have a problem with urine stains on feet and tail. To remove them, make a paste of equal parts vinegar and water mixed with cornstarch. Rub into the stained areas and leave overnight. Brush out thoroughly in the morning.

CONDITIONING

Obviously, proper conditioning for superior appearance in the ring is the result of good diet, plenty of exercise, close weight watch and general attention to the dog's health. Uncomfortable travel arrangements will also take their toll, so be sure the dog is comfortable on its way to a show, especially if it must be shipped by air. The airline crate should be properly roomy, and should have a water supply either during hot weather or for long distances: Fill a rabbit/ guinea pig water bottle and attach it to the crate door so that water will drip into the plastic dish that is usually attached to the door. Movement of the crate will allow the water supply to drip gradually, or the dog can lick the tip of the water bottle.

Frozen cold packs wrapped in freezer bags beneath the crate's floor covering will also help in warm weather.

16

Beagle Rescue

THE PUREBRED DOG population has exploded during the
last twenty-five years. An unfortunate side effect is the growing number of
purebreds abandoned or turned in to humane societies. In an attempt to save
these dogs from extermination, many breed clubs have developed a "rescue
service" for their specific breeds. Attempts are made to locate the owner of the
dog if the animal has been lost; if relinquished, the dog, after neutering or
spaying, is placed in a new home through the efforts of the rescue service.

Individual Beagle rescue efforts have been made over the years by some.
One East Coast breeder, when aware that the owner of a certain kennel had
become incapacitated, placed the dogs for the owner, and also rescued a
number of Beagles from another kennel when their owner abandoned them.

Beagle rescue became organized in 1977 when the Southern California
Beagle Club developed a program that included picking up, housing and
placing homeless or rejected Beagles. At the same time, Mary Powell and
Trudi Reveira (Powveira Beagles, Sunnyvale, California) established the
Northern California Beagle Rescue.

These organized efforts have been costly, exhausting and, both heartbreaking and rewarding. In 1985 the Southern California Beagle Rescue found
itself overwhelmed. Too much of the Club's manpower and funds were needed
to support the program. Janet and Bill Nieland of Nieland's Beagles placed the
remaining rescue Beagles over the next year, at which time the service closed.

The Northern California Beagle Rescue has continued to operate, handled by Mary and Trudi. The following, written by Mary, is a summary of its
activities. The statistics are appalling.

177

Beagle Rescue really began in 1966 when McGillicutty Beagle wandered to our door. His owner was lost and never found. McGillicutty moved in and stayed.

In 1973 Sam, tied up by his owner for a year, was taken into custody by the Humane Society and placed with us. Sam had a collar so tight around his neck it required surgical removal. We obtained his American Kennel Club papers, showed him both in Conformation and Obedience, where he gained his CD and CDX degrees.

Between 1966 and 1977 when we started the Northern California Beagle Rescue, we placed approximately 150 Beagles, all from area animal shelters. From 1977 through 1988, 520 Beagles were placed. Of these, 50 percent came from animal shelters; 40 percent were turned in by their owners directly to us; 10 percent were held by their owners until placed in new homes.

Of the 50 percent turned in or held by original owners until placed, 20 percent were bred by local breeders and 30 percent initially purchased from pet stores. The majority (90 percent) of the Beagles from the shelters were definitely pet-store quality, complete with dewclaws.

We are grateful to the Blossom Valley Beagle Club and its membership for their support over the years.

Prospective homes are carefully screened; the most important question asked is "Where will the Beagle sleep?" A recent placement was an unusual one. An eight-year-old rescue Beagle now joins his new owner and a young Beagle bitch sailing out to an island where both hounds can run free for the day. At night they sleep in the boat. Protective netting keeps the Beagles from falling overboard in choppy seas.

Could you ask for more?

17

Genetics: How Can I Use What I Don't Understand?

WELL, the happy news is that you don't have to be a geneticist to use the principles of genetics. The purpose of this chapter is to give the breeder a way to work with the principles of heredity in a practical way.

Remember as you read that the key to the system hinges on consistency and focus. In other words, figure out what you want and adhere to it, and don't try to solve all your problems at once.

BREEDING CO-OPS

Since most of us are limited in our breeding facilities, I recommend the idea of a co-op breeding program. The idea would be to link up with two or three others who agree with your ideas of what the perfect dog should be, establish a list of priorities and work on them together. One or two good studs and several bitches can not only increase your chances of success, but also accelerate your time frame considerably.

All of these dogs should have the same general conformation or "type,"

Ch. Fulmont's Fail Safe, thirteen inches, multiple Group winner (Ch. Page Mill On the Road Again ex Ch. Swan Lake Fulmont Foolproof), owned by Dr. and Mrs. William Fulkerson.   *Sabrina*

Ch. Hewley Easter, fifteen inches, Best of Opposite Sex to Best of Breed, National Beagle Club Specialty, 1988, and winner of multiple Group Firsts (Ch. Johjean Crackerjack ex Hewley Eastland), owned by Ed Jenner.

Ashbey

and should be appealing to all the breeders involved. If you could cut and paste, you *must* be able to make the perfect dog with these starter dogs. That is, no one fault should appear in all of the dogs. After the first or second round of breeding you should be able to determine which of your bitches are going to be the best producers.

CULLING ETHICS AND BREEDER RESPONSIBILITY

The greatest problem for the breeder is not in selecting the good puppies, but in culling out the puppies with the undesirable traits. It seems to be our cross to bear that we get a gorgeous puppy with at least one ghastly fault or inherited defect, or a not-so-great puppy that has a spectacular virtue. This is the hardest part of breeding, because our hearts are so in control of our heads. If all we are going to do is neuter these puppies, keep them and love them, fine. But if we lose control of our plan, the improvement of the breed is never going to become a reality.

Most breeds have some hereditary problems that their breeders would rather not deal with at all, and Beagles are no exception. But conscientious breeders meet the challenge of hereditary defects head on. They look for straight answers from their veterinarians and consultants on the nature of these defects in their breeding programs. A failure to face hereditary problems as they arise can only lead to more trouble in the future. We are all tempted to overlook a fault in a "superpup," particularly if he only carries it recessively, or it is not visible. However, linebreeders and especially inbreeders must be heartless and dedicated cullers.

In the canine world as a whole, and the Beagle world in particular, there is a general unwillingness to admit that genetic problems exist. There can be no upgrading with regard to a problem if owners and breeders refuse to admit there are problems. It is all well and good to talk about the promotion and improvement of Beagles, but we can do this only if the owners are honest in their dealings with one another.

Among the factors that will retard progress in reducing the incidence of genetic problems are:

- Ignoring the problem
- Rationalizing the inheritability of a problem
- Basing a breeding program on insufficient or incorrect data
- Dishonesty about the carrier status of one's dogs
- Breaking down honest communication by gossiping and witch-hunting

With early detection of affected dogs and their removal from the breeding population, we can reduce the chance of increasing the problem. The avoidance of breeding the affected dogs must inevitably result in fewer carrier dogs being born, and in the lower number of affected puppies being produced.

Ch. Saga Critic's Choice, fifteen inches, Best in Sweepstakes, Southern California Beagle Club Specialty, 1987 (Ch. Saga Top Cat ex Ch. Saga Sally Goodin), owned by Ada T. Lueke. *Missy Yuhl*

Ch. The Whim's Rule the Roost, thirteen inches, Group and BIS winner (Ch. The Whim's Cock of the Walk ex Ch. The Whim's Maker's Mark), owned by Mrs. A. C. Musladin. *Fox Foto*

Even when the exact mode of inheritance for a particular trait is a puzzle to the breeder, the principle of heredity can be followed with a well-thought-out plan and specific goals to accomplish.

A BREEDING SYSTEM

Given that only a small number of gene pairs that produce the qualities breeders are interested in have been identified and their mode of inheritance worked out, and given the number of puppies it would take to get the qualities we as breeders desire, there are no easy answers. How—or maybe the question should be why—then should breeders make use of their genetic knowledge?

First, keep in mind that all of our dogs are more or less inbred, or we could be getting St. Bernards instead of Beagles when we have a litter. This makes the job a little easier.

Second, the breeder has three very powerful tools at his disposal: inbreeding, outcrossing and selection. Linebreeding is a form of inbreeding. With a well-thought-out program these three devices can improve the quality of your stock rather rapidly.

The system:

1. Make a list of traits and decide which are essential and which are intolerable. Rank these traits in order of importance.
2. Be clear in your mind what it is you are looking for in a particular breeding, and stick with it until you get it. In other words, set clear goals.
3. Develop a scoring system that can easily be carried out.
4. Linebreed or inbreed to the best animal produced until a better one in respect to the qualities that you have given top priority comes along. Then breed to that one.

That's the whole thing in a nutshell—everything else is ruffles and flourishes on that theme.

The steps to getting what you want are easy. It's the implementation that gets tough because of the sheer volume of records and the strict need for objectivity.

One should plan a breeding program in a positive manner, breeding for desired traits. However, faults can spoil an otherwise promising breeding animal, so the breeder must give them attention as well.

I suggest that you start with dogs of overall correct English Foxhound type. Then decide what single or at most two faults you wish to eliminate or improve upon and work to that end while maintaining the overall correct appearance. After all, you do have to live with these dogs on a daily basis, and they might as well be pleasing to the eye while you have them!

The genotype, or genetic constitution of an organism including genes without visible manifestation, is determined partially by what we see and by

Ch. Saga Sally Goodin, fifteen inches, Best in Sweepstakes, Southern California Beagle Club Specialty, 1978; dam of three champions (Ch. Saga's Cinderfeller ex Ch. Don's Irish Peggy O'Edlaine), owned by Ada T. Lueke.
Henry C. Schley

Ch. Saga's Cinderfeller, fifteen inches (Ch. The Whim's On Target ex Ch. The Whim's Plum Pudding), owned by Ada T. Lueke.
Ludwig

Ch. The Whim's Brujita, thirteen inches (Ch. Suntree's Beef Wellington ex Ch. The Whim's Top Drawer), owned by Mrs. A. C. Musladin.
Mitchell

what the animal produces, as well as the growing number of diseases that can be tested for in the laboratory.

Try to keep your goals simple. Your chances for success will be greater if you don't try to breed for or against too many qualities all at once. The ideal would be to select for one thing at a time. This is what agricultural breeders do, and so should you. Unfortunately, we are not looking for just one quality, such as egg production or quantity of meat on the hoof, but the idea is the same. If you get and keep these one or two traits in successive generations, consider yourself very lucky.

For selection purposes a minimum acceptable level must be established, and all dogs kept as breeding stock must be above the minimum accepted standard that you have established for all traits being considered. However, there must be some flexibility, to assure that you have enough replacement dogs to maintain a stable population size.

Selection is probably the most important single tool you will use. You must cull your puppies based on objectivity, not sentimentality. You need patience, high tolerance for frustration, scrupulous ethics and a tough skin.

If your bitch puppies are no better than their mom, or the dog puppies no better than their dad, then you have made no progress.

Keep only those puppies that are better than their sire or dam. By better I mean better in the one or two characteristics that you have decided to select for first. Remember that there is no point in selecting dogs that are inferior to the ones you already have. They can still be fun to show, but you have not improved your line until the puppies are better than their parents.

When you do get improvement, use these younger dogs as your next key breeders. Keep their parents in reserve in case you find that your new selections are producing some unsuspected and unfortunate results.

This brings up the question of whether the breeder wants to carry along these defects in his breeding program. If he decides that he does not, then the answer is simply to not breed any affected dogs, their parents or their siblings. That, of course, is not an easy choice to make because we are all so emotionally wrapped up in the good qualities of our dogs. This is where a thoroughly thought out plan, recommended at the beginning of this section, will pay off.

If the breeder decides to deal with a particular problem in his line he might be able, through selective breedings, to eliminate it. These selective breedings are also called test breedings or progeny testing.

To improve his breeding stock, the breeder must spend many hours researching his dogs' pedigrees. Not only should he ask questions about the dogs listed on the pedigree, but he should also ask about each of their siblings. It would be ideal if one could get all this information by making phone calls and writing letters to the owners, but the fact is that most breeder-owners are quite reluctant to give out information that they feel reflects badly on their dogs or their breeding program. Therefore, a good portion of the information will come in the form of gossip and hearsay and must be scrupulously filtered.

Start by making detailed notes on each dog in your pedigree. For our purposes, three generations are probably sufficient, provided you have full information. It is better to fill out these fourteen dogs than it is to have bits of information on other dogs in a six-generation pedigree. Gather as complete a picture on as many characteristics as possible on these dogs and their littermates as you can. You will need information on their conformation, inherited health problems and assets, temperament, etc. You will usually find it easier to gather information on the males because the number of puppies they produce is much greater than that of the bitches.

Your next step is to do a pedigree analysis.

PEDIGREE ANALYSIS

Each animal in a pedigree can be analyzed phenotypically, based on the genetic nature revealed by physical characteristics, and to a certain extent genotypically. This can become cumbersome with respect to paperwork, but is essential to achieving your goal of stock improvement.

The fancy term "pedigree analysis" simply means an in-depth study of all of the dogs in your pedigrees and their siblings. You probably already know a great deal about the dogs in your pedigrees, but have never thought of calling it pedigree analysis. That is just what it is. When you have asked questions and gotten answers about specific problems, the next step is to put it into usable form.

As you are gathering information, look at the pedigrees in terms of your information, rather than in terms of the dogs' names, so you won't be influenced by a dog's record for high wins alone, which is sometimes, but not always, more a reflection of the owner's status than the quality of the dog or bitch.

To do an actual pedigree analysis, put your information in a concise form on a card or individual evaluation sheet (see example). In addition to descriptive adjectives you might add a placement as if the dog were in the ring and was being judged against the ideal. Using the tail as an example:

set: O.K. (not perfect), somewhat low—2nd place
brush: good—1st place
length: longer than desired—3rd place

The placement technique simplifies the process of choosing breeding partners. You want a breeding where both dog and bitch don't have the same fault, at the same time allowing for acceptable levels of imperfection.

While looking at the pedigree, determine if there is a pattern to the inheritance of the trait you are studying. In other words, does it come up in every generation or does it skip a generation or more and show up again later? The rules for inheritance are that a dominant trait will never skip a generation but a recessive trait may or may not. Keep in mind that some of us have bred the same bad traits for so many generations that our recessive problems are beginning to appear like dominant traits.

186

Name: Height:

Owner: Weight:

Age: Parents:

Head   Eye   Ear
 Skull: Color: Shape:
 Muzzle: Haws: Placement:
 Underjaw: Shape: Thickness:
 Flews: Mascara: Length:
 Eye placement: Eyelashes:

Teeth   Neck   Expression
 Bite: Length:
 Color: Thickness:
                         Throatiness:

Body   Shoulder   Rear
 Topline: Angulation: Angulation:
 Back length: Layback: Muscling:
 Rib spring: Muscling: Width:
 Chest depth: Hock/stifle:
 Forechest:
 Tuckup:

Legs   Feet   Tail
 Dewclaws: Cat's paw: Set:
 Pasterns: Nail color: Brush:
 Bone: Pad color: Length:
 Wrist/growth: Pad thickness:
 Elbow/chestline: Pad texture:

Coat   Movement   Temperament
 Pigment: Front:
 Texture: Rear: Intelligence
 Length: Side: Trainability
 Markings:

OVERALL EVALUATION

If you are unable to determine the mode of inheritance (recessive or dominant), assume that the trait is a recessive and work with the genetics for recessive traits.

Once you have gathered your information, several considerations are involved in making a breeding decision: what you have to work with (maybe deciding to start with new stock); how willing you are to cull your mistakes, or, for that matter, to admit that you made a mistake; and what tools you have available. Again, the tools are inbreeding, outcrossing and selection.

The next step is to inbreed or linebreed to the best animal available that presents the one or two qualities that are at the top of your list.

Inbreeding and its less severe partner linebreeding are the tools that have much more fear associated with them than any other facet of dog breeding.

Homozygosity, the carrying of two of either the dominant or recessive

Ch. Teloca Navan Pruf O' The Puddin', CD, thirteen inches, multiple Group winner, sire of thirty-five champions (Ch. Teloca Puddin' An' Tame, CD, ex Ch. Navan's You Light Up My Life), owned by Maria Shuart. *Graham*

Ch. Stonebridge All Aglow, thirteen inches, ranked in Top Ten, thirteen-inch Beagles, 1988 (Ch. Craigwood's Murphy ex Ch. Summerhill Serendipity), owned by Judy Formisano. *Kurtis*

188

genes of a pair of alleles, increases with more intense inbreeding regardless of how the genes express themselves phenotypically. Thus dominant, recessive, polygenic, qualitative or quantitative genes are more homozygous. The increase in homozygosity is estimated from the inbreeding coefficient, a formula that can be found in any good genetics book.

Inbred dogs when bred to unrelated dogs will tend to breed better than they look. On the other hand, outcrossed dogs tend to look better than they breed.

Inbreeding depression will occur eventually and cause loss of vigor, smaller litters with more puppies dying at an earlier age; the time at which this occurs will differ for different lines. Therefore, the breeder can judge for himself when to back off if he keeps track of the coefficient of inbreeding for all his dogs. There is evidence from some studies that if inbreeding is continued, there will be a breakthrough, but most of us aren't tough enough to hold out this long.

There is a general feeling that inbreeding is dangerous and to be avoided and that linebreeding is totally safe. If the breeder will think about this in the light of our knowledge of genetics, it will be clear that this is illogical. Assuming that appropriate stock is available, whatever good can come of linebreeding will be obtained more quickly through inbreeding.

Inbreeding can be used to fix desirable genes, it does not create them. Neither does it create undesirable genes. The faults in the inbred animal are faults already in the line, and once identified can then be eliminated. It simply reduces the number of heterozygotes and increases the number of homozygotes.

I do not mean to imply that inbreeding is harmless. It should not be used by the ignorant or the foolhardy. Neither should it be used by those of us who cannot accept responsibility for the results and won't cull properly.

Outcrossing is a method that has the least to recommend it. It is normally used to bring in new genetic material. The only time you want to do this is when there is no dog in your line that carries the trait for which you are looking.

One of the reasons I don't like outcrossing is that in one breeding your puppies' carefully planned inheritance has been diluted by as much as half.

Another reason I don't like outcrossing is that you might, and probably will, open a Pandora's box of new genetic problems with which you will have to deal.

If you do choose to outcross, breed back to your line once the desired trait appears and work to maintain the qualities of your line, as well as the new trait. It may take several generations to recoup from this one breeding. Be prepared that you may bring in new unwanted genes as well as the one you do want.

A better way to do this might be to breed to a dog that is the result of an outcross to your line. In other words, half of that dog's pedigree includes your line.

If there is no such dog as just described, then you might outcross to a dog that is phenotypically similar to your dogs. The rationale for this is that if two dogs look alike, it took similar genes to make them that way. This, at least, gives you new genes without losing type.

There comes a time when the breeder needs to know whether his dogs are heterozygous for a particular trait. To eliminate a recessive gene, all the homozygous recessive individuals must be culled, as well as the affected individuals. This requires a breeding test.

It is an important point to understand that every animal derives 50 percent of its heritage from each parent, even though the contributions from each of the ancestors will vary. The old theory that each parent contributes 50 percent, the grandparents 25 percent and the great-grandparents 12.5 percent has been disproved. The genes passed through the generations do not always occur in fixed percentages. There may even be ancestors who contributed little or no genes to the progeny due to independent assortment.

PROGENY TESTING

A recessive gene may skip not just one generation but several. If a dog or bitch is bred only a limited number of times, then we may never know if that dog carries a particular gene. The most certain way to ascertain if a dog carries the recessive gene in question is to breed that dog to a homozygous mate. Remember that only dogs who carry two recessive genes will show that trait. Therefore, it is unfair to blame only one of the parents when an undesirable trait appears.

Now, the formula for progeny testing is used for single gene inheritance, and most of the characteristics we are looking for are inherited in a more complex manner, but the formula should help guide you somewhat.

The easiest test for our recessive genes is to mate the dog in question to one who already has the characteristic you suspect he may carry. In other words, breed your suspect dog that doesn't have the characteristic to a dog that does. This works whether the characteristic is desirable or detrimental.

Before you do your breeding, you should decide how certain you want to be that your dog does or does not carry the gene, so you don't have to breed those dogs into their respective eternities. Mathematicians call this certainty "level of significance." For example, if you want to be 95 percent certain, then this leaves only a 5 percent chance that your dog will produce without throwing any homozygous pups if he is a carrier. Please note that there is no such thing as 100 percent certainty. With this in mind, we can use the general formula for calculating how many puppies you need to give you 95 percent certainty that your dog is not a carrier. The formula is:

$$S^n = P$$

"S" is the number of times that your assumed carrier dog does not throw the recessive gene when bred to a homozygous dog. Thus, as an example:

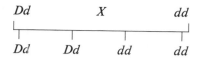

Don't panic! Read on!

In this case, half of the puppies will theoretically be carriers of the recessive gene but will be phenotypically normal, and the other half will be homozygous for the recessive gene and will manifest the trait. In other words, we can assign to the letter S the number 0.5 (half the puppies).

Furthermore, P represents the probability that the dog will produce only puppies that are heterozygous for the trait, in spite of the fact that he carries the gene himself. This takes into consideration the fact that Beagles, being the sneaky little creatures that they are, might try this one on for a new trick. In our test case we can be cautious and be 95 percent sure, and then P can equal 0.5, or we can be supercautious and be 99 percent sure, then P equals 0.1.

The letter n represents the number of puppies that your dog will have to produce to give you 95 or 99 percent assurance that the dog does not carry the factor.

The calculations for this formula will upset some of you, since n has been calculated by using logarithms. Don't despair! I have done the work for you. If you wish to be 95 percent certain that your dog is not a carrier, then 4.3 puppies must be produced (5.0 puppies would be less messy). If you are of a conservative nature and wish to be 99 percent certain, then 6.6 (7.0 puppies) will be necessary. If you are fortunate, you will get all seven puppies in your first litter. It will take two litters from this identical breeding for most of us.

DOMINANT INHERITANCE

Oh, would that all of our genetic problems and solutions were the result of single gene inheritance!

The purpose of showing ratios is to give you an idea of what you might expect for any characteristic, good or bad, whose inheritance you think might be due to a single gene.

To illustrate single-gene inheritance, I will use von Willebrand's disease (VWD). Although there have not been many documented cases in Beagles, there have been some, and since most of us are not testing for the problem, there is a chance the disease is increasing and will be a greater problem for the breed in the future.

Von Willebrand's disease is the result of abnormalities in the blood-clotting system. One of the factors involved is the reduced activity of Factor VII, and one of the symptoms is a slow clotting time when a nail has been cut too far back into the quick. If clotting does not take place within two to five minutes, there might be reason for concern, and a subsequent test should be made by your veterinarian's reference laboratory. For some reason the disease will improve with age and is associated with hypothyroidism. This disease is one that

Ch. Plain & Fancy's Clover, fifteen inches (Ch. Mitey Cute Just Like Daddy ex Plain & Fancy's Miss Muffet), multiple BIS and Group winner in the United States and Canada, is the only bitch to win Best of Breed at the National Beagle Club Specialty. She is owned by Ray Scott.
Klein

Am./Can. Ch. Chardon Ancient Mariner, fifteen inches, BIS and Group winner (Am./Can. Ch. Chardon Weekend Warrior ex Ch. Chardon Regatta), owned by Charles and Donna Mitchell. *Earl Graham*

seems to have a great deal of variability, possibly due to modifying genes.

The genetics for von Willebrand's disease has already been worked out. Normal to normal produces no affected pups, while every dog that has the disease had at least one affected parent. When an affected dog was bred to an unaffected dog, the ratios of affected to unaffected was approximately 1:1—the ratio expected for a dominant gene. Therefore, von Willebrand's disease is due to a dominant gene.

Using Punnett's Square to illustrate the products of a mating of an affected dog *(Vv)* to an unaffected dog *(vv)*, the results would be

	v	v
V	Vv	Vv
v	vv	vv

We can see from this illustration that 50 percent of the puppies will be affected. The unaffected puppies do not carry the gene at all, since the dominant gene will always manifest itself.

RECESSIVE INHERITANCE

To refresh your memory, it takes two genes, one from the father and one from the mother, to produce a characteristic that is inherited recessively. There are not many characteristics in the Beagle that have this inheritance, and so to illustrate it I will have to borrow from some other breeds, and use cleft palates as my example. You could replace cleft palates with epilepsy, if you believe my anecdotal evidence that epilepsy can be followed as a simple recessive.

Again, using Punnett's Square to show what the expected ratios will be if two dogs are mated, both of which carry the gene *(c)* for cleft palate *(cc)* but are themselves normal in appearance

	C	c
C	CC	Cc
c	Cc	cc

producing three normal (two carriers) and one affected.

This follows the normal 3:1 phenotype with the 1:2:1 genotype. When you are dealing with genetic traits, the first step is to decide how they are inherited. Are you dealing with a single pair of genes or is there more than one pair involved? Is the trait you want dominant or recessive? Is it one whose mode of inheritance has been worked out or must you try to do this yourself?

The rules for determining whether a trait is dominant or recessive are:

Dominant factors never skip a generation. Once a dominant factor disappears it is gone for good unless it is reintroduced from outside. The puppies that exhibit the trait whether they are homozygous or heterozygous carry the gene. If we are dealing with a single pair of genes and a dog exhibits the dominant trait but does not reproduce it in every puppy, we know he is heterozygous for that trait.

POLYGENIC TRAITS

Most of the desirable characteristics that we seek, such as good shoulder layback, correct movement and good temperament, are the result of many genes, with other factors influencing their expression. Some of the other influences are incomplete penetrance, the presence of modifying genes or poor environmental conditions.

Polygenic traits result from the cumulative effect of a number of different genes. Different traits probably have different numbers of genes involved. They can mimic either recessive or dominant inheritance and, therefore, create incorrect conclusions. This is also complicated by the fact that polygenic traits are especially subject to environmental influences.

More traits are polygenic than are controlled by a single gene pair. The problem is that some traits that are desirable are desirable in the heterozygous state. When this is the case, no matter how hard you try to "fix" the trait by breeding correct individual to individual, you will still get some dogs (even after many generations of selective breeding) that do not have the desired trait.

For example, the genetic makeup that produces the correct shoulder will not breed true. No matter how many generations of correct shoulders are in your pedigrees, there will continue to be individuals that will have a short upper arm to go with well laid back shoulder, or a long upper arm with a steep shoulder.

Even if knowledge of certain hybrid traits doesn't exactly speed you to your goals, at least you will know that certain "failures" go with the territory. But don't relax vigilance in selecting for desirable traits that experience has shown do not breed true.

Temperament is another trait that cannot be "fixed" in dogs. Fixed means generations of selected breeding so that an entire population or strain has identical genetic makeup and breeds true for the trait, generation after generation.

The proper combination of intenseness, stubbornness, independence, sense of humor and pack cooperativeness are contradictory characteristics.

Recessive traits, whether simple or polygenic, are difficult to eliminate from the population. These pesky traits get into a population, usually through a top-producing stud dog, and before anyone realizes there is a problem, anywhere from 20 to 90 percent of the dogs are carriers.

Eliminating affected individuals with a dominant trait will reduce the incidence to zero in one generation. Eliminating affected individuals with a recessive or polygenic trait will *never* reduce the incidence to zero, and it might take as many as fifty generations to get the incidence below 1 percent, depending on how high the carrier rate was to begin with.

18

Genetics and Your Beagle's Health

SEE NO EVIL

Compared with humans, dogs have poor close-up vision, less focusing ability and are relatively colorblind. Evidence as cited in *DVM,* March 1986, indicates that dogs may see the color red. Their pupils, however, give them superior peripheral vision and night vision.

The Beagle, though relatively free of many of the major genetic eye problems afflicting other breeds, does have its own set of difficulties.

Cherry Eye

Your promising three-month-old puppy suddenly develops a small, red cherry-like swelling in the inner corner of the lower lid. Ugly! What is it?

Definition: This condition is simply an enlargement of the gland of the third eyelid with resultant prolapse. It is thought to be due to either inflammation and/or a lack of connective tissue bands which hold the gland in place. It is unsightly but probably does not bother the dog much.

This small gland provides about 30 percent of the aqueous portion of the tear film, so surgical removal, which in the past was the treatment, leaves the dog more susceptible to developing dry eye syndrome if the remainder of the tear production is compromised.

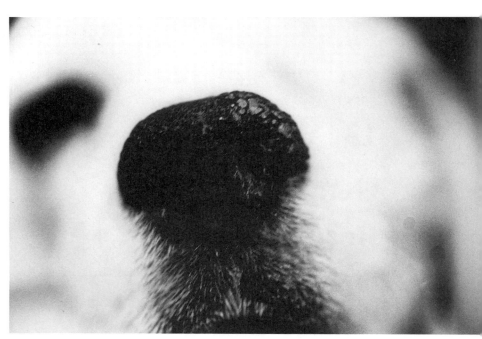

Dry nostril, left, in Beagle with dry eye.

Prominent right eye, secondary to acute glaucoma.

The incidence of cherry eye in the current conformation Beagle population is significant. Occasionally, an entire litter is affected. Not enough data have been reported to date to determine the mode of transmission. There is some indication that it functions as a simple recessive.

Management: Occasionally the simple application of an ophthalmic ointment containing both antibiotic and a potent steroid will reduce the gland. Recurrence can occur. If the protrusion persists, the gland should be sutured back in place by your veterinarian. When properly done (and it is not always easy!), the gland remains intact and your little Beagle regains its pretty expression.

Under no circumstances should the gland be totally removed, unless it is affected by cancer, which is rare.

Dry Eye Syndrome (Keratoconjunctivitis Sicca)

One of your Beagle's normally bright, shiny eyes suddenly appears dry and lusterless. In the mornings a thick, stringy discharge accumulates over the eye. Several days or weeks later, that eye, if not treated, is red, squinty and very painful.

This is a serious disease. Painful for the Beagle, KCS can result in severe ulceration and scarring of the cornea and blindness, and may eventually require removal of the eyeball.

Cause: Drying of the cornea results from inadequate tear production. Tear glands may be defective as a result of severe systemic infection, such as canine parvovirus or canine distemper. Surgical removal of the third eyelid gland may be at fault. Some oral sulfa medications have triggered KCS.

If the nerves to the tear glands are not functioning properly, the Beagle may also have a dry nostril on one side. A young Beagle with a dry nostril should be watched carefully for the first indication of dry eye.

Plugged tear ducts can cause dry eye, but the preceding two factors are the most common mechanisms in Beagles.

Recent reports indicate that dogs with dry eye may occasionally be hypothyroid. While supplementation of such dogs with thyroid does not increase tear production, it has been shown to improve the health of the eye tissues. Thus all dogs with dry eye should be tested for thyroid function.*

It has also been reported that KCS can be an autoimmune disease in which there is a reaction to the dog's own tear glands. Successful experimental treatment has consisted of cyclosporin drops as an immunosuppressant.

Diagnosis: Run, don't walk, to your nearest veterinary ophthalmologist (eye specialist). A paper-strip test indicating reduced tear flow makes the diagnosis.

*Alan Brightman, *Washington State University Animal Health Notice,* 9:1; 1987.

Treatment: Your veterinarian will try to find the underlying causes while placing the Beagle on a regimen of eyedrops and ointments to lubricate the eye, preventing infection and inflammation, along with oral medication to stimulate tear production. Transplant of a salivary-gland duct to drain into the eye works well when medicating the eye alone is insufficient.

In those Beagles we have followed for years, fluctuations in the production of tears occur. As a result, frequency of administration of treating agents needs to be adjusted from time to time.

Of course, any underlying disease, such as hypothyroidism, requires treatment as well.

Glaucoma

Definition: Glaucoma is an eye problem that researchers have found Beagles, as well as other breeds, to be prone to developing. The problem results when the normal fluids within the eyeball fail to drain normally back into the bloodstream. When this happens, too much pressure builds up in the eye. The pressure increases to above normal levels and can eventually cause damage to the optic nerve. The condition seems to show up more in the older dog.

Symptoms and signs: Signs of glaucoma can appear gradually or suddenly. As pressure builds up, the retina and optic nerve become damaged, eventually leading to blindness.

Chronic glaucoma is not always easy to recognize, and usually one must use an instrument called a tonometer to measure the intraocular pressure. Other clues are changes in the eye's appearance and possibly the dog's behavior.

Signs of glaucoma include discomfort, tearing, inflammation of the white part of the eye, a cloudy cornea and enlargement of the eyeball. Left untreated, an eye with glaucoma may eventually bulge to the point where the eyelids can no longer cover the eye. This can cause the cornea to dry out and ulcers to form, making surgical removal of the eye necessary.

Treatment: In many cases medical treatment is possible. Your veterinarian may be able to decrease the fluid production and increase drainage with medication.

Because the exact dosage of medication is a delicate balance, the dog may have to be hospitalized for several days. After that, the owner must treat the dog religiously for the medication to be effective. Rechecks with the veterinarian, of course, are a requirement.

Most cases of glaucoma cannot be treated medically forever, and surgery may become necessary to control the disease. Several techniques are available, and if you have access to a board-certified ophthalmologist, one of the techniques can be employed.

Cyclocryosurgery is one of the methods in which the eye's fluid-producing tissue is frozen to eliminate future pressure buildup. Another method is to evacuate a blind eyeball and insert a prosthesis, making the eye look fairly normal. Sometimes the eyeball is simply removed.

Nothing can be done to prevent glaucoma.

It is generally accepted that it is hereditary, since it is prevalent in certain breeds like the Beagle.

One study showed that prophylactic treatment of glaucoma in one eye may delay the onset of glaucoma in the other eye (bilateral glaucoma). Several breeds were studied. Beagles, among others, were shown to have a significantly higher risk of developing the condition than other breeds.

However, unlike other breeds, these breeds responded well to prophylactic treatments such as timolol, dichlorphenamide and/or echothiophate, used to delay the development of glaucoma in the second eye. The average time lengthened from five to ten months.

Although the disease is generally considered to be bilateral, it does not necessarily develop into a bilateral condition.

In the Beagle, glaucoma is inherited as an autosomal recessive trait. To date in the conformation Beagle population, only one line has reported seven cases of glaucoma. Four occurred in offspring of one bitch, three from a daughter of this bitch. In all of these cases, a weakness of the tissue holding the lens in place was at fault.

White Haws

The dog has three eyelids: an upper, a lower and a third (or nictitating membrane). Constructed of elastic cartilage covered by conjunctiva, the third eyelid is located where the upper and lower eyelids converge at the inner corner of the eye. It protects the eye in a similar fashion as the other two lids, but it also acts as a wiper to remove pollen, dust and other irritants from the eye. This membrane also contains an important tear gland in dogs.

The third eyelid's main portion is covered by a pink-colored mucous membrane, usually showing a dark-brown edge where it is visible. This pigmentation is considered normal. On occasion, the brown edge is only lightly pigmented, appearing white. It is not serious, but contrasts with the iris, giving a less than pleasing expression. The condition may be present on one or both sides and is not an anatomical deformity but genetic in origin.

Cataracts

Opacity of the lens of the eye is a common condition in older Beagles, as it is in many breeds. Usually a milky look to the eye is noticed when the hound reaches eleven or twelve years of age. In some Beagle lines, cataracts may appear at younger ages.

Chrondrodystrophic Beagles frequently develop an early cataract in the left eye.

Vision decreases gradually. Dogs can accommodate very well to a slow loss of vision unless moved into new surroundings. Cataract can be surgically treated by removal of the lens. Lens implants, which have worked so well in people, are available for dogs now, too.

Juvenile cataract, an inheritable disease that produces the condition in very young dogs, is, fortunately, not a problem in Beagles.

"WE DON'T HAVE ANY EPILEPSY HERE . . ."

Your sleeping Beagle is startled awake. Within a few seconds you notice the dog staggering about, looking confused. Muscular twitching, contractions of the legs, salivation and unresponsiveness to the environment may follow. You pick him up to find him stiff. The muscular contractions subside within a very few minutes, and shortly, the Beagle is alert, coordinated and responsive again. . . .

The eleven-week Beagle litter is coming along nicely. The second set of vaccinations has been given a week or so ago and they are ready for their new homes. Suddenly, one puppy begins to look alarmed, staggers about, falls to the ground and begins convulsing. Legs contract, breathing may stop for a few seconds and involuntary urination may occur. Within a few minutes, the pup regains consciousness and is able to walk, but circles aimlessly for several more minutes, seemingly unseeing.

Over the past few years there has been a growing concern among Beagle breeders over the increased incidence of epilepsy in our breed. It is the intent of this section to describe the syndrome and its genetic significance. The reader can find further information in the bibliography at the end. On a few occasions in the following I have voiced opinions, and I hope that it is clear when this indulgence was used.

Although epilepsy has been identified in many breeds, those most afflicted are all three varieties of Poodles, Keeshonden, German Shepherds, Belgian Sheepdogs, Golden Retrievers and Beagles.

Definition

Epilepsy is a dysfunction of the brain that manifests itself with some type of seizure. The seizures may vary from mild to severe, in some cases causing death.

Many terms have been used to mean seizure, such as "convulsion," "fit" or "epileptic attack." These terms are used to describe the abnormal behavior that occurs at any one time, whereas epilepsy is the term that applies to the syndrome itself.

A convulsive seizure is evidence of an electrical storm in the brain. This abnormal electrical activity is a phenomenon caused by the physical and chemical makeup of the discharging cells in the brain. The overactivity of these cells produces disturbances in consciousness and in muscular coordination. Therefore, the primary cause is chemical, or more appropriately, electrophysiochemical. But the chain of events leading up to the brain's chemical reaction can be infinitely varied. This variation is what makes veterinarians so cautious about giving pat answers.

Epilepsy is not a specific disease but, rather, a set of symptoms that can result from many causes.

There are three main types of seizures, and if your dog has appeared to have any of them, he is a strong candidate for epilepsy.

Types

One of the less common forms of epilepsy is called petit mal. The seizure is quite brief in duration, and only very subtle changes in behavior can be seen, such as staring, stumbling, etc. It is possible that these seizures do not seem to be as serious as others. Their causes are probably the same.

The second and most common type of seizure is called grand mal. This is the classical form of epilepsy and has three phases. The first phase may or may not be seen and immediately precedes the actual seizure. This phase is called the aura, during which the dog seems to sense the onset of the seizure and has brief changes in behavior such as staring, stumbling or psychological depression. Often the dog will try to get to its owner. This phase lasts only a few seconds and is therefore missed.

The second phase is the actual seizure, with falling, trembling in the limbs, running movements, loss of consciousness and frequent loss of bowel and bladder control. If this stage of seizure becomes prolonged, it is called status epilepticus and can lead to injury or even death.

The third phase is the recovery period and can last from a few minutes to an hour, depending on the severity of the seizure itself.

The third type of epilepsy is called psychomotor.

Causes

Epilepsy can be either genetic or acquired.

Acquired epilepsy can be caused by infections (viruses such as distemper, bacteria, fungi and protozoa such as toxoplasmosis); blood chemistry imbalances (oxygen, sugar, salts, vitamins and toxic wastes); toxins (insecticides, lead, mercury, insect or snake bites); trauma (head injury or electrocution); and tumors of the skull or brain and its coverings.

By far the most common is idiopathic epilepsy, a condition for which the cause is unknown, although many cases are known to be inherited.

Manifestation

The usual age of onset is eighteen months to two years. In Beagles it has been seen as early as three months and as late as nine years. Occasionally a reaction to a second vaccination results in transient episodes of swelling of the brain tissue, which will precipitate seizures. Stress is often the trigger mechanism.

There is nothing in the dog's health history to cause suspicion. Laboratory tests and electroencephalography (brain-wave study) are normal, but if your dog has ancestors or relatives with epilepsy and abnormal behavior as described above, there is reason to suspect genetic rather than acquired causes. Although both acquired and genetic epilepsy manifest themselves similarly, and are treated in the same manner, it is the genetic type with which this section is most concerned.

Beagles seem to have a couple of variations on the classic epilepsy described above. Although most canine seizures seem to occur around the age of eighteen months to two years, Beagles seem to have them at any age, late onset being almost as common as the classic type, with early onset running third in number of first occurrences.

A second variation is that Beagles seem to have seizures that vary from mild to moderate in intensity. Very few have severe occurrences. Severe seizures are relatively common in other breeds, such as the Poodle, especially the miniature variety.

Treatment

Since the cause of most epilepsies is unknown, treatment must be based on the clinical signs. Genetic epilepsy is incurable, but in our breed totally manageable. When required, the most effective treatment is anticonvulsant medications. There are a number of anticonvulsants that are quite effective in controlling the number and severity of seizures. Currently three most commonly used drugs are diphenylhydantoin (Dilantin), phenobarbital and primadone (Mysoline). Most of the epileptic Beagles I know do quite well with no medication at all, and have only occasional seizures during their lifetime. By comparison, I know of a miniature Poodle that was having as many as six seizures per day and is now doing quite nicely at the age of ten years on rather large doses of Mysoline. When medication becomes necessary, it usually must be continued for the life of the dog.

Genetics of Epilepsy

The genetics of epilepsy in dogs has received some attention from the scientific world, but no clear-cut mode of inheritance has been established. Some of the possibilities that have been postulated and some thoughts follow.

Autosomal recessive inheritance: This is the most commonly held belief for inheritance. It simply means that only two genes are necessary to show seizures, one inherited from the sire and one from the dam.

Polygenic inheritance: This is present when many sets of alleles are needed to determine a trait. In such cases, if the parents were at two extremes of a trait, such as epilepsy with variations in age of onset and in severity of expression, the puppies would probably fall somewhere between the parents in expression.

Simple recessive inheritance with additive genes: This is one researcher's explanation for the early onset of seizures. That is, as dogs (specifically British Alsatians) become more inbred, more genes that influence the inheritance of epilepsy are added onto the heredity of the dog, causing earlier onset. It was discovered that by selecting for dogs with epilepsy, the researchers automatically selected dogs that were more inbred than their control group.

In following the Beagle lines for which I have the most information, this held in the sense that early-onset puppies were more inbred than the average, but their siblings who had the same coefficient of inbreeding, and had seizures, did not necessarily have them earlier than would be expected normally.

This study group of Alsatians also had a statistically significant difference in the ratio of males to females having seizures. This has been observed by other researchers, but with the pedigrees I have studied, this is not very convincing.

Switch genes: Another possible explanation for the variability in age is what are called switch genes. These genes cause changes in developmental pathways. If switch genes, of which there are various types, are the cause, they lend credence to the supposition that epilepsy alleles fit into the category of polygenic, not simple.

Genocopies: Yet another explanation for the age difference may be that epilepsy has genocopies—that it is not a single disease, but rather a set of diseases, each with a different set of genes responsible for its manifestation. It is possible that late-appearing seizures, classic eighteen-month epilepsy and early appearing epilepsy may be genocopies, nonallelic and therefore completely separate genetic diseases.

If genocopies are involved, the genetics will be quite complex and difficult to study.

Modifying genes or suppressor genes: Since seizures are sometimes not seen in a dog that one would expect to have, based on his pedigree, there might be a possibility of modifying genes or suppressor genes. Modifying genes do exactly what the name implies—they modify or change the expression of a trait in some way. A suppressor gene actually suppresses mutant genes so that the normal phenotype can be expressed. If either of these types of genes is present, it could be responsible for the differences we see.

It has been suggested that all epilepsy may be environmentally caused, since it seems to be triggered by stress and can be caused by trauma. It is my opinion that the widespread incidence of seizures that we see in canines cannot be caused by environmental deficiencies or excesses.

The breeder who refuses to accept the genetic basis for epilepsy, and continually treats his dogs with nutritional supplements with the hope of finding the "magic potion" that will "cure" epilepsy, is in for much heartache. On the other hand, I am of the opinion that there are no traits that are purely genetic in their expression; that is, environment can and does influence even the most dominant trait. Therefore, it is important to give your dogs the most optimal environment that you are able. Even superior genes cannot cope with a poor environment.

Happily, the breeder does not actually have to know the mode of inheritance for epilepsy. Regardless of the real mode, the inheritance can be followed as a single recessive in the great majority of pedigrees we have studied. That is not to say that the different forms are not real, but in all cases, whether late or early onset, the parents carried the genes for some form of epilepsy. It is this mode of inheritance the breeder can use for selection.

Although epilepsy should not be taken lightly, neither should it be considered the Great American Tragedy. The epileptic Beagle can and does lead a normal life, often without medication.

A good deal of our knowledge of canine epilepsy has been inferred from studies done with humans. Approximately 10 percent of the human population has a predisposition to seizures but may never know it, because the contributing factors are never present.

In recent years attitudes toward human epileptics have supposedly improved, with ostracism, social rejection and downright discrimination becoming things of the past. However, if the unseemly fear and lack of understanding of canine epilepsy are indications of our progress, human epileptics must still be under a great psychological strain.

HYPOTHYROIDISM

Since the incidence of hypothyroidism is on the increase in Beagles, as well as the general purebred dog population, the following section is particularly detailed. The better informed we are, the better breeders we will be.

Definition

Hypothyroidism is the generalized metabolic disease resulting from a deficiency of the thyroid hormones, tetraiodothyronine or thyroxine (T4) and/or triiodothyronine (T3).

The disease develops gradually after the onset of puberty, and typical signs tend to occur in midlife. In nearly 90 percent of cases, the cause of canine hypothyroidism is autoimmune thyroiditis (like human Hashimoto's disease); the remainder have thyroid atrophy of unknown cause.

Sometimes a transient thyroid problem occurs in conjunction with another disease or secondary to use of a drug being given to treat another condition and will clear if thyroid function has not been suppressed too long.

Physiology

The principal hormone produced by the thyroid gland is thyroxine, commonly referred to as T4. Thyroid function begins with the hypothalamus in the brain, which releases thyroid-releasing hormone (TRH). This hormone, in turn, stimulates secretion of thyroid-stimulating hormone (TSH) from the pituitary gland. The primary function of TSH released into the bloodstream is to cause the thyroid gland to release T4. T4 is then converted to triiodothyronine, better known as T3, within the cells of the thyroid gland.

T3 is the most biologically active form of thyroid hormone, and most of it remains intracellularly, where it is readily used. The half-life of T3 is extremely short (five to six hours).

The complex process of thyroid hormonal function summarized above is controlled by a biofeedback system of checks and balances that turns on the various parts of the circuit as needed.

Signs and Symptoms

If the thyroid gland is not producing enough hormonal material, an animal becomes affected with a wide variety of physical problems.

The clinical signs and symptoms of hypothyroidism in most dogs include: lethargy; fatigue; reduced alertness; excitability; poor appetite; weight gain; dry sparse coat; skin infections and flea allergy; food allergy; smelly and greasy skin that becomes blackened or thickened and scaly (elephant skin); arthritis and stiff gait; smelly ears due to excessive wax production and ear infections; dry eye syndrome; anemia; a bleeding tendency; mild chronic liver, kidney, pancreas or adrenal dysfunction; seizures; muscle weakness and reproductive problems.

Usually a dog won't show all of these symptoms, but most will show several. If the problem is left untreated, the condition will progress until more severe and persistent symptoms develop that can be fatal.

Normal thyroid function is essential to reproduction. Both sterility in the dog and infertility in the bitch may indicate thyroid dysfunction or imbalance.

While the skin is usually not itchy, a lowered resistance to infection accompanies thyroid disease, allowing secondary bacterial infections, demodectic mange or flea allergy dermatitis to take hold. An intensely itchy and hypersensitivity dermatitis often will result.

Diagnosis

Diagnosis of the early stages of thyroiditis or clinically evident hypothyroidism is determined either by blood tests that measure circulating thyroid hormone levels (minimally total T4 and total T3, but preferably also free or unbound T4 and optionally free T3 as well) or by a four- to six-week clinical response trial of twice daily L-thyroxine treatment. This regimen consists of 0.1 mg per ten pounds of body weight given twice daily.

Another test called the thyroid stimulating hormone (TSH) response test is also commonly used. However, this test measures thyroid hormonal reserve and can therefore be normal in early stages of thyroid disease. Thus, an abnormal TSH response test (poor response) is diagnostic of hypothyroidism, but a normal or equivocal test result does not rule out thyroid disease.

Treatment

Most affected dogs respond well to twice daily treatment with L-thyroxine. It is important to split the total daily requirement into two treatments because the half-life of the hormone is very short in the dog (ten to twelve hours) unlike in humans (several days).

Once treated adequately, the dog's prognosis is excellent.

Regular monitoring once or twice yearly with a complete thyroid test panel is needed to ensure that treatment dosages are proper to maintain thyroid levels within the upper half of the normal range. Blood should be drawn four to six hours after the morning treatment to measure peak circulating levels of hormones.

Practical Aspects

The three principal functions of the thyroid hormones are (1) to ensure that body cells take up and burn oxygen effectively; (2) to generate enough heat to enable body cells to maintain the proper temperature; and (3) to maintain metabolic activity. Thyroid hormones either alone or in conjunction with other hormones are involved in protein, fat and carbohydrate metabolism, growth and maturation, normal libido and reproduction and normal skin functions.

As an aside, there may be problems associated with choice of laboratories for testing thyroid levels. Most veterinarians feel that only measuring a T4 level is insufficient, since false negatives are more likely to occur. T4 levels can also be affected by other illnesses and some drugs. Hence, a T3 should be obtained as well.

There is also some evidence that only a few laboratories are qualified to obtain proper canine values. Human laboratories that are sometimes used for this test cannot read the lower levels of circulating thyroid hormone levels in dogs accurately without recalibrating their standard assay curves to suit this species.

It is very important that your veterinarian use a laboratory that has good standards for canines and can properly evaluate the test.

The results of these tests plus the clinical symptoms will enable your veterinarian to make a diagnosis. If the dog is hypothyroid, the veterinarian will probably select one of the synthetic forms of thyroid for treatment, since the "natural" version has proven to be unreliable in some cases. Although generic drugs are usually quite satisfactory for most medical problems, they do not seem to work as well in the dog with thyroid deficiency.

You should see a difference in your Beagle in a week as to how "perky" he feels, but other associated problems will take six weeks or longer to resolve.

If your dog is diagnosed as hypothyroid, he will probably be on medication for the rest of his life. Dosage may also need to be readjusted from time to time; hence, the need for periodic tests. Fortunately, in spite of the many areas of the body this disease can affect, with treatment the life span of the dog is usually not affected.

Hypothyroidism can occur in any breed, including mixed, but some fifty breeds seem to be especially predisposed to this condition. There seems to be a growing number of Beagles that have been diagnosed as hypothyroid. The hereditary nature of this disease has been established in humans and dogs, though it appears to be the predisposition to developing thyroid disease that is inherited. The prevalence of primary thyroid dysfunction seems to be on the increase in both purebred and mixed-breed dogs.

In addition to an apparent genetic predisposition, nutritional factors, viral infections and immunologic mechanisms may play a role. At the same time the proportion of primary hypothyroidism of the familial immune-mediated type has increased over the last decade from about 50 percent to nearly 90 percent today.

Thyroid deficiency also plays a major role in bone marrow hypoplasia (decreased or failed blood-cell formation) associated with immune-mediated blood diseases, as well as increasing the risk of bleeding in von Willebrand's disease (see pages 191–93 and 223).

Although it is not always possible to determine the exact cause of the condition, hypothyroidism is most often the result of autoimmune destruction, where the affected animal's body is forming antibodies against its own tissues. In these cases, the thyroid is destroyed, and as a result thyroid hormones are no longer produced.

Several environmental factors have recently been implicated in triggering autoimmune diseases, thyroid disease in particular, in both humans and other animals. These include retrovirus and parvovirus infections, use of certain drugs or toxicants, increased pollution and use of pesticides, nutritional imbalances and the increased use of single and combined live virus vaccines.

In the pedigrees that are available to us (the authors), there is evidence that hypothyroidism is hereditary. At the very least, the problems seem to run in certain families.

Since there doesn't seem to be any published conclusions about the mode of inheritance of thyroid disease in dogs, the breeder can work with it as if it were a simple recessive, selecting breeding partners carefully and doing test breeding when the problem seems to be cleared up. Please keep in mind that this problem often does not show up until the dog is middle-aged.

So save your celebrating until the get have reached that age and all have been tested and found to have thyroid hormone levels well within the midportion of the so-called normal range!

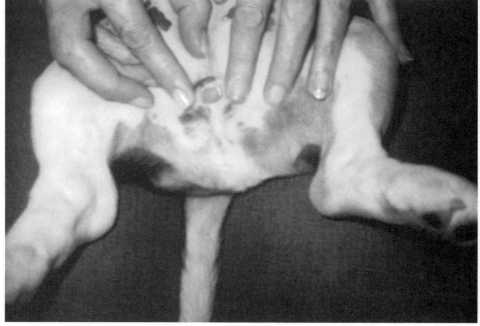

Four-month-old Beagle puppy showing enlarged clitoris protruding from the vagina. Laboratory studies and subsequent spaying confirmed diagnosis of intersex.

PROBLEMS WITH THE REPRODUCTIVE SYSTEM

Intersex

You are trimming the excess hair around the rump of your eight-month-old Beagle bitch, preparatory to a show. Suddenly, you notice a growth protruding from the vulva. Upon closer examination, it seems to resemble the tip of a penis! How can this be? Why, she even had her first season the month before.

Definition: An intersex is an animal or person who has the internal reproductive organs (ovaries and testes) of both sexes. This condition, formerly known as hermaphroditism, is to be differentiated from pseudohermaphroditism, which is the presence of external genitalia of one sex and the internal gonads of the other. This latter condition is thought to be a congenital defect (a noninheritable abnormality that occurs *in utero* while the embryo is developing) due to some noxious influence during pregnancy—drugs, toxins, etc. An enlarged clitoris may result, giving the appearance of male genitalia in a female. In the true intersex, both ovarian and testicular tissue are present.

Developmentally, the normal fetus begins as a female with differentiation into male occurring as a result of male-determining genes. The rudimentary female reproductive tract is replaced by the developing male reproductive system. If there is a disruption in this normal process, an intersex results.

Occurrence in Beagles: To date, in the current families of conformation Beagles, five apparent females have been diagnosed as intersex, and there is a report of one male with malformed external male genitalia.

One, a newborn, had a normal-appearing vagina and an enlarged clitoris, resembling a penis, and was put down. Another was discovered when an attempted breeding was unsuccessful and the examining veterinarian found an enlarged clitoris obstructing the vaginal canal. A third was diagnosed at twelve weeks with the appearance of an enlarged clitoris. Two more were diagnosed at four and one-half and eight months of age. Each affected Beagle was from a different litter, and all litters had one common ancestor within a few generations. There is one deceased male common to all pedigrees.

Genetics of intersex: A genetic study* was done on a family of American Cocker Spaniels in which nine true intersex and two XXY males (males with two female sex chromosomes) occurred in ten separate but related litters.

Eight of the females also had enlarged clitores.

The parents of these litters were related within a few generations through at least one common denominator. All were related to one deceased male ancestor. Cellular, serological, anatomical and genetic studies were done, with

---

*J. R. Selden et al. "Inherited XX Sex Reversal in the Cocker Spaniel Dog," *Human Genetics* 67 (1984):62–69.

the conclusion that transmission is most likely through the mode of an autosomal recessive gene, originally a mutant.

No studies have been published on Beagles to date, but most likely the transmission is the same for our breed.

Management: First, a correct diagnosis must be made to differentiate between the true intersex and the pseudohermaphrodite. A fasting blood level of testosterone, the male hormone, is compared with the level following injection of human chorionic gonadotropin, a hormone that stimulates the testes to produce testosterone. The normal female will have some testosterone in the blood. However, if testicular tissue is present, there will be a marked rise in the testosterone level after injection of human chorionic gonadotropin.

If this study proves your Beagle to be a true intersex, then she should be spayed. The enlarged clitoris may recede somewhat, or it may be removed if it protrudes so far that infection or injury are likely.

If your Beagle proves to be a pseudohermaphrodite, then a careful review of the management of the bitch's pregnancies is in order. Special attention needs to be given as to whether and what kinds of antibiotics are used at the time of breeding and early in pregnancy, as well as other drugs, toxins, sprays, etc.

Unfortunately, there is no test available outside research centers to check for carrier status in the siblings. Natural selection will play a part. Not all females are bred, and though there are reports of litters born to intersex dogs, these are obviously rare.

Sterility in the Male Beagle

Over the past twenty years several incidents of sterility in male Beagles have occurred. There is suggestive evidence that this condition may be inherited. If it is, obviously it will be self-limiting. We won't have to worry about it any more. Some lines report a higher proportion of sterile males than others, but this may be a function of varying practices of reporting among Beagle breeders.

It is heartbreaking to discover that a promising stud has stopped producing viable sperm.

The typical history is that a young dog that had sired one to three litters then became infertile. Extensive work-ups at diagnostic centers in several cases failed to account for the arrest of spermatogenesis (sperm formation). Some of these Beagles have had decreased levels of circulating thyroxine, the hormone produced by the thyroid gland, but thyroid supplementation did not restore fertility.

Suggested causative factors include hypothyroidism, chronic low-grade infection of the prostate gland and immune-related problems. These are in addition to obvious causes, such as brucellosis or an acute infection of the testes.

A temporary drop in fertility may occur with stress, particular medications or a severe illness from which the dog recovers. In these cases sperm production will return.

Not enough data are available to date to draw any conclusions. The condition has been known to occur in all breeds and continues to be a puzzle.

My personal hunch is that some lines may be more prone to immune-deficient problems, with specific target organs determined genetically. In this case, the target organs would be the testes.

Undescended Testicle

Monorchidism, the failure of one testicle to descend into the scrotum (the external sac that holds the testicles), is a commonly reported phenomenon in beagles. Cryptorchidism, the failure of both to descend, is rare.

In most dogs, testicles normally descend into the scrotum before birth. In Beagles, frequently this does not occur until after birth. Sometimes they are difficult to feel, for they are so small. A testicle that moves up and down from groin to scrotum is not unusual. Puppies can retract them in play and when cold or frightened. So don't worry if your pup's testicle behaves like a yo-yo.

One heaves a sigh of relief if both little testicles are neatly in place by six to eight weeks of age. If you have a particularly promising male puppy with an undescended testicle still at twelve weeks, don't give up on him. We have seen the second come down nicely at between four and five months of age. One nice male dropped his at eight months, with full normal development of the testicle by ten months.

If the testicle can be felt in the groin but does not move, a short cord is the most likely cause. Some breeders report that *gentle* regular stretching of the cord and testicle while the pup lies on its back will succeed in lengthening the cord. Others have achieved success with a course of hormone injections prescribed by their veterinarian. It may be that these testicles simply needed a bit more time to descend.

A late-descending testicle does not appear to affect fertility in the adult Beagle.

Since monorchidism is an inherited condition, the adult Beagle with only one descended testicle should never be used for breeding. Your veterinarian should be consulted about the advisability of castration (removal of both testicles) in these cases.

DEM BONES

Hip Dysplasia

Hip dysplasia, defective hip-joint structure due to either bony abnormality or muscle/ligament dysfunction, is a problem that is not well publicized among Beagles.

Most Beagle breeders are of the opinion that hip dysplasia is nonexistent

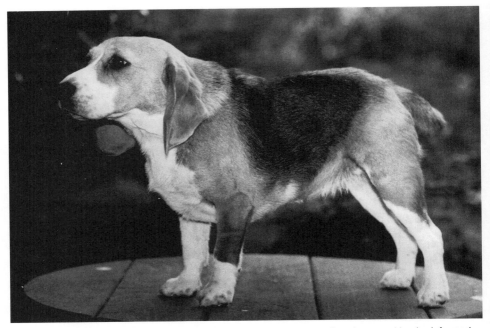

Lil' Sis, adult Beagle with severe chondrodystrophy. Note shortened neck, curved back, deformed front and rear legs.   *Diane Quenell*

Lil' Sis; note position of front legs.
Diane Quenell

in the breed. It is a fallacy that because hip dysplasia usually occurs in large breeds that we do not have this problem. There have been a few cases, and if we looked closer, we might find more. If you don't check, surely you won't know!

Hip dysplasia does have the advantage that it can be diagnosed clinically with radiographs. The drawback is that there is increasing evidence that hip dysplasia is part of a systemic disorder, part of a series of interrelated problems affecting other joints.

Screening by X ray of one joint may miss some incipient cases of a generalized involvement. A Cornell University study found that among ninety-two dogs with joint abnormalities, 71 percent involved the hip, 38 percent the shoulder, 22 percent the stifle and 40 percent were multiply involved. This may, in part, explain why selective breedings based on pelvic radiographs alone have reduced the occurrence of hip dysplasia only 30 percent.

Many years ago I heard of a Beagle that was diagnosed as having shoulder dysplasia. It would have been interesting to have seen if the line had a tendency to come up with other bony or joint problems, such as hip dysplasia.

Chondrodystrophy, or "The Funnies"

Your litter has arrived. The smallest pup seems slow to nurse and less vigorous than his siblings. Supplemental feeding is needed, and soon you have to contend with diarrhea as well. After a week or ten days of fluid supplementation and antibiotics, he seems to be catching up and is nursing along with the rest. Development seems to be normal. Up on his feet by three weeks, he is hiking around the whelping box. One night he starts to scream and is unable to put weight on one of his forelegs. You assume that he twisted it somehow, and try to make him comfortable. Within a day or two all seems well. But not so!

By about four weeks, he seems to be having difficulty getting up on his feet and moves with a shuffling gait. Plucky, very responsive and affectionate, the puppy becomes special. Visits to your veterinarian, treatment of various kinds, a variety of diagnoses become the story of this pup's early weeks.

Reaching four to six months of age, he seems completely comfortable and the condition has stabilized. At this point he is small, has crooked front legs, a roach to his back, walks with a limp and shows weak and cow-hocked rearquarters. Skin is frequently itchy, and he will rub his back just above the tail on whatever is available. Intelligent, affectionate and less active than the usual, he makes a marvelous companion.

Definition: Chondrodystrophy, or multiple epiphyseal dysplasia as it has been known in the veterinary literature, is a disease affecting the long bones and vertebral bodies in which there is pathological enchondral growth. This means there is a failure in the growth centers within the cartilage precursors and bones, resulting in stunted, twisted limbs and shortened, deformed vertebrae, the latter producing signs associated with intervertebral disc disease.

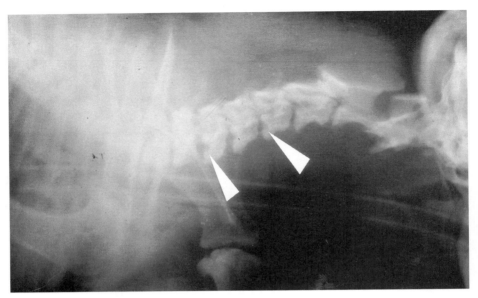

Radiograph of cervical spine, Lil' Sis, taken at nine months of age. Note the erosion of the endplates of the vertebral bodies and joint changes in the upper cervical spine.

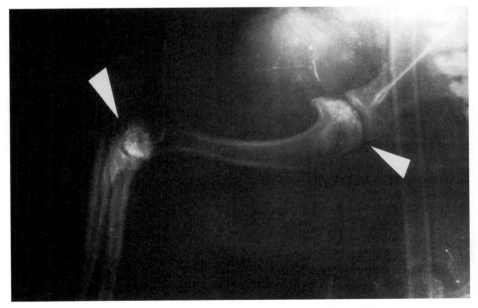

Radiograph of shoulder and elbow joints, Lil' Sis, nine months of age. Note the irregularity of the joint surface of the upper arm, spotty densities and bone erosion. Similar changes are present in the elbow joint.

214

Some of the purebred breeds of dogs belong to the achondroplastic group, characterized as disproportionate dwarfs. Members of this group are the Pekingese, Basset Hound, Dachshund and, to a lesser extent, the Boston Terrier and King Charles Spaniel. The Beagle, too, is considered basically to belong in this general category. Most likely, as the forebears of the modern Beagle were bred down in size to function more efficiently on rabbit and hare, certain genetic traits were incorporated that predispose to achondroplastic characteristics—short legs, large head, crooked front extremities, etc.

Genetics: An autosomal recessive mode of transmission is cited in the available veterinary literature. More likely it is more complicated than that. As with any genetic predisposition, extrauterine influences, such as illness, nutrition, drugs, toxins etc., may determine the severity of the process in the developing puppies. Thus one can see pups that are so severely affected they die, as well as pups that are only mildly affected.

The principle of multiplicity of genetic defects seems to apply to these pups. Often seen in conjunction with this condition are failure to thrive, bad bites, predisposition to dental disease, early left eye cataract, increased vulnerability to infection, etc.

Diagnosis: In addition to the clinical signs mentioned above, X rays in the early stages (three weeks of age) reveal abnormal epiphyseal ossification centers, which are the bony growth centers at the ends of long bones and in the vertebral bodies, in some or all of the limb bones and vertebrae. At two months, the best age to make the diagnosis, the growth centers are mottled and frayed, with some irregular spots of calcification present. By four to six months of age, these changes have disappeared and the growth centers are incorporated into the bone. At this point the osteoarthritic changes that involve the joints obscure the original disease process. Degenerative joint disease or osteoarthritis is frequently seen in the joints of the shoulder, hip and elbow.

Occurrence in Beagles: Over the past twenty-five years, twenty-nine Beagles with pedigrees have been reported to us, along with oral reports of others without specific identification, that most likely had or have chondrodystrophy. It was only during the period 1987–88 that a diagnosis of these "funnies," as they are affectionately known, was made. These cases range in severity from a fourteen-day-old puppy put down for failure to thrive and inability to get around to a mildly affected five-year-old that has a slight roach and a rear-quarter limp. All degrees of involvement lie between these extremes.

Generally, one affected pup may appear in a litter; in one instance, three pups were affected. Repeat breedings have produced normal puppies. In our kennel the pattern is one in which the C-6 and L-7 vertebrae seem especially targeted. I would suspect that it varies from line to line.

Management: Obviously, those Beagles surviving to a comfortable adult life should be neutered or spayed. Because they are especially bright and

215

Boom Boom; note deformity of hind legs.

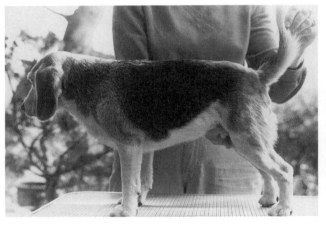

Banty; adult with less severe form of chondrodystrophy.

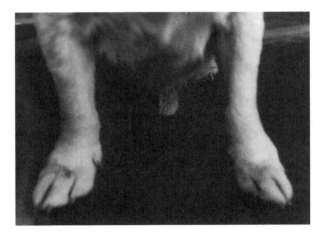

Banty; front legs show typical deformity.

responsive, probably due to the extra handling and care required during the first few months of life, they make wonderful companions. So affliction does not automatically mean euthanasia. Normal siblings when bred may never produce an affected puppy.

It is important to be able to recognize these puppies, for misdiagnosis can be terribly discouraging. For the first twenty-five years those produced in our kennel were variously diagnosed as having vitamin D deficiency, septicemia of the newborn or injury to one or more of the joints and a variety of treatments suggested.

Pain relief (aspirin works nicely) and protection from injury can see the plucky little ones through the acute phase of the process, and their lifespan is no different from the usual.

Slipped Kneecap

Any leg problem is generally a subject that is carefully ignored by breeders as being unimportant. Not so! It is very important, and information regarding it is rarely passed on to novice breeders.

Definition: The common name for this disorder is "slipping" or "slipped stifles," resulting from either subluxation (partial dislocation) or complete dislocation of the patella, or kneecap.

It is seen more often in small dogs than large ones. In the dog, intermittent or recurrent subluxations are characterized by the animal appearing normal one minute and carrying a hind limb the next. The dog generally does not appear in pain and examining the limb is not resented.

Subluxation usually is medial—that is, toward the midline of the body— with the stifle adducted (pulled or drawn to the midline) and the hock rotated outward. Lateral displacement is infrequent and usually the result of severe trauma. Bilateral involvement is rare and is evidenced by difficulty standing and walking with a hopping movement.

Treatment: In all cases surgical treatment, consisting of ligament and tendon repair, is indicated.

Genetics: Genetically speaking, I don't have enough pedigrees to give an opinion as to the nature of this condition's heritability, but since there seems to be a tendency for certain Beagle families to have had more than one example in the show ring over the years, I would have to jump to the conclusion that the problem can be inherited.

If you have had the problem more than once, it would be helpful for you to gather all of your pedigrees and do some detective work. By following the rules of recessive versus dominant inheritance, you can at least sort things out in a simple way. As to whether it is a simple recessive or something more complex, that will take a great deal more pedigree information than most individuals have available to them.

217

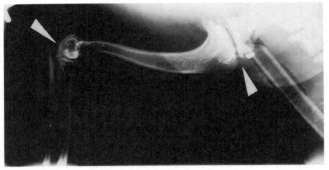

Radiograph of Banty's left shoulder and elbow showing degenerative joint disease of the shoulder and misshapen elbow joint.

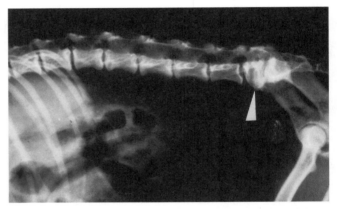

Radiograph of Banty's lumbar spine at age six, showing wedge-shaped deformed L7 vertebra and decreased disc spaces between vertebrae.

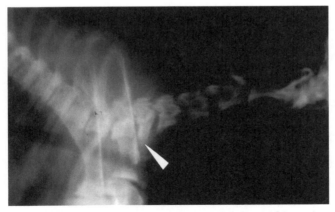

Radiograph of Banty's cervical spine with wedge-shaped C6 vertebra and narrowed intervertebral disc spaces.

218

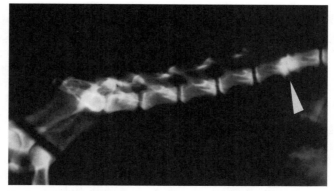

Radiograph of lumbar spine in nonaffected adult Beagle demonstrating normal shape of vertebral bodies and intervertebral disc thickness. Marker points to site of intervertebral disc disease.

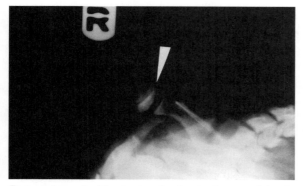

Red—radiograph of front extremity showing increased density of the upper end of the upper arm bone (humerus) at six weeks of age. Best time for X-ray diagnosis is at eight weeks.

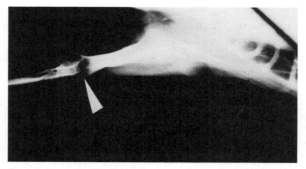

Red at six weeks. Radiograph shows destruction of the elbow joint including the upper end of the forearm bone (ulna) and the lower end of the humerus.

219

Breeders and owners seem to have difficulty differentiating between three groups of problems that may affect a dog's limbs: (1) genetic or hereditary; (2) problems secondary to true accidents and (3) changes secondary to aging.

When one repeatedly breeds to a genetic problem, one increases its incidence and possibly worsens it. A genetic problem cannot correct itself except through the almost nonexistent chance of a mutation occurring. Thus, it is never wise to ignore a genetic problem.

Common sense should tell one when true accidents have occurred. An accident in the birth canal due to improper positioning will not necessarily recur when the bitch is bred again.

A sound-limbed puppy or adult who suffers an injury that results in a damaged extremity may not be a candidate for the show ring, but this would have nothing to do with the dog's genetic makeup.

With age, dogs develop degenerative osteoarthritis, much as humans do. The degree of involvement may vary from one line to the other.

Short Chest or Pigeon Breast

The Beagle with this condition presents a shortened and markedly curved sternum or breastbone. The number of ribs is normal. It is most easily discovered by the feel of the puppy when it is held with one hand under the chest. With the dog standing in profile, if one looks carefully, it is evidenced as a "tuck-up" that is closer to the front end of the Beagle than normal.

There are not enough data yet to speculate on the mode of transmission. However, because it has occurred in two generations, it is a genetic defect.

Posing no health problems for the dog, it should be considered a defect for breeding purposes.

Short Outer Toes on the Front Feet

This is not an uncommon occurrence. Usually found in a very tight small foot with very straight pasterns, the outer toe is foreshortened. There have been reports from breeders of a rare occurrence of more than one toe on a foot being short as well as additional toes and pads (supernumerary) on the top of an otherwise normal-looking foot.

There are not enough data to speculate on the mode of transmission, except to say that this condition seems to occur in certain lines.

Intervertebral Disc Disease

Intervertebral discs are little "cushions" between the vertebral bodies that function basically as shock absorbers and to produce mobility of the spinal column. With age, there is a slow degeneration, which can cause problems when a prolapse of the disc material occurs, producing pressure on the adjacent spinal cord or spinal nerve roots.

"Pigeon breast."

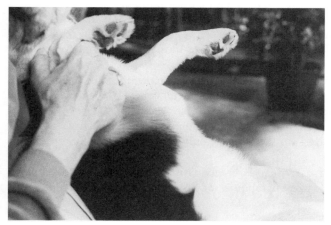

"Pigeon breast," more apparent in this position.

Note short outer toe.

221

Symptoms usually involve pain and varying degrees of difficulty with locomotion.

Because Beagles fall under the category of achondroplastic breeds, degeneration of intervertebral discs begins earlier and progresses more rapidly than in nonachondroplastic breeds. Hence, it is not unusual to see the disease manifested as early as three to six years of age.

We have found in our kennel that most of the Beagle's symptoms will subside with crate rest and corticosteroids. A veterinarian should always be consulted. Rarely, when signs of nerve compression progress, neurosurgical intervention is required. Although the latter is expensive and requires careful follow-up care, the Beagle can have many years of active and happy life remaining.

Crooked Tails

Occasionally one sees Beagle tails with an obvious bend or angle in the line of the tail vertebrae, giving the appearance of a "kink" in the tail.

X rays of such a tail show that two vertebrae are fused together, reducing the natural flexible curve. This condition occurs most commonly at the base and tip of the tail.

A good, full brush obscures the small bony deformity, which is most easily discovered by running your hand along the full course of the tail. When the fusion occurs at the base, the tail may appear "gay."

Some Beagle lines have had several offspring with fused vertebrae at the base of the tail, but, once again, the data are only suggestive of an inheritable condition.

Usually this slight deformity is barely visible and certainly does not detract from the Beagle's working abilities or his Conformation ring appearance.

Bites

Occasional reports of bad bites crop up each year. Most of these occur in only one puppy in a litter. Rarely is an entire litter affected, although it has happened.

Overbites are more common than underbites, and each appears to be relatively line specific. A wry bite—one side scissors, the other undershot and open—also occurs in Beagles.

OTHER PROBLEM AREAS

Teeth

Beagles have a reputation for early development of tartar (brown stains), calculus (layers of tartar) and gum disease. Some conformation lines show a greater tendency toward this condition.

Occasionally pitting and staining of the permanent teeth occur. Though commonly known as distemper teeth, this destruction of the tooth enamel can occur as the result of a high fever or use of certain antibiotics such as tetracycline in a puppy at the time of permanent tooth formation.

We have seen this condition develop in young Beagles with *no* history of high fever or exposure to antibiotics. Breeders of Standard Poodles and Miniature Schnauzers have reported similar experiences.

At least in the affected Beagle population, the pattern of distribution strongly suggests an inherited tendency.

Begun early, good preventive dental hygiene delays the onset of tooth and gum problems. But regular cleaning by your veterinarian will be required.

Bleeding Tendency

Von Willebrand's disease (VWD), an inherited bleeding disorder, commonly occurs in a number of dog breeds.

Though an occasional case of von Willebrand's disease in Beagles has been reported, the disease does not appear to be a serious threat at this time.

However, any Beagle that demonstrates slow clotting time should be tested by a veterinarian. Any cut or bleeding toenail that does not clot within two to three minutes indicates an increased clotting time.

For a fuller discussion of von Willebrand's disease, see pages 191–93.

Umbilical Hernia

This condition, a protrusion through an opening in the abdominal wall at the site of the umbilical cord, is caused by a genetic predisposition for delayed closure of the abdominal ring.

Small umbilical hernias are common in Beagles and require no treatment. If large enough to admit a fingertip through the ring, surgical repair will be required.

Ch. Kamelot's The Strumpet, fifteen inches (Plain & Fancy's Duke Gemini ex Ch. Plain & Fancy's Clover), owned by Janet E. Wolfley. *Fox/Cook*

Am./Bda. Ch. The Tavern's Riunite, thirteen inches (Ch. Brantwood's Bounty Hunter ex Am./Bda. Ch. The Tavern's Popcorn, Am./Bda. CD), owned by Linda Forrest. *John Ashbey*

19

Coat Color Inheritance

GENETICISTS have postulated many coat-color genes, but I will deal mainly with the four colors of greatest interest to Beaglers: (1) tricolor, (2) lemon or red and white, (3) blue and (4) liver or chocolate. In the following explanation I have leaned heavily on Clarence C. Little's *Inheritance of Coat Color in Dogs* (New York: Howell Book House, 1957).

The degree of expression of a gene may vary from animal to animal. This may be due to other genes modifying the effect of the genes in question. Difference in expression may also be due to other alleles (either of two genes that occupy the same locus). The case in which the effects of a gene are expressed in some animals and not in others is termed incomplete penetrance. Also, there are many genes that have small modifying effects on color or patterns, sometimes acting at different ages, tending to obscure the effects of the major genes.

While only two alleles can be present at a locus in one animal, multiple alleles often exist in the population as a whole. The locus involved in the coat color of the Beagle is an example of this. Listed below are these loci and their various allelic possibilities. This information can be seen with other color patterns in Little's book.

Because of the complexity and the difficulty in determining the various fine shades of color, I have eliminated detailed information concerning inheritance of different degrees of redness, tanness, the various grades of spotting or intensity of coat colors, etc.

GENES FOR COLOR BELIEVED PRESENT IN BEAGLES

Each individual will have two genes for each locus; the highest ranking member at any locus will be seen in the phenotype.

The genes Beagles are believed to carry are listed in order of relative dominance, top to bottom, at each locus. When only one gene is shown at a locus, it indicates that the Beagle is homozygous for that gene. By "relative dominance" we mean that certain genes, whether they are dominant or recessive, are more dominant than others at the same locus and, therefore, have a higher rank from top to bottom.

A^s (rare)	B (common)	C (common)	D (common)	E m	S (rare)	T
a^y (rare)	b (rare)	c^{ch} (rare)	d (rare)	e	s^i	t
a^t (common)					s^p	
					s^w	

Locus A: Allows or restricts formation of dark (black or brown) pigment.

A^s: Allows distribution of dark pigment over whole body (self, or solid color) as in the Newfoundland; rare in Beagles.

a^y: Restricts dark pigment greatly, and in most complete expression produces a clear sable or tan dog, as in the Basenji. This type of red, tan or sable is doubtful or rare in Beagles, most clear yellows or tans being the ee type, which is described below.

a^t: Produces tan points (black and tan, liver and tan, etc.). To the best of our knowledge, all Beagles are homozygous for a^t, no matter what their color, even lemon and white.

aw: This gene is not included under Beagles in Little's book, but since I have had a few dogs with this hair pattern, I have included it for your information. "Wild color," this gene allows for a banded type of hair. In a^t type dogs the banded hair is restricted to certain areas, usually along the neck in Beagles.

Locus B: Determines whether dark pigment formed at A will be black or brown, brown including liver and chocolate. Tricolored Beagles are Bb or BB. Liver- or chocolate-colored Beagles are bb.

Locus C: Basic factor for color, as distinguished from albinism.

C: Rich pigmentation, resulting in dark tan or red areas and absolute black or liver areas.

c^{ch}: Reduces richness of pigmentation, but usually its effect is visible to the eye only on red, tan or yellow pigment areas, which become lighter in shade toward lemon, buff or cream.

Locus D: The dilution factor for dark pigment.

D: Causes black or brown to remain black or brown.

d: Dilutes black to so-called Maltese blue (actually, gray) and brown to

Ch. Birchwood Land-O-Lakes, fifteen inches, and get out of Ch. Birchwood Juice Newton: Ch. Wenric One If By Land, thirteen inches, Winners Dog at National Beagle Club Specialty, 1988, owned by Nancy Youngdahl and Linda Lindberg, and Wenric One Good Turn, thirteen inches, owned by Jo Wilson.

Ch. Burnbridge Marci Daisyrun, fifteen inches, finished her championship with a Hound Group First (Ch. Meadowcrest's Fireside Chap ex Ch. Daisyrun Ben-brae Dauntless, CDX), owned by Nadine and Rene Chicoine. *Kernan*

227

silvery, as in Weimaraners. The dog must be *dd* to be "blue," that is, both parents contributed a gene for color to appear.

Locus *E:* The extension factor for dark pigment.

E: Allows dark pigment (black, brown or their diluted forms if affected by *dd*) to extend throughout the areas where produced.

e: Prevents extension of dark pigment, leaving the animal clear red, tan or yellow in pigmented (non-white) areas. The dog must be "ee" to be lemon or red and white.

Locus *M:* The dominant merle (*m*) factor, as in Collies. This has not been observed in Beagles; therefore, they are presumed to be of the formula *mm* (nonmerle).

Locus *S:* The spotting factor.

S: Causes pigmentation of the entire surface—no white, except possibly an isolated spot, as on chest; rare in Beagles.

s^i: Irish spotting; white feet, legs, chest, blaze; a pretty definite pattern, as in the Basenji.

s^P: Piebald spotting. Colored head and blanket, rest of surface being white, the usual distribution in Beagles. There is a whole range of spotting, which is described in Little's book.

s^w: Extreme white piebald spotting; dog is almost pure white, except for dark patches at the eye, ear or near the base of the tail. As there is considerable variation in amount of spotting, it is sometimes difficult to differentiate between the low extreme of a higher type and the high extreme of a lower type except by breeding tests to check progeny.

Locus *T:* The ticking factor.

T: Allows ticks of the dog's dark pigment color to appear in white areas.

t: Absence of ticks in white areas.

These loci have been named after the traits they represent, and to simplify the notations, they have been abbreviated. Thus, for example, *D* stands for the dilution factor. If there are more than a few alleles, then another letter is added to help describe the trait, as in a^t, the allele that allows for tan points. The inheritance of pigmentation, including color and patterns, is generally complex. Also, many genes have small modifying effects on color or patterns, sometimes acting at different ages, tending to obscure the effects of the major genes.

In addition, genes that are dominant are written as capital letters and those that are recessive are written in lower case. In the Beagle all the loci involving coat color exist, but are never expressed in their dominant forms. For example, the gene A^s would produce a completely black Beagle, and none has ever been recorded, or at the *M* locus, which would produce a merle dog. The point of all this is that the Beagle does carry two genes at these loci, but that the traits they represent are never seen.

With respect to the genes *A, B, D* and *E*, it can be seen that one Beagle can carry the genes for all four of the coat colors under discussion. It should also be apparent that the term "dominant for tri" is a misnomer, since the gene for tri-ness is actually recessive.

You can also see that blues are simply tri dogs that are homozygous for the dilution factor. They will have the genes $a^t a^t$ dd E?. The question mark means that the other gene at the locus can be either E or e, as the dominant form will mask any e gene.

In the same vein, you can see that the lemon and white Beagle is a homozygous tri that is also homozygous for the recessive form of the E gene. This dog will have the genes $a^t a^t$ D? ee. Again, the question mark represents the idea that the gene at this locus can be either D or d.

Have you ever seen a red, white and blue Beagle? Believe it or not, they do exist. This dog will have the genes $a^t a^t$ dd ee and will generally look like a lemon and white, but the tan points will be duller in color than you normally get.

The next question for the breeder interested in the color of his dogs is how carriers of these recessive genes can be detected. The answer is by test breeding. The breeder can now refer to the section on progeny testing (chapter 17) to see how a test breeding is done and what the chances are for getting any one of the colors that breeders can get.

SAMPLE COLORS AND GENETIC PATTERN

$a^t a^t$ B? C? D? E? mm s^p? tt: tricolor (black blanket, tan points, no ticking)

$a^t a^t$ bb C? D? E? mm s^p? tt: tricolor (liver blanket, tan points, no ticking)

$a^t a^t$ B? C? dd E? mm s^p? tt: tricolor (blue blanket, dull yellow points)

$a^t a^t$ B? C? D? ee mm s^p? tt: red and white (white dog with varying degrees of tan or red patches). If the genotype at the C locus was C^{ch}, the dog would have rich pigment but could throw pups whose tan was reduced to buff.

$a^t a^t$ B? chch ee mm s^p?: lemon and white (white dog with lemon or buff patches)

$a^t a^t$ B? C? dd ee mm s^p?: red, white and blue (very patriotic—the dog would look like a lemon and white with dull, buff points, light nose and eye pigment)

Where question marks appear, the other gene of the pair for the locus may be either dominant or recessive—only test breeding will tell.

As an example, let us say that you have a liver (chocolate) maiden bitch that you wish to breed to a tricolor male that has produced lemon and white puppies, and you want to know what your chances will be of getting tricolor puppies.

We know a little about your bitch's genotype because of her unusual color. It is $a^t a^t$ bb C? D? E? mm s^p? tt. We are not concerned with the D, M, S or T loci at this time, so we can disregard them for now.

We also know that the bitch is homozygous for a^t (she is tricolor) and b (her color is liver). The possible combinations for the bitch during segregation are:

Ch. Teloca Play with Fire, CD, thirteen inches (Ch. Teloca Navan Satisfaction, CD, ex Ch. Teloca Sunspun Dazzlin' Delite), owned by Anne Schaefer. *Booth*

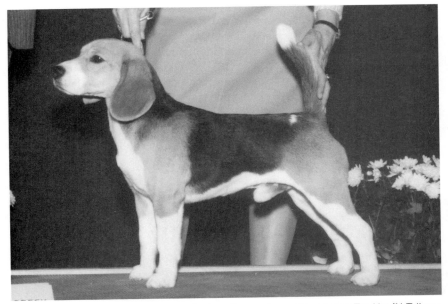

RD's Salute and Charge Ollie, thirteen inches, Group placer (Ch. Lanbur Top Hat 'N Tails ex Ch. RD's Odds on Favorite), owned by Ardie Haydon. *Wayne Cott*

a^tbCE a^tbCe
a^tbcE a^tbce

Because of the male's color and the puppies he has produced, we also know something about his genotype. It is a^ta^t $B?$ $C?$ $D?$ Ee mm $sP?$ tt. We know that the dog is homozygous for a^t (he is tricolored) and he has produced lemon and white puppies. The possible combinations for the dog during segregation are:

a^tBCE a^tBCe
a^tBcE a^tBce
a^tbCE a^tbCe
a^tbcE a^tbce

Using Punnett's Square:

BITCH

DOG	a^tbCE	a^tbCe	a^tbcE	a^tbce
a^tBCE	$a^ta^tBbCCEE$ tricolor	a^ta^tCCEe tricolor	$a^ta^tBbCcEE$ tricolor	$a^ta^tBbCcEe$ tricolor
a^tBCe	$a^ta^tBbCCEe$ tricolor	$a^ta^tBbCCee$ red & white	$a^ta^tBbCcEe$ tricolor	$a^ta^tBbCcee$ red & white
a^tBcE	a^ta^tbCcEE tricolor	$a^ta^tBbCcEe$ tricolor	$a^ta^tBBccEE$ tricolor buff points	$aaBbccEe$ tricolor buff points
a^tBce	$a^ta^tBbCcEe$ tricolor	$a^ta^tBbCcee$ red & white	$a^ta^tBbccEe$ tricolor buff points	$a^ta^tBbccee$ lemon & white
a^tbCE	$a^ta^tbbccee$ liver	$a^ta^tbbCCEe$ liver	$a^ta^tbbCcEE$ liver	$a^ta^tbbCcEe$ liver
a^tbCe	$a^ta^tbbCCEe$ liver	$a^ta^tbbCCee$ red & white w/bb color?	$a^ta^tbbCcEe$ liver	$a^ta^tbbCcee$ red & white
a^tbcE	$a^ta^tbbCcEE$ liver	$a^ta^tbbCcEe$ liver	$a^ta^tbbccEE$ liver buff points	$a^ta^tbbccEe$ liver buff points
a^tbce	$a^ta^tbbCcEe$ liver	$a^ta^tbbCcee$ red & white w/bb color?	$a^ta^tbbccEe$ liver buff points	$a^ta^tbbccee$ lemon & white buff points bb masked?

If the male carried the gene for liver and the female the gene for lemon and white, your statistical possibilities would be 12 tri: 12 liver: 6 red and white: 2 lemon and white. Your chances of getting a tri are 12 out of 32, or 37.5 percent. Remember the numbers for progeny testing: if out of six puppies none are red and white, there is a 95 percent chance that the bitch does not carry that gene. If there are no liver puppies, there is a 95 percent chance that the dog does not carry that gene.

Normally, with three genes there would be sixty-four possible combinations, so you can see how knowing more information about these dogs would simplify our probabilities. You could also have eliminated the C gene to simplify it further.

In brief, the tricolor coat, although inherited as a recessive, is dominant (less recessive) over the lemon or red and white gene, which is also inherited recessively.

The blue color is not a color at all, but a dilution of one of the other colors. We usually see a tri Beagle with the dilution factor. This gives the black saddle a bluish color and the tan points a duller, less bright cast. However, a lemon and white or liver and white can also have this diluted effect.

As far as the importance of the colors themselves, please refer to the Beagle Standard. However, there are some interesting points that might be considered. According to one author, there is evidence that Collies that are homozygous for the dilution factor dd have lower intelligence and are less resistant to infections. It should be noted that the dilution effect in Collies and Beagles is not the same as merling (also known as dappling). The merle pattern consists of an irregular patchwork of two contrasting colors, such as black with blue-gray. The blue Beagles that I have been acquainted with have thinner coats than our Standard calls for and seem to be more susceptible to skin problems.

On the other hand, lemon and white dogs would be expected to be more resistant to the ill effects of a hot, sunny day than the darker-coated dogs.

Punnett's Square is a sure and graphic way to illustrate how gene pairs might be inherited. However, it becomes unwieldy very quickly when we do three-gene pairs that have sixty-four possible combinations.

This, however, brings up the main problem in breeding dogs. With an average of four to five puppies per litter, it is not possible for more than half the possible nine combinations in a two-gene pair characteristic to occur. It would probably take several litters before a desired recessive will turn up. This might even be the case for a characteristic inherited through a one-gene pair. Given these poor odds, it should become obvious why we have so much difficulty getting or keeping a quality such as good movement, which probably has many genes involved in its creation.

To complete your frustration, there is the case of chromosomal inheritance. The dog has thirty-nine chromosome pairs—humans have only twenty-three. During reduction division, the chromosome pairs separate, one of each pair going into one or the other side of the nucleus. The nucleus then divides, leaving each half with thirty-nine chromosomes, one of each kind. The key to this is that, as far as we know, it is pure chance how the chromosomes line up before cell division, and consequently the proportion of contribution from each grandparent will vary.

A method to illustrate this for you has been suggested by Anne Paramoure in *Breeding and Genetics of the Dog* (Middleburg, Va.: Denlinger, 1959).

Take two sets of poker chips or paper, for example, red and white poker chips. Number each set from 1 to 39. Mix them together in a bowl and then draw them out one at a time. Arrange them in two piles through 39.

When you have finished, you will have two piles numbering thirty-nine each. But they will not be all the same color in either pile. (Well, they could, but it is extremely unlikely.)

You can let red represent the sire and white the dam, and the two piles will represent the two halves of the germ cell in reduction division.

This can be enlarged by setting up another group with blue and yellow chips representing your bitch (be sure to discard one pile, which would represent the polar body that is discarded in reduction division of the female). Now add the male chromosomes, giving you seventy-eight chromosomes, or thirty-nine pairs.

Now set up two equal piles. Each pile represents just one of the possible chromosome combinations your puppies might inherit. How many chips represent each of the grandparents? If you keep selecting different combinations, you will see that it is possible that one of the grandparents might not be represented at all.

Now put all the chips back and do it again. No matter what you got the first time, it will be different the second time. Even if the colors were the same, you would find that the chromosome numbers are different.

Again, the exception to this is when a mutation occurs—let's hope you all find the equivalent of the Morgan horse in your kennel!

Ch. Wilkat's Teddy Caboose, fifteen inches, multiple Group placer (Ch. Whisper's Double Tough ex Cejay Lee's Sweet 'n' Sassy), owned by Bruce and Shirley Irwin.

John Ashbey

Ch. Hare Hollow's One for the Road, fifteen inches, Best of Variety from the classes at ten months of age (Ch. Page Mill On the Road Again ex Ch. Starbuck's High Falutin'), owned by Karen Crary.

Callea

20

Life Cycle of a Dog Fancier

DOG FANCIERS don't just happen—they don't just burst forth full-grown like Athena from Zeus's forehead. Either they are born to the fancy or acquire the passion in later years. Growing up with parents who spend weekends showing or running their dogs can have a powerful impact on children. Some will love it and continue to be involved in their adult life. Others resent it and are only too glad to be free of it. For those who stumble into organized dog activities later in life, the process is similar to falling in love. The initial attraction either fizzles out, since the average life of a dog exhibitor is about five years, or develops into a lifetime commitment.

Man, like the dog, is a highly territorial and competitive animal. Feelings can run high in a sport where there is only one Best of Breed. Even the most civilized people can be reduced to sore losers.

When dog activities are the only leisure interest, even more of one's self becomes centered on the outcome of shows. "Love me, love my dog" is the rule of the day. Involvement in at least one or two other unrelated interests helps.

If both spouses in a family are not comfortable with dog activities, then trouble may lie ahead. Both need not be equally involved, but the "passive" partner needs to support his/her spouse's interest. Often both are required to handle the associated work load.

Competition exerts tremendous pressure on friendships within the sport. Everyone loves a loser. The consistent winner inspires at least feelings of

Ch. Starcrest's Warlock, fifteen inches, Specialty winner (Ch. Starcrest's Jason ex Ch. Hera of Starcrest), owned by Louise Merrill.   *Fox/Cook*

Ch. Sun Valley's Rowdy Free Agent, fifteen inches (Ch. Sun Valley's Big Spender ex Ch. Sun Valley's Page Two), among Top Ten 15″ Beagles, 1984, and one of the top producers in both varieties in 1986, owned by Ray and Sue Jackson and Michael Kurtzner.   *Fox/Cook*

ambivalence. Joint breeding programs and co-ownerships can help. However, delicate nurturing of special friendships will require tact and empathy.

Let's face it. Dog shows are not like a golf game.

IN THE BEGINNING

Most of us start with a pet dog. Some go to a local dog show to look at various breeds prior to making a family pet purchase. That first contact with dog activities may snap the trap. If people are having fun, if the dogs are good-looking and happy, if the exhibitor/breeder approached for information is helpful and persuasive, then a decision may be made to invest in a good show prospect.

Once the investment is made and the new puppy is home, training should begin. Contact with the original breeder, other Beaglers and attendance at puppy matches fuel the excitement. If the puppy is good enough and you work hard to learn good handling techniques, wins will come at all-breed shows. Usually it takes longer for the novice exhibitor to finish his dog to its championship. The fun of handling your own dog makes the additional time and effort worth it.

Dog-show days become social occasions where people discuss dogs endlessly. Indeed, the mark of a "real" dog person is an ability to discuss every detail of his Beagle's ancestry, appearance, personality, digestive tract functions, wins and losses *ad nauseam*. This typical form of communication is highly recognizable.

Along the way you may try some obedience work with your Beagle and most likely will join either a local breed or all-breed club if one is available.

Your Beagle has acquired its championship. The next major decision must now be made. If your Beagle is a bitch, should you breed her and begin again with a new puppy? Or should you campaign your Beagle as a Special (that class of an American Kennel Club show for dogs that have achieved their championships)? Obviously, the decision about male dogs is not affected by breeding.

THE CAMPAIGN

"Specialing" your Beagle is a totally different ballgame. Wins at Variety level are exciting, but competition at the Group and Best-in-Show levels are the "big high." The excitement can truly become addictive as you work for the top prize. Competition at this level requires several essentials: a good Beagle, time, a good handler and money.

Certainly not all Beagles that are campaigned successfully are exceptional representatives of the breed, but they all have one thing in common. They are "show dogs." These are dogs that love to please, love to show and will give their all in the ring. They have a "look at me" attitude.

Campaigning a Special does not mean showing at an occasional show.

Can. Ch. Terwillegar's Hit the roof, fifteen inches, a Group winner (Ch. Page Mill on the Road Again ex Ch. The Whim's Raise the Roof), owned by Mrs. G. R. Lloyd. *Mikron*

Ch. Someday's Pork Belly, thirteen inches, Best Puppy and Reserve Winners Bitch, National Beagle Club Specialty, 1988 (Ch. Surelow's Portfolio ex Ch. SureLuv's Gizmo), owned by Dr. & Mrs. John R. Frazier. *Alverson*

It means exhibiting at most of the shows in your geographical area and often beyond. If you handle your own dog, it requires travel almost every weekend of the year. Early mornings, long drives, difficult airline connections, time lost at home, long hours of grooming and caring for your Beagle are part of the package. Even if you hire a professional handler, the dog must be transported to and from the handler. Of course, many of the shows you will attend as well.

Our experience has taught us that the Beagles that do not return home frequently for contact with their normal routine and surroundings do not enjoy the shows after a time as much as those that do so. They also need the rest and relaxation, much as humans do. The demands on owner, handler and dog are very stressful. During intensive campaigning, physiological changes can result in reduced sperm counts in dogs and delayed seasons in bitches.

Along with direct involvement in shows, time is also needed for peripheral dog activities. Remember that most owners of successful show dogs belong to their local all-breed kennel club and frequently to their national breed club. Making a contribution of time and work is an important part of the dog-show scene. Club meetings, days of preparation for the all-breed show, special projects are demanding but rewarding. As a working club member you have opportunities to meet exhibitors and breeders of other breeds, American Kennel Club personnel, and last but not least, judges! All have much to teach.

Time is a precious and finite commodity. How we choose to spend it is a highly personal decision. When spent on dog activities, less is available for families, children and other interests.

THE HANDLER

If you are not handling your Beagle yourself, you will need a professional dog handler. Selecting the proper person for your needs will require some research. Of first concern will be the quality of care that will be given your Beagle. Cleanliness, good health and proper grooming make for proper presentation. Also, will your Beagle be happy and safe? Communication between owner and handler must be clear and open. Competition is stressful. You need someone who can lose as well as win gracefully, is respected by his or her peers and who preferably will give you "first call" in the Hound Group.

A special rapport develops between handler and dog in a successful team. Also, the client/handler relationship can develop into a special friendship, one more reward in the dog game.

MONEY

Campaigning your Beagle is a costly business. When making the decision, consider that entries at roughly sixty shows a year will run about $900 and that handling fees and travel expenses can run into the thousands. Don't

Ch. Jabrwoki's Jyro Gearloose, fifteen inches (Ch. Buglair Dismal Creek Bandit ex Ch. Jabrwoki's Hex on You), owned by Shawn and Barbara Robblee. *Bergman*

Ch. Merry Song's High Performance, fifteen inches, BIS National Beagle Club Specialty, 1988, and multiple Group winner (Ch. Starbuck's Hang 'Em High ex Ch. Merry Song's Ms Sunshine), owned by Mara Baun and Nancy Bergstrom. *Olson*

forget the advertising in dog-fancy magazines and newspapers. Regular exposure, at least monthly if not more often, helps increase your dog's chances of recognition in the show ring. Photographs of your Beagle's win run about $25 to $30 per show. Campaigning is not for everyone.

THE NEXT GENERATION

The next stage, breeding, definitely requires two people.

Decisions about breeding, raising of litters, placement of puppies, servicing either your own or visiting bitches are tasks that come with this stage of the development of the breeder. Requests for stud service are the natural consequence of a successful campaign, and one of the reasons for it.

Frankness about your stud's virtues, faults, genetic makeup is essential.

Extensive correspondence, time-consuming phone calls, trips to airports, struggles with frightened bitches and sometimes difficult owners are standard. It may seem as though bitches are receptive only on Christmas or during family holidays. Weekends and evenings are frequently interrupted by enthusiastic owners, complete with relatives and children, as well as their bitches in season.

Once we dealt with the owner of a bitch, an elderly grandmother who spoke only Russian, and the owner's eight-year-old granddaughter, who played the piano in the living room for the duration of the breeding. Her parting shot was a request for a quarter along with an invitation to my husband to marry her. Fortunately, laughter eases difficult times.

Each litter sired by your stud becomes part of your extended dog family. What happens to them in part happens to you, too.

Delivering and raising a litter can be one of the joys of life with Beagles. Newborns are a marvel with their instinct for survival. Maternal behavior is astonishing to observe. Nothing is more fetching than six-week-old Beagle puppies. Born clowns, they tumble, cuddle, roughhouse and are always appealing. A good breeding produces promising puppies. What a thrill it is to watch a good puppy grow into an excellent adult!

But things do not always go well. Missed breedings, difficult deliveries, Caesarean sections in the middle of the night under less than ideal conditions and weak and failing puppies confront us all. If that were not enough, there are always some puppies that are lost either in delivery or during the neonatal period, the uncovering of genetic defects theretofore undisclosed and the worry about infectious diseases. Sleepless nights spent feeding weak puppies, cleaning up after mother and offspring, and visits to the veterinarian all take their toll. And finally, there is the emotional trauma when loved puppies leave for new homes.

Visits from prospective puppy owners bring unusual opportunities to observe family interaction. You've probably met them: the nice people who don't want to touch the dogs; the delightful young couple whose nine-year-old

Ch. Jo Lee's Six Pack, fifteen inches, multiple Group winner and Best of Opposite Sex to Best of Breed, National Beagle Club Specialty, 1986 (Ch. Starbuck's Full Count ex Norman's Sugar VCC), owned by Harry L. and JoAnn Schoo.   *Graham*

Ch. Birchwood's Jack Daniels, fifteen-inch blue Beagle (Ch. Linven's Super Star ex Ch. Meado Glo Birchwood's Holly), owned by Linda Lindberg.   *John Ashbey*

attempts to strangle his little friend behind the kitchen counter while the five-year-old sneakily pushes the little puppies over; the family that must have a puppy day before yesterday—and when arrangements are finalized to have the puppy available in two weeks, the family has had a change of heart.

Most original homes are neither designed for dog breeders nor situated in appropriate neighborhoods. Inevitably, the search for country property begins with plans for a "real kennel." As a result of the burgeoning dog population and worry about potential complaints from neighbors, a major move is in order. Sometimes this involves becoming experts in septic systems, private water supplies and roadbuilding, and dealing with the threat of mud slides and forest fires.

Hard Times

Your time will come! In any breeding program, lean times are inevitable. Breedings that look marvelous on paper sometimes produce disappointing puppies. The appearance of previously unidentified genetic defects, breakthroughs in your vaccination program, loss of litters, missed breedings will test the most hardy of breeders. Outcrosses made to increase vigor and fertility often bring new problems as well.

Fortunately, there is an ever-increasing reservoir of information related to many of the problems encountered by the conscientious breeder. Consultation with knowledgeable professionals and other breeders offers new approaches. Don't be shy about asking for help.

The Golden Years, or Life Is Not Over

You are now twenty or thirty years into your life as a breeder. Wiser, less positive about many of the aspects of Beagling than you once were, you begin to cut back a little.

It is said that old age is a time of losses. This is true for an aging breeder as well. Your life apart from dogs presents new tasks and challenges to handle. Also, by this time, a collection of aging Beagles requires special time and attention. You attend fewer shows, breed an occasional litter, and wonder what life would be like without the dogs.

You may spend time pursuing a career in judging. For those who enjoy organization, more time can be devoted to their local all-breed club. Volunteer service at the local Society for the Prevention of Cruelty to Animals is always needed. Who is better qualified than an experienced breeder or dog lover?

Or you can always write a book!

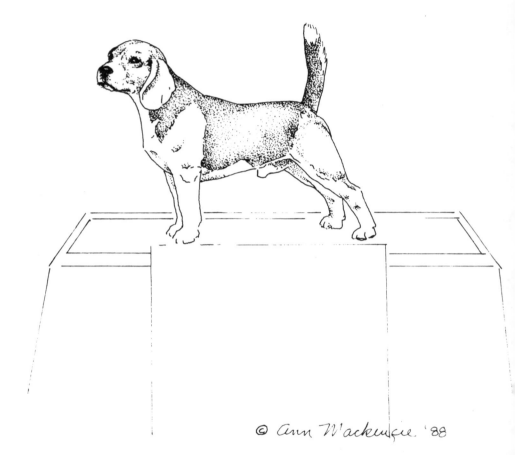

© Ann Mackenzie '88

244

21

Top Producing
Sires and Dams

$\mathbf{A}$ BEAGLE, just like any other life form, is the sum total of its genetic parts. Every tangible and intangible factor that contributes to the makeup of the unique individual that is the Beagle before you is fixed at conception. One of those factors is its ability to pass the genetic "baton" to its offspring.

Of course, some Beagles are more blessed than others. A great show dog is not always an equally great producer, and many wonderful producers have never set the world within the ring ropes on fire. On the pages that follow, we present a group of top producers, including many who did have a strong impact in the show ring as well as on the breed's later generations.

With the photos of these hounds appear their pedigrees. These "road maps of heredity" offer an intriguing picture of the families of these standouts. May they help enhance your association with the breed and further familiarize you with the source of some of the breed's best.

Ch. Starbuck's Hang 'Em High, fifteen inches, top Beagle sire of all time with 118 champions; top winning Beagle with twenty-three Bests in Show and eleven Specialty Bests of Breed; winner of the National Beagle Club Award for Top Sire, 1980–84, and Beagle of the Year, 1980. Owned by David and Linda Hiltz. *Missy Yuhl*

Ch. Page Mill Whirlwind

Ch. Wandering Wind

Ch. Wandering Sue

Ch. The Whim's Buckeye

Ch. Page Mill Trademark

The Whim's Firecracker

Ch. Page Mill Wildfire

CH. STARBUCK'S HANG 'EM HIGH

Ch. Validay Show Biz

Ch. Elsy's Jack Frost

Ch. Elsy's Joyful Jennifer

Ch. Elsy's Shooting Star

Ch. Wagon Wheels Winter Sport

Ch. Colegren Elsy's Lucky Star

Ch. Johjean's Bill Jamboree Jubal

Ch. The Whim's Buckeye, thirteen inches, sire of 99 champions; winner of ten Bests in Show; top Beagle, all systems, 1971 and 1972; top hound, all systems, 1972. Sire of ten top producers. Owned by Mrs. A. C. Musladin.

Ch. Page Mill Downbeat
Ch. Page Mill Whirlwind
Ch. Page Mill Night Mist
Ch. Wandering Wind
Ch. Pine Lane Powerhouse
Ch. Wandering Sue
Johnston's Joyful Judy
CH. THE WHIM'S BUCKEYE
Ch. Page Mill Whirlwind
Ch. Page Mill Trademark
Ch. White Acres Lady Slipper
The Whim's Firecracker
Ch. Wandering Wind
Ch. Page Mill Wildfire
Ch. Oakwood Silky Sue

Ch. Teloca Patches Littl' Dickens, thirteen inches, sire of 85 champions; top-winning thirteen-inch Beagle of all time; winner of the National Beagle Club Awards for thirteen-inch Beagle, 1986, and Beagle of the Year, 1984 and 1985; Sire of the Year 1985 and 1986. Owned by Wade Burns and Jon Woodring. *Earl Graham*

Ch. The Whim's Cock of the Walk
Ch. Teloca Puddin' An' Tame, CD
Ch. Teloca Red's Me Too
Ch. Teloca Patches On Target, CD
Ch. Teloca Marshall Arts
Ch. Centurian's Jingle
Ch. Teloca Cookie Too of Belbravo
CH. TELOCA PATCHES LITTL' DICKENS
Ch. The Whim's Cock of the Walk
Ch. Teloca Puddin' An' Tame, CD
Ch. Teloca Red's Me Too
Ch. Teloca Upstage Bann'd in Boston, CD
Ch. Kings Creek Triple Threat
Ch. Teloca Red's Middle Child, CD
Ch. Robin's Red of Honey Hill. CD

Ch. Busch's Nuts to You of Brendons, fifteen inches, sire of 83 champions. Multiple Best in Show winner. Owned by William and Fitzi Busch. *Darrell Gwinup*

Ch. Wor-Lu's Crown Royal

Ch. Johjean Joker of Do Mor

Ch. Do Mor Debutante

Ch. Busch's Bonnie Prince Charlie

Ch. Clark's Lackawana Tony

Hoffman's Maggie

Bollinger's Linda

CH. BUSCH'S NUTS TO YOU OF BRENDONS

Ch. Page Mill Whirlwind

Ch. Wandering Wind

Ch. Wandering Sue

Ch. Lawndale's Gusty Wind

Ch. Wor-Lu's Comet

Ch. Sunnymede Little Doll

Ch. Devonridge Gay Girl

Ch. Kings Creek Triple Threat, fifteen inches, sire of 78 champions. First Best of Breed at the National Beagle Club Specialty; four times Best of Variety, fifteen inches, Westminster Kennel Club; Multiple Best in Show winner. Owned by Marcia Foy. *Evelyn Shafer*

Ch. Graphite of Walnut Hall
Ch. Snelling's Dapple John
Ch. Gay Boy's Faith
Ch. Kings Creek Stagerlee
Takakkaw Merryman
Ch. C.S. Charmer's Princess
C.S. Charmer
CH. KINGS CREEK TRIPLE THREAT
Security Serenader
Ch. Security Black Gold
C.S. Faultless
Security Susie Black Flash
C.S. Strike III
C.S. Flash
Williamson's Gay Girl

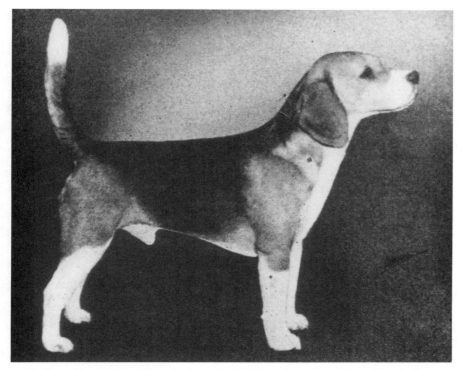

Ch. Thornridge Wrinkles, fifteen inches, sire of 76 champions. Specialty and Best in Show winner. Owned by Sam Granata.

Ch. Delco Minor

Ch. Muirland's Micky

Dwan's Twin

Ch. Eberle's Mickey II

Ch. Thornridge Toney

Ch. Eberle's Princess

Ch. Eberle's Little Lady

CH. THORNRIDGE WRINKLES

Interlaken Lasher

Ch. Thornridge Toney

Nancy Hanks III

Ch. Joyful of Culver Hill

Ch. Madden's Minor

Ch. Captina Charmer

Nellie Flash

Ch. Rockaplenty's Wild Oats, fifteen inches, sire of 59 champions, as well as second of three generations of the National Beagle Club Specialty Best of Breed winners; top Beagle, 1973; sire of top winning Beagle bitch, Ch. Kamelot's Queen Bee. Owned by Anna Katherine Nicholas. *John Ashbey*

Ch. Snelling's Dapple John

Ch. Kings Creek Stagerlee

Ch. C.S. Charmer's Princess

Ch. Kings Creek Triple Threat

Ch. Security Black Gold

Security Susie Black Flash

C.S. Flash

CH. ROCKAPLENTY'S WILD OATS

Ch. Page Mill Trademark

Ch. Page Mill Hallmark

Ch. Page Mill Starlet

Ch. Page Mill Call Girl

Ch. Wandering Wind

Ch. Page Mill Fantasy

Ch. White Acres Pansy

252

Ch. Navan's Triple Trouble Rick, fifteen inches, sire of 55 champions. Multiple Best in Show winner; Best of Breed, the National Beagle Club Specialty, 1975. Owned by Nancy Vanstrum Cannon. *John Ashbey*

                    Ch. Snelling's Dapple John
              Ch. Kings Creek Stagerlee
                    Ch. C.S. Charmer's Princess
        Ch. Kings Creek Triple Threat
                    Ch. Security Black Gold
              Security Susie Black Flash
                    C.S. Flash
CH. NAVAN'S TRIPLE TROUBLE RICK
                    Ch. Kings Creek Merry Go Boy
              Trailside Midnight Sun
                    Ch. Kings Creek Miss Fire
        Ch. Navan's Penny a Go-Go, CD
                    Ch. Kings Creek Merry Go Boy
              Carwood Carrie A Go-Go
                    Celtic Coquette

Ch. The Whim's Cock of the Walk, thirteen inches, sire of 42 champions. Top thirteen-inch Beagle, 1975; Specialty and Best in Show winner. Owned by Mrs. A. C. Musladin.

Jayne Langdon

Ch. Page Mill Whirlwind

Ch. Wandering Wind

Ch. Wandering Sue

Ch. The Whim's Buckeye

Ch. Page Mill Trademark

The Whim's Firecracker

Ch. Page Mill Wildfire

CH. THE WHIM'S COCK OF THE WALK

Ch. Seven Hills Gold Toke

Ch. Seven Hills Black Gold

Sailaway Sailbright

Ch. The Whim's Chatterbox

Ch. Wandering Wind

Ch. The Whim's Priscilla Mullins

The Whim's Firecracker

Ch. Chardon Kentucky Derby, fifteen inches, sire of 38 champions. Winner of five Bests in Show and three Specialty Bests of Breed; top fifteen-inch Beagle, 1981 and 1982. Owned by Charles and Donna Kitchell.   *Ralph Karley*

Ch. Wandering Wind

Ch. The Whim's Buckeye

The Whim's Firecracker

Ch. Starbuck's Hang 'Em High

Ch. Elsy's Jack Frost

Ch. Elsy's Shooting Star

Ch. Colegren Elsy's Lucky Star

CH. CHARDON KENTUCKY DERBY

Ch. Busch's Nuts to You of Brendons

Ch. Busch's Gin Rickey

Ch. Busch's Dixie Debutante

Ch. Busch's Truly Fair

Ch. Busch's Nuts to You of Brendons

Ch. Busch's Black Eyed Susan

Ch. Busch's Dixie Dynamo

Ch. Kinsman High Jinks, fifteen inches, sire of 38 champions. Owned by Lee Wade.

<pre>
                        Ch. Foxcatcher Merryman
              Ch. Little Merryman
                        Ch. Charmac Fancy of Beascot
         Ch. Kinsman Little Merryman
                   Veach's Minor
              Ch. Kinsman Jinny
                   McWethy's Show Girl
CH. KINSMAN HIGH JINKS
                        Ch. Walridge Sapper
              Ch. Kinsman Sapper
                        Ch. Walridge Columbine
         Kinsman Prim
                        Ch. Muirland's Micky
              Ch. Osborne's Prim
                        Randall's Mellowstone
</pre>

Ch. Plain & Fancy's Delilah, fifteen inches, top Beagle dam of all time with 22 champions out of 25 get. A son, out of Ch. Starbuck's Hang 'Em High, Ch. Graadtre's Hot Pursuit of Rossut, was a top winning Beagle and top producer in England. Owned by Mary Hammes.

Ch. Wandering Wind
Ch. The Whim's Buckeye
The Whim's Firecracker
Ch. Mitey Cute Just Like Daddy
Ch. Page Mill Hallmark
Ch. South Spring Ample Answer
Ch. South Spring May Morn
CH. PLAIN & FANCY'S DELILAH
Ch. Lynnhaven's Gallant Fox
Ch. Sunnymeade Captain Gun
Meado-Glo Mina Tonka
Ch. Plain & Fancy's Pixie Image
Ch. Johnson's Fancy Boots
Little Lady III
Felty's Gay Gidget

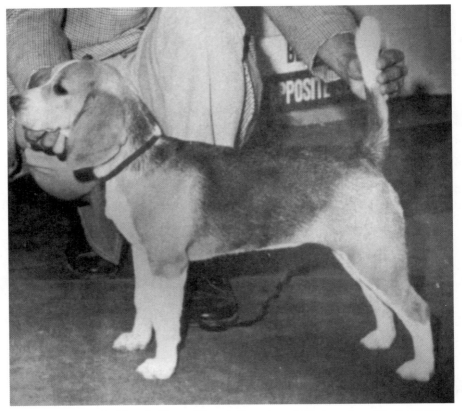

Ch. J's Bonnie V of Beagle Chase, fifteen inches, dam of 18 champions. Winner of the National Beagle Club Dam of the Year Award, 1980. Owned by Dick Johnson.

Ch. Nottowa's Amigo
Ch. Windmar's Tom Thumb
Ch. Char-Mar Becky Sharp
Ch. Hi Spirit JC
Ch. South Paw Senor Amigo
Hi Spirit Jin
Ch. Hi Spirit Jill
CH. J'S BONNIE V OF BEAGLE CHASE
Yaupon Row Lugan
Ch. S.K. Rough Rider
Ch. Ell-Gee's Fair Lady
Ch. Ruff's Pixie V of Beagle Chase
Ch. Gladewind's Great Caesar
Duerr's Tip Top Tammy
Carwood Cheerful Commotion

Ch. Junior's Fun Machine, thirteen inches, dam of 18 champions. Winner of the National Beagle Club Dam of the Year Award, 1983 and 1986. Owned by Dick Johnson. *Graham*

Ch. Wandering Wind

Ch. The Whim's Buckeye

The Whim's Firecracker

Ch. Jana Pagent

Ch. Page Mill Hallmark

Ch. Jana Will O Wisp

Ch. Bowmanor's Prima Donna

CH. JUNIOR'S FUN MACHINE

Ch. Windmar's Tom Thumb

Ch. Hi Spirit JC

Hi Spirit Jin

Ch. J's Bonnie V of Beagle Chase

Ch. S.K. Rough Rider

Ch. Ruff's Pixie V of Beagle Chase

Duerr's Tip Top Tammy

Ch. Junior's Belle Starr, fifteen inches, dam of 15 champions. Owned by Dick Johnson.

```
                              Ch. Nottowa's Amigo
                    Ch. Windmar's Tom Thumb
                              Ch. Char-Mar Becky Sharp
          Ch. Hi Spirit JC
                              Ch. South Paw Senor Amigo
                    Hi Spirit Jin
                              Ch. Hi Spirit Jill
CH. JUNIOR'S BELLE STARR, CDX
                              Ch. Page Mill Whirlwind
                    Ch. Page Mill Trademark
                              Ch. White Acres Lady Slipper
          Ch. Page Mill Shamrock
                              Ch. Page Mill Whirlwind
                    Ch. Page Mill Nutmeg
                              Ch. Oakwood Silky Sue
```

Ch. Johjean's Bill Jamboree Jubal, fifteen inches, dam of 14 champions. Owned by Mrs. William Coleman.

<pre>
                              Ch. Jim Dandy of Pine Lodge
                    Ch. DoMor Director
                              Ch. DoMor Patrolette
        Johjean Jamboree Jake
                              Ch. Security Salute
                    Ch. Forest Festivity
                              Ch. Jacobi's Jewel
CH. JOHJEAN'S BILL JAMBOREE JUBAL
                              Ch. DoMor Director
                    DoMor Director's Duplicate
                              Ch. Thornridge Gaiety
        Ch. Lady Wrinkles of Perk's DoMor
                              Ch. Altopa Atom II
                    Ch. Ginger of Perk's DoMor
                              Ch. DoMor's Faith Flash
</pre>

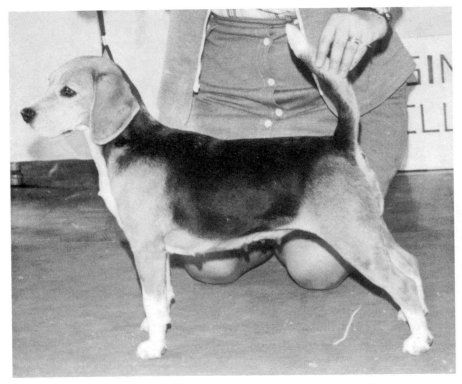

Ch. Meado Glo Birchwood's Holly, fifteen inches, dam of 14 champions. Owned by Linda Lindberg.

Ch. Ralph's Julius Caesar
Ch. Meado Glo Pinto
Meado Glo Mini Ho Ho
Ch. Meado Glo Dancer
Ch. Lo Na's Jack
Meado Glo Ponda
Ch. Sunnymede Gay Lady
CH. MEADO GLO BIRCHWOOD'S HOLLY
Ch. Meado Glo Gallant Magoo
Ch. Meado Glo Captain
Meado Glo Cindy Lou
Meado Glo Katie Did
Ch. Johjean Jubal
Meado Glo Princess Lu
Meado Glo Lula Bell

Ch. Robin's Red of Honey Hill, CD, fifteen inches, dam of 14 champions. Group-winning bitch owned by Marie Shuart.

Ch. Kings Creek Stagerlee

Ch. Kings Creek Merry Go Boy

Ch. Kings Creek Merrianne

Trailside Midnight Sun

Ch. Kings Creek Stagerlee

Ch. Kings Creek Miss Fire

Thornridge Bambi

CH. ROBIN'S RED OF HONEY HILL, CD

Ch. Kings Creek Stagerlee

Ch. Kings Creek Merry Go Boy

Ch. Kings Creek Merrianne

Lady Susan of Camelot, CD

Kings Creek Gunsmoke

Ch. Kings Creek Into Everything

Thornridge Toots

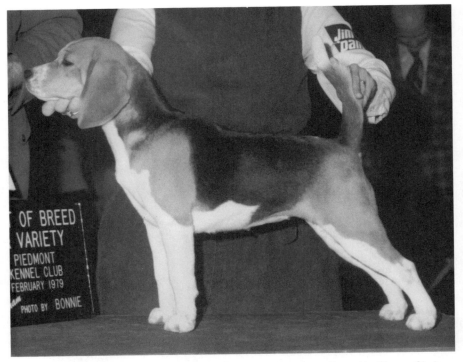

Ch. Swan Lake's I Declare, fifteen inches, dam of 14 champions. Owned by Sharon Clark.
Graham

Ch. Wandering Wind
Ch. The Whim's Buckeye
The Whim's Firecracker
Colegren's Peter of Craigwood
Ch. Jennie's Johnnie Junior
Ch. Colegren's Carbon Copy
Ch. Johjean's Bill Jamboree Jubal
CH. SWAN LAKE'S I DECLARE
Ch. Pin Oak's Little Tom Thumb
Ch. Pin Oak's Charming Don Juan
Ch. Pin Oak's Performing Gay Lady
Ch. Funny Face of Beagle Chase
Ch. Hi Spirit JC
Ch. J's Gay Lady of Beagle Chase
Ch. Ruff's Pixie of Beagle Chase

264

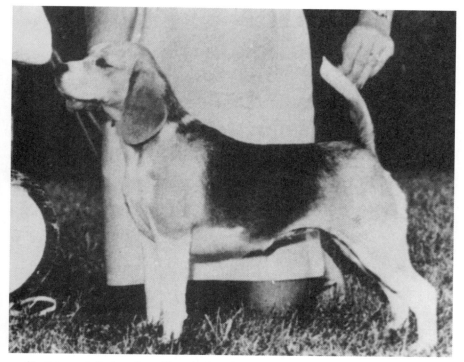

Ch. Colegren's Carbon Copy, fifteen inches, dam of 13 champions. Owned by Mrs. William Coleman.

Ch. Beau A Black Bomber
Ch. Johjean Gentle John Janzoom
Ch. Socum Tammy
Ch. Jennie's Johnnie Junior
Ch. Johjean Jock
Penjock Jennie
Johjean Penelope
CH. COLEGREN'S CARBON COPY
Ch. DoMor Director
Johjean Jamboree Jake
Ch. Forest Festivity
Ch. Johjean's Bill Jamboree Jubal
DoMor Director's Duplicate
Ch. Lady Wrinkles of Perks DoMor
Ch. Ginger of Perks DoMor

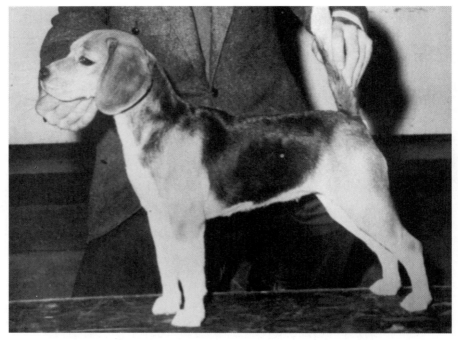

Ch. Garber's Cupcake, fifteen inches, dam of 13 champions. Winner of the National Beagle Club Specialty Best of Breed, 1973. Owned by Marcia Foy and Virginia Flowers.

                      Ch. Foster's Shorty
             Ch. Jacobi's Journeyman
                      Ch. Jacobi's Jennifer
        Ch. Wagon Wheels Winter Sport
                      Ch. Belair Jerry
             Ch. Wagon Wheels White Hope
                      Ch. Dalecarlia's Gay Doll
CH. GARBER'S CUPCAKE
                          Ch. Waldor's Flying Dutchman
             Ch. Walloping Windowblind, CD
                          Ch. Wagon Wheels Warbler
        Garber's Determined Beauty
                          Fd. Ch. Twink-L-Hill Timmy
             Neatline Lynn
                          Ch. Enoka Sheba

Bibliography

Acton, C.R. *The Modern Foxhound.* New York: Winward House, 1936.

American Kennel Club. *The Complete Dog Book.* New York: Howell Book House, 1987.

American Kennel Club, 1884–1984: A Source Book. New York: American Kennel Club, 1985.

Anderson, Allen C. *The Beagle as an Experimental Dog.* Ames: Iowa State University Press, 1970.

Ashmont [J. Frank Perry]. *Kennel Secrets.* Boston: Little Brown & Company, 1904.

Bedford, P.G., "The Aetiology of Canine Glaucoma," *Vet. Rec.* July 1980. 26:107: 76–82.

———. "The Treatment of Canine Glaucoma," *Vet. Rec.* August 1980. 26:107: 101–4.

Berndt, Robert J. *Your Beagle.* Fairfax, Va.: Denlingers Publishers, 1976.

Brightman, A.H. "Keratoconjunctivitis Sicca," *J. Am. Vet. Med. Assoc.* Apr 15, 1980. 176 (8): 710–1.

Brown, S. Gary. "Skeletal Disease." In *Textbook of Veterinary Internal Medicine,* vol. 2, edited by Ettinger. Philadelphia: W. B. Saunders, 1975.

Canine Medicine. 2nd ed. American Veterinary Publications, 1959.

Carlson, Delbert G, D.V.M., and Giffin, James M., D.V.M. *Dog Owner's Home Veterinary Handbook,* New York: Howell Book House, 1980.

Clark, Ross D., D.V.M., and Stainer, John R. *Medical and Genetic Aspects of Purebred Dogs.* Edwardsville, Kan.: Veterinary Medicine Publishing Company, 1983.

Colombo, Henry J., et al. *The New Complete Beagle.* New York: Howell Book House, 1966.

Concannon, Patrick W., Ph.D., and Lein, Donald H., Ph.D. "Canine Reproductive Biology." *Proceedings for Veterinary Technicians at Western Veterinary Conference,* 1986.

Dalziel, Hugh. *British Dogs.* London: L. Upcott Gill, 1988.

Davies, C. J. *The Theory and Practice of Breeding to Type,* Our Dogs Publishing Company, n.d.

Denlinger, William. *The Complete Beagle.* Fairfax, Va.: Denlingers Publishers, 1956.

Dodds, W. Jean, D.V.M. *Proceedings of the Fifty-sixth Annual Meeting of the Animal Association, April 1989* (St. Louis), pp. 603–24.

Elliott, Rachel Page. *Dogs Steps: Illustrated Gait at a Glance.* New York: Howell Book House, 1973.

————. *The New Dog Steps,* New York: Howell Book House, 1985.

Emily, Peter, D.V.M. "Canine Dentition Syllabus." Santa Clara Valley Kennel Club Seminar, 1985.

Fisher, Sir Ronald A. *The Theory of Inbreeding,* New York: Academic Press, 1985.

Foy, Marcia, and Nicholas, Anna Katherine. *The Beagle.* Neptune City, N.J.: TFH Publications, 1985.

Gelatt, K.N., and Gum, G.G. "Inheritance of Primary Glaucoma in the Beagle." *An. J. Vet. Res.* October 1981. 42:1691–3.

Gould, George M., M.D. *Gould's Pocket Pronouncing Medical Dictionary,* Philadelphia: Blakiston Co., 1941.

Holst, Phyllis A., M.S., D.V.M. *Canine Reproduction,* Loveland, Colo.: Alpine Publications, Inc., 1985.

Hutt, Frederick B. *Animal Genetics,* New York: The Ronald Press Company, 1964.

————. *Genetics for Dog Breeders.* New York: W. H. Freeman & Co., 1979.

Johansson, Ivar, and Johansson, Rendel. *Genetics and Animal Breeding,* Edinburgh and London: Oliver and Boyd, 1968.

Kirk, Robert W., D.V.M. *Current Veterinary Therapy VI,* Philadelphia: W. B. Saunders, 1977.

Krook, Leonard. "Short Summary of Metabolic and Skeletal Disease," Special Pathology Lectures, New York Veterinary College, Cornell University, 1973.

Lentilhon, Eugene. *Forty Years Beagling in the United States.* New York: E. P. Dutton, 1921.

Lerner, Michael, and Donald, H. P. *Modern Developments in Animal Breeding,* New York: Academic Press, 1966.

Little, Clarence C. *Inheritance of Coat Color in Dogs.* New York: Howell Book House, 1957.

Lush, Jay L. *Animal Breeding Plans,* Iowa State College Press, 1958.

Lyon, McDowell. *The Dog in Action,* New York: Howell Book House, 1963.

Merck Veterinary Manual. 6th ed. Rahway, N.J.: Merck & Co., 1986.

Migliorini, Mario. *Beagles,* New York: Arco Publishing Company, 1976.

Mosier, Jacob, D.V.M. "Canine Neonatology and Pediatrics Syllabus," Santa Clara Valley Kennel Club Seminar, 1987.

Nelson, R.W. "Hypothyroidism in Dogs and Cats: A Difficult Deficiency to Diagnose." *Veterinary Medicine,* January 1987.

Nicholas, Anna Katherine, and Brearley, Joan. *The Wonderful World of Beagles and Beagling.* Neptune City, N.J.: TFH Publications, 1975.

Olson, Patricia N., D.V.M., Ph.D.; Behrendt, Michelle D., and Weiss, Deborah E., M.S., D.V.M. "Reproductive Problems in the Bitch: Finding Answers Through Vaginal Cytology," *Veterinary Medicine,* 1987.

Paramoure, Anne Fitzgerald. *Breeding and Genetics of the Dog.* Middlebury, Va.: Denlinger, 1959.

Patterson, Donald F. "A Catalog of Genetic Disorders of the Dog." In *Current Veterinary Therapy VI.* Edited by R. W. Kirk. Philadelphia: W.B. Saunders, 1977.

Peake, Harry C. *Practical Dog Breeding.* New York: Macmillan Company, 1948.

Povey, C. "Canine Distemper Vaccination Failure." *University Veterinary Medical Extension.* Iowa State University, 1987.

Prentice, H. W., *The Beagle in America and England.* De Kalb, Ill.: H. W. Prentice and W. A. Powell, 1920.

Rasmussen, Paul G. "Multiple Epiphyseal Dysplasia in Beagle Puppies," Small Animal Clinic, The Royal Veterinary and Agricultural University, Copenhagen, Denmark, 1982.

Seldon, J. R., et al. "Inherited XX Sex Reversal in the Cocker Spaniel Dog." *Human Genetics* 67 (1984):62–69.

Smith, Jones, and Hunt. *Veterinary Pathology,* Philadelphia: Lea & Febiger, 1972.

Stockner, Priscilla, D.V.M. "Canine Reproduction Syllabus." Santa Clara Valley Kennel Club Seminar, 1988.

Stonehenge. *The Dogs of Great Britain and America.* New York: Orange Judd Co., 1881.

Watson, James. *The Dog Book,* Vol II, New York: Doubleday, Page & Co., 1906.

———. *The Dog Book.* New York: Doubleday, Page & Co., 1916.

Youatt, William. *The Dog,* London: Longmans, Green & Co., 1879.

© ann Mackenzie '88

270